State and Local
Affordable-Housing Programs

A Rich Tapestry

Michael A. Stegman

**Urban Land
Institute**

About ULI–
the Urban Land Institute

ULI–the Urban Land Institute is a nonprofit education and research institute that is supported and directed by its members. Its mission is to provide responsible leadership in the use of land in order to enhance the total environment.

ULI sponsors education programs and forums to encourage an open international exchange of ideas and sharing of experiences; initiates research that anticipates emerging land use trends and issues and proposes creative solutions based on that research; provides advisory services; and publishes a wide variety of materials to disseminate information on land use and development. Established in 1936, the Institute today has more than 15,000 members and associates from more than 50 countries representing the entire spectrum of the land use and development disciplines.

Richard M. Rosan
President

Recommended bibliographic listing:
Stegman, Michael A. *State and Local Affordable-Housing Programs: A Rich Tapestry.* Washington, D.C.: ULI–the Urban Land Institute, 1999.

ULI Catalog Number: N05
International Standard Book Number:
  0-87420-829-7
Library of Congress Catalog Card Number:
  99-66866

ULI Project Staff

Rachelle L. Levitt
Senior Vice President, Policy and Practice
Publisher

Marta Goldsmith
Vice President, Land Use Policy
Project Director

Diane R. Suchman
Project Editor

Jennifer LeFurgy
Senior Associate, Urban Development

Nancy H. Stewart
Director, Book Program

Sandy Chizinsky
Manuscript Editor

Betsy VanBuskirk
Art Director

Meg Batdorff
Graphic Artist

Martha Loomis
Desktop Publishing Specialist

Diann Stanley-Austin
Associate Director of Publishing Operations

Cover photo: Park View Terrace is a 92-unit affordable housing apartment complex in Poway, San Diego County, California. Serving families and seniors, the project was made possible through local government subsidies, California's redevelopment tax-increment program, and federal low-income housing tax credits. It was developed through a joint venture between Community Housing of North County and Central Pacific Housing Development.

Photographer: John Durant

About the Author

Michael A. Stegman holds three posts at the University of North Carolina at Chapel Hill: Duncan MacRae '09 and Rebecca Kyle MacRae Professor of Public Policy and Business; chairman of the Public Policy Analysis Curriculum; and director of the Center for Community Capitalism, Frank Hawkins Kenan Institute of Private Enterprise, Kenan-Flagler Business School. From January 1992 to June 1996, Stegman was the Cary C. Boshamer Professor of City and Regional Planning at UNC; he also served as the chairman of the department from 1983 to 1993 and was the founding chair of UNC's Ph.D. Public Policy Analysis Curriculum, serving in that capacity from July 1990 through June 1993.

In February 1993, President Clinton nominated Stegman to be Assistant Secretary for Policy Development and Research at the U.S. Department of Housing and Urban Development (HUD), a post he held through June 1997.

Stegman was elected a fellow of the Urban Land Institute in June 1998. He is a member of the Federal Home Loan Mortgage Corporation's Affordable Housing Advisory Council and a consultant to the U.S. Department of the Treasury's Community Development Financial Institutions Fund and to the U.S. General Accounting Office. Stegman is a member of the board of directors of the World Trade Center North Carolina; a member of the national board of directors of the Initiative for Competitive Inner Cities; a member of the national advisory board of the Center on Urban and Metropolitan Policy at the Brookings Institution; and immediate past vice president of the Association for Public Policy and Management (APPAM) and member of APPAM's Policy Council and Executive Committee.

In 1998, Stegman received the Robert W. Ponte Award from the New York chapter of the American Planning Association. In 1995, he received both the Distinguished Educator Award from the Washington chapter of Lambda Alpha International and the Richard T. Ely Distinguished Educator Award from Lambda Alpha International. The June 14, 1997, issue of *National Journal* named Stegman one of Washington's 100 most influential decision makers.

Stegman has written extensively on housing and urban policy. While at HUD, he became the founding editor of *Cityscape*, a new journal of urban policy research. Among the books he has written are *Savings for the Poor: The Hidden Assets of Electronic Banking* (Brookings Institution Press, 1999), *More Housing, More Fairly* (20th Century Fund Press, 1991), and *Nonfederal Housing Programs: How States and Localities Are Responding to Federal Cutbacks in Low-Income Housing* (ULI–the Urban Land Institute, 1987).

About the Sponsor

Fannie Mae Foundation, a private nonprofit organization, transforms communities through innovative partnerships and initiatives that revitalize neighborhoods and create affordable homeownership and housing opportunities across America. The Foundation conducts and sponsors research on housing and community development issues; publishes two highly regarded journals, *Housing Policy Debate* and *Journal of Housing Research*; and sponsors research roundtables and conferences including, the Annual Housing Conference. The Foundation's sole source of support is Fannie Mae. The Fannie Mae Foundation is head-quartered in Washington, D.C., with regional offices in Atlanta, Chicago, Dallas, Pasadena, and Philadelphia.

State and Local Affordable-Housing Programs: A Rich Tapestry

More than a quarter of a century separated the tenures of Robert C. Weaver and Henry G. Cisneros, but their reflections upon leaving office as secretary of the U.S. Department of Housing and Urban Development (HUD) define the challenges facing housing and urban policy as the 20th century draws to a close.

Frustrated that many of his initiatives had been seriously compromised by military escalation in Vietnam, then terminated by a hostile Nixon administration, Weaver departed in 1968, after four years on the job, convinced that the nation's unfinished business centered on its cities.

> [The] resolution of the urban crisis turns on resolving problems of poverty, race, citizen participation, proliferation of local governments, and municipal finance. Putting a floor under income . . . breaking segregated racial patterns, increasing the citizen's role in decision making, developing more effective instruments of local government, providing tax-sharing or some other form of substantial aid to local governments—these are some of the major issues that the nation must tackle.[1]

Nearly thirty years later, as HUD's eleventh secretary, Cisneros set out to tackle some of these same issues. Believing that the problems of distressed cities and older suburbs had been put on the back burner by the previous Republican administrations, Cisneros urged Americans to resist blaming the cities for the growing social disorder in many low-income neighborhoods. He promised to seek ways to "bind the wounds of racism and discrimination, to take this nation to higher heights, and to bequeath a more peaceful, civil, and prosperous future to our children."[2] To achieve these goals, he fought passionately within the Clinton administration for an ambitious urban agenda.

Under Cisneros, HUD developed a blueprint for investing in neighborhoods, in housing, and in people that was based upon the belief that no one can possibly care more about a city or its neighborhoods than the people who live there. Cisneros understood that for HUD to become a stronger force in community development, the department's resources had to offer more support to local visions, local ideas, and local strategies, and his reinvention and reform agenda for HUD put maximum authority into the hands of local decision makers. As assistant secretary for policy development and research, I was privileged to work with him in planting the seeds of opportunity in our communities.

Housing, Cisneros believed, should be a springboard to a better life, and housing assistance should do more than simply ameliorate a symptom of poverty: it should help families move up the ladder of opportunity. When families are assured of decent housing, they can stop worrying about leaking pipes or about whether they will be evicted—and focus instead on developing their potential.

Cisneros believed that public housing worked for most families in most places, but he recognized that it was not working in some cities. These were the cities overrun by drugs, poverty, and despair, where public housing residents were forced to live as virtual prisoners in their own homes. He was passionately committed to transforming public housing, and two years after his departure, it continues to be one of HUD's highest priorities.

When he left office in January of 1997, Cisneros said that he had found no "silver bullet" that could fix public housing or heal the problems of "place and race": "The truth is, after all the comprehensive solutions and sweeping ideas, I've learned that the way to solve the biggest problems is block by block, neighborhood by neighborhood, city by city. There is no substitute for the magic of persistent, untiring, day-to-day work."[3] Like Weaver, Cisneros never lost sight of what the day-to-day work was all about:

> Despite all its promise, the America of our hopes and dreams cannot *be* if we accept the level of poverty that we have in this country today. It cannot *be* if we accept the sight of men and women in rags, with their homes bulging out of garbage bags beside them on our street corners. It cannot *be* if we accept inner-city despair. It cannot *be* if we accept hunger among children. It cannot *be* if we accept these things, if God forbid, we come to expect these things, as some sort of unavoidable byproduct of modern society.[4]

Origins of *State and Local Affordable-Housing Programs: A Rich Tapestry*

In the summer of 1997, shortly after leaving HUD to return to university life, I received a call from Rachelle Levitt, senior vice president of the Urban Land Institute. Ten years earlier, I had written a book for ULI entitled *Nonfederal Housing Programs: How States and Localities Are Responding to Federal Cutbacks in Low-Income Housing*. That volume, a compilation of local programs and an assessment of the revenue sources that supported them, was aimed at helping local policy makers adjust to the draconian budget cuts of the Reagan administration.

This time, Levitt said, ULI was interested in how state and local governments were adjusting to a more decentralized federal policy environment. The new enterprise would have a much broader purpose than the earlier one: it would examine how local affordable-housing delivery systems put in place in the 1980s had matured and stood the tests of time, as well as how states and communities were responding to a number of important issues: welfare and public housing reform; the crisis of Section 8 contract renewals; homeownership for lower-income families; the balanced budget agreement, which put a cap on total federal spending; and the continuing decline in new federal commitments for affordable housing.

I welcomed the opportunity to take on this project because I thought that it would help communities develop better policies and programs and help me broaden my own perspective—which, of necessity, had been focused for four years on a handful of critical HUD issues. *Nonfederal Housing Programs* was a basic primer for affordable-housing policies as well as a call to arms; *A Rich Tapestry* moves beyond that work to celebrate the coming of age of state and local housing policies. It documents how affordable-housing issues are now more routinely incorporated into state and local government policy and budgetary processes; it highlights the growing sophistication of nonfederal housing policies and programs; and it discusses important developments in the private sector and in the secondary market that have made it possible to leverage scarce public resources.

A Rich Tapestry does share one important goal with its predecessor: by describing a rich array of nonfederal programs in some detail, both books seek to inform and educate local policy makers and to broaden policy horizons. Like its predecessor, *A Rich Tapestry* includes contact information in each profile to enable readers to obtain additional information about programs of particular interest.

Descriptions of more than 100 programs are organized into eight chapters that span the full range of affordable-housing concerns. The first two chapters address ways to help more families of modest means buy a home. Chapter 1 focuses on local homeownership partnerships and other time-tested efforts to close the homeownership gap. Chapter 2 reviews the use of means other than second mortgages to close the downpayment gap. The reader is introduced to local individual development account (IDA) programs and to savings incentive programs sponsored by the Federal Housing Finance Board, both of which help families save for a downpayment. IDAs were given a major boost in the closing days of the 105th Congress, when the Assets for Independence Act established a national IDA pilot program funded with $10 million during the first year and with a total of $125 million over five years.

Although national homeownership rates reached an all-time record high in 1998, not all Americans have the desire or the ability to own a home. Recognizing that fact, the next four chapters address issues associated with affordable rental housing. Now that developers as well as state and local governments have had more experience with the low-income housing tax credit (LIHTC), it has become the single most powerful force driving the production of affordable rental housing in this country today.

Chapter 3 shows how states use their federal tax credit allocation plans to accomplish strategic housing goals, and it underscores the importance—for housing advocates and local policy makers who hope to influence their state's tax credit priorities—of participation in the allocation planning process. Chapter 4 describes a variety of programs that help finance affordable rental housing. Some, like state-funded LIHTCs that "piggy-back" on the federal credit, leverage the federal LIHTC; others, like 501(c)(3) bonds, supplement it.

Chapter 5 is concerned not with increasing the supply of affordable rental housing but with preserving what already exists. For a variety of reasons, the inventory of affordable rentals has decreased sharply in many communities. The two principal causes are (1) the expiration of long-term subsidy contracts on HUD-assisted rental projects and (2) the deterioration in market conditions, which has made it much more difficult to earn a living as an inner-city landlord. The programs described in Chapter 5 are divided into those that are designed to preserve HUD-assisted housing and those that are designed to shore up the lower end of the unsubsidized rental market.

The tenant-based rental assistance programs described in Chapter 6 are designed to help welfare recipients make a successful transition to the world of work. Like child care and transportation, housing is a critical element in a single parent's ability to find and keep a job. Significantly, these locally funded housing assistance efforts were the first such efforts to be time limited.

Chapter 7 highlights innovations in the secondary-mortgage market that are designed to increase the amount of capital available for affordable housing. Although most of these programs were created by the private sector, they are included here because local housing advocates and policy makers need to learn how to use these exciting new tools to leverage available capital.

Borrowing generously from and updating Mary Brooks's excellent treatise on housing trust funds, *A Rich Tapestry* concludes with a retrospective on these most flexible of all affordable-housing finance programs. While most housing trust funds may not be as well capitalized as their supporters had hoped, their flexibility enables them to make the most of their limited dollars and to leverage other, more restricted funds. All in all, a housing trust fund remains a good way for communities to support affordable housing.

A Note on the Research Process

The initiatives described in this book were culled from a much larger number of nonfederal programs; we obtained information about those programs through a national survey of large cities; a sample survey of smaller communities; and a canvass of countless Web sites, housing trade publications, and other specialized publications and materials. When one of these secondary sources revealed an interesting program, we telephoned local program officials with a request for more detailed information. Once that information was in hand, we typically followed up with additional phone interviews to clarify particulars such as program requirements, to pin down the level of program activity, and to obtain more information on funding levels and sources.

This book is not a compilation of best practices, although some of the programs included here have received important recognition for their outstanding accomplishments. Most best-practice awards and publications recognize excellence in projects, not programs; this book, in contrast, focuses on replicable programs that have the potential to achieve scale. Moreover, what makes an undertaking such as this most interesting is the author's freedom to decide which programs to include in the book. For better or worse, I accept full responsibility for these decisions. Although an extraordinarily able group of research assistants and I tried our best to accurately portray the programs included here, we had neither the time nor the resources to send all draft descriptions to program officials for their review and suggestions. However, to address queries raised in the editorial process, we did contact many program officials, who clarified specific points and approved our program summaries. Nevertheless, I accept full responsibility for any errors or omissions and apologize to those whose admirable efforts may have been misreported or overlooked.

Two organizational issues require some explanation: (1) how it was determined in which chapter a particular program would appear and (2) how the program descriptions were arranged within individual chapters. The first issue arises because, as all of us in the field appreciate, many affordable-housing programs try to do more than one thing. For example, some bond programs finance both sales and rental housing; a community development financial institution may provide home loans to first-time buyers in addition to buying portfolios of Community Reinvestment Act loans from mainstream banks. In deciding where to place a program that served more than one purpose, I used "a preponderance of activity" rule. If the program's center of gravity was homeownership, even though it also financed some rental development, I placed it with programs that were devoted exclusively to homeownership. I handled the second issue more objectively. Within each chapter, state and local programs appear in alphabetical order: first by state, then by city, county, or program title. The few programs that operate on a regional or a national scale—and not many do—are located at the end of the chapter.

Finally, I want to acknowledge the assistance of those who worked with me at various times during the two years that I worked on this project. As a second-year graduate student in city and regional planning at the University of North Carolina (UNC), Patrick Wagner helped me frame the book, collect program materials, and prepare first drafts of many program descriptions. When Patrick went on to a well-earned position with the Enterprise Social Investment Corporation, Nancy Thall and Allison Freeman joined the research staff. Thanks to her experience as a state housing and community development professional, Nancy (now a doctoral candidate in public policy analysis at UNC) provided a steady hand and keen insights, serving as my chief research assistant and drafting most of the program descriptions. Allison, a graduate student in city and regional planning at UNC, took charge of the housing trust fund chapter.

I was also very fortunate to have a terrific collaborator assigned to this project by ULI. Diane Suchman, a longtime friend and colleague, served as reviewer and chief editor. I have so much confidence in Diane's judgment and writing skills that she was the first person I hired when I joined the Clinton administration. Diane's penetrating review of each abstract led to a round of revisions resulting in clearer, more accurate, and up-to-date program descriptions. I also want to acknowledge the assistance of Eleanor Howe, who edited the chapter introductions and preface; and Karen Danielsen, ULI director of residential development, who reviewed the draft and offered valuable insights. Thanks, too, to Marta Goldsmith, ULI's vice president for land use policy, for keeping me and this project on a tight schedule, and seeing it through to publication. Lastly, ULI and I express our appreciation to the Fannie Mae Foundation for its financial contribution to support the publication of this book.

Notes

1 E. Zisch, Paul H. Douglas, and Robert C. Weaver, editors, *The Urban Environment: How It Can Be Improved* (New York: New York University Press, 1969), 87–88.

2 Confirmation hearing for Henry G. Cisneros, January, 1993.

3 Henry G. Cisneros, speech at the National Press Club, Washington, D.C., January 7, 1997.

4 Ibid.

Contents

Affordable Homeownership Comes of Age

Most Americans want to own a home. According to a 1998 survey by the Federal National Mortgage Association—Fannie Mae—"six in ten renters say that buying a home ranks between being a very important priority and their number one priority in life, an all-time high."[1] By purchasing a home, a family acquires not only a place to live but also a valuable asset—equity that can someday be used to move to a larger home in a more desirable location, to finance retirement, to pay for a child's college education, or to start a business.

Overview

Home equity—the value of a home minus the amount owed on the mortgage—represents an important source of household wealth, and for homeowners in the lowest income brackets, it is *the* most important source of wealth. While half of all homeowners in 1995 held at least 50 percent of their net worth in home equity, among those with incomes under $20,000, half held nearly 72 percent of their wealth in home equity.[2] Equity represents an even greater share—more than 80 percent—of African American and Hispanic homeowners' net wealth, which makes the 20 percent gap in homeownership rates for minorities and non-Hispanic whites so troublesome and the financial and social costs of discriminatory lending practices so pernicious.[3] Perhaps even more telling is the difference in net wealth between owners and renters: in 1995, homeowners had a median net wealth of more than $102,000, compared with just $4,750 for renters.

Homeownership also seems to foster a sense of family responsibility and community investment, promote self-sufficiency, create opportunities and choices, and give homeowners a firm foothold on the ladder of economic opportunity. The recent work of Denise DiPasquale and Edward Glaeser, for example, suggests that homeownership strengthens social capital by encouraging greater civic involvement and political awareness,[4] and Greene and White have found other social benefits of owning a home: other things being equal, children of homeowners are more likely to stay in school past age 17, and daughters of homeowners are less likely to have a child before the age of 18.[5]

Homeownership is also important to economic development and to the quality of life in communities. Enterprising individuals often use home equity as their primary source of capital to start a small business. In communities where homeownership rates are low, revitalization is generally harder to accomplish: if low-income renters fear that improvements will bring unaffordable rent increases, revitalization projects may limp along without the full engagement or support of the community. In contrast, a resurgence of homeownership in a neighborhood may stimulate commercial reinvestment because owners of commercial properties take investment cues from the improvement or decline of the surrounding area. Successful neighborhood revitalization, particularly through targeted efforts to increase homeownership, invites private sector investment in the supporting commercial sectors.

Compared with the 1980s—or with any postwar decade—these are extraordinarily good times for housing. Thanks to sustained economic growth, negligible inflation, and low interest rates, Americans have gone on a homebuying spree. The national homeownership rate has reached an all-time high—66.8 percent as of the third quarter of 1998—and the addition of 4 million new homeowners between 1994 and 1997 set a record for any consecutive three-year period in history.[6] Moreover, in the first 11 months of 1998, builders sold more new homes—823,000—than in any *full* year ever.[7]

The lowest unemployment rate in a generation—along with aggressive outreach on the part of conventional lenders, national intermediaries, and community-based affordable homeownership programs—has also made the 1990s good years for minority and first-time homebuyers. Local homeownership partnerships like those described in this chapter provide a variety of important services, including pre- and postpurchase counseling, subsidized downpayment and second mortgage programs, and affordable housing that is financed by mainstream banks. Although they account for only 17 percent of all homeowners, minorities were responsible for a 42 percent share of the increase in the number of owners between 1994 and 1997.[8] Over this same period, lending to minority buyers increased by 45 percent, compared with only 14 percent for non-Hispanic white buyers. Lending to low- and moderate-income borrowers, regardless of race, rose by 30 percent, compared with just 20 percent for upper-income buyers.[9]

This good news notwithstanding, at least four areas need more targeted attention. First, immigrants remain a major untapped market in many of our cities. According to a 1995 Fannie Mae survey, these newcomers are almost three times as likely as other renters to list buying a home as their highest priority. However, HUD researchers have found that, as a group, immigrants are nearly twice as likely to be renters—despite the fact that their incomes make them as financially capable of buying a home as the population at large.[10]

Second, although the strong economy has enabled many young people to buy their first homes, wages have been stagnant for large numbers of 25- to 34-year-olds with high school educations. Without subsidies of some kind, young people in this group will not have sufficient income or savings to purchase homes.

Third, we need to increase homeownership rates in our central cities. The surge in minority homebuying is impressive, and the lending boom that supports it speaks well for racial progress; both trends, however, are primarily suburban phenomena: central-city homeownership rates have scarcely budged. Between 1995 and 1997, central-city homeownership rates edged up less than half a percentage point, to 49.9 percent, while suburban rates climbed from 71.2 percent to 72.5 percent.[11]

Finally, mortgage loans continue to be in relatively short supply in rural communities, where credit facilities and homeownership support systems are limited. With their small staffs and primarily local orientation, rural banks and credit unions also have less familiarity with—and access to—the secondary mortgage market.

In response to the continuing need for targeted intervention in even the strongest and most buoyant housing markets, many one-dimensional local homeownership assistance programs have given way to the broader-based, more comprehensive partnerships featured in this chapter. Many of these local partnerships work in cooperation with HUD's National Partners in Homeownership program, which was established by President Clinton in 1994. The goal of the partnership is to help the national homeownership rate continue to climb by coordinating and sharing information on the efforts of hundreds of local, state, and national homeownership organizations. About 65 national organizations and over 100 local and state groups are now part of this network.

In general, local partners, including many of those featured here, try to address one or more barriers to affordable homeownership and neighborhood improvement:[12]

• Insufficient stock of affordable housing;
• Restricted availability of financing at affordable terms;
• Neighborhood disinvestment;
• Racial and ethnic discrimination in access to mortgages;
• Unprepared, inexperienced buyers;
• Prospective buyers' lack of information on homeownership issues and opportunities.

It is important to emphasize that neither the partnerships discussed here nor their counterparts across the country are in the business of helping to put people into homes who are not prepared to be homeowners. The partnerships' reason for being is the large pool of potential homebuyers that the market, unaided and unsupported, simply does not effectively serve, even though the risks of doing so are reasonable. That such a pool exists has been amply demonstrated: according to a 1996 HUD research report undertaken by the Urban Institute,

> a large number of current renters have a higher likelihood of becoming owners than many former renter households that actually achieved homeownership. Of 20.3 million households having low or moderate incomes, roughly 16 percent had a higher probability of homeownership than one-half of the renter households that actually became homeowners over the sample period. Looking also at the likelihood of default relative to the average expected for renters who become homeowners, 10.6 percent or 2.15 million low- and moderate-income renters had a lower than average likelihood of default assuming the purchase of a home priced at or below median area home price.[13]

In describing affordable homeownership partnerships and other targeted efforts to close the downpayment gap, this chapter is rich with possibilities for communities that are poised to act.

Partnerships in Support of Homeownership

Operation HOPE Banking Center
Los Angeles, California

The Operation HOPE Banking Center (OHBC) is a multibank collaborative community banking center unlike any of the other partnerships discussed in this chapter: OHBC provides a banking center staffed by its own employees and those of member banks; offers automated teller machine (ATM) services; accepts utility payments; and meets a wide range of banking needs beyond those directly associated with homeownership. OHBC seeks to establish itself as the prototypical "banker's bank," in and for underserved but viable communities in south central Los Angeles.

Participants

OHBC is the result of an innovative partnership between Operation HOPE, Inc., America's first nonprofit investment banking organization, members of the local lending community, and other private and public sector partners. The center grew out of efforts led by Operation HOPE, Inc.; Rebuild LA; the First African Methodist Episcopal Church; and other organizations that banded together to restore and revitalize south central Los Angeles following the civil unrest of 1992.

Program Description

The intent and range of services provided by OHBC are much broader than those of the typical homeownership partnership. Products and services include economic education for both homeownership and business development; ATM access points and interbank deposits; affordable check cashing; dropoff sites for payment of utility bills and payments on loans held by participating lenders; secured credit cards; investment services; and a full range of consumer, business, and home lending products.

OHBC offers comprehensive homeownership assistance through its Operation HOPE Home Loan Center, whose mission is to "prepare, qualify, and fund prospective borrowers seeking to finance new home purchases in underserved areas of Los Angeles." In its seven programs—described briefly in the sections that follow—the home loan center capitalizes on a synergistic relationship between the community, the center itself, and private sector lenders.

Rotating Lender Pool. Six member lenders—Fidelity Federal Bank, First Federal Bank of California, First Republic Thrift and Loan, Southern Pacific Thrift and Loan, Union Bank, and City National Bank—participate in the center's rotating pool. The pool is designed to increase potential borrowers' access to lending services in underserved markets; to increase technical assistance to potential borrowers and leverage their ability to become homeowners; and to create an environment that provides an incentive for lenders to adjust to market demands.

Member lenders may provide the center with one of their own trained loan officers or use a trained community loan officer employed by the center. In addition to participating in the center's overall marketing and outreach programs, the loan officer works in the target community, conducting market and business development activities for his or her member institution.

Member banks receive loan referrals from the center's staff on a rotating basis. Loan applicants who are declined may reapply to other member lenders, but they must first meet with the executive director of the center, who documents the problems with the application and works with borrowers to address them before application can be made to the next lender. (In some instances, applicants may instead be referred to the case management program, described below.) Prospective borrowers benefit from having access to multiple lenders "under one roof" and from technical assistance in resolving barriers to loan approval. Most important, proximity fosters competition: with the banks working side by side, borrowers are assured that lenders have greater incentive to adjust to market demands.

First-Time Homebuyer Workshops. Using curriculum materials created in house, banking center staff lead homebuyer counseling seminars on a range of topics, including estimating what clients can afford to pay for a home, calculating monthly payments, home inspection, loan closing, and personal budgeting.

Case Management. Applicants who are declined for a loan but have the potential to qualify later (after correcting problems identified in the application) are referred to the case management program for six to 12 months. During this period, borrowers commit to (1) setting aside enough savings each month to yield the minimum amount required for a downpayment and (2) maintaining an on-time credit history with all creditors.

Downpayment Assistance Loans. Through a lending consortium of Operation HOPE, Inc., member lenders, qualified homebuyers may receive loans to assist with their downpayments. Eligible borrowers are identified by center staff during the preapplication process for the first loan. The downpayment loan is in the form of a secured second deed of trust, payable over seven years. Loan amounts range from $2,000 to $5,000 and carry an interest rate of prime plus 1 percent. Operation HOPE, Inc., serves as the fund manager for the program, and the loans are serviced by First Federal Bank of California.

Each participating lender commits $25,000 to the loan pool along with a $2,500 management fee. (Applicants also pay a one-time processing and packaging fee of $250, which they are permitted to draw from their loan funds.)

Once an applicant for downpayment assistance receives loan approval from the first deed of trust lender, the center forwards the proposed package of loans (and documentation) to that lender, to a participating downpayment loan lender, and to First Federal. The participating lender decides within three days whether to grant the second deed of trust.

Hawthorne HOPE Matching Grant Program. The Hawthorne HOPE Matching Grant Program is a matching savings program for homeownership savings accounts. In brief, the program matches dollar for dollar (up to $5,000) the savings accumulated by participants to be used for a downpayment on a home. Borrowers must meet income, property location, and economic literacy requirements. (This program is described in more detail in Chapter 2 of this volume.)

The Vision Fund. The Vision Fund is used to grant loans to applicants who successfully complete their six- to 12-month commitment in the case management program. Each member institution agrees to provide up to 20 percent of its total annual loan volume to an OHBC combined loan pool and to share the risk of participation in this program. Although Vision Fund loans are nontraditional in structure and approach, the home loan center believes that the combined commitments of the center, the borrower, and the lender make the Vision Fund portfolio even stronger than a traditional mortgage loan portfolio.

Marketing and Business Development. OHBC recognizes the need to reach out to a population that, by and large, does not perceive homeownership to be within its reach. The center's comprehensive marketing plan includes donated bus and billboard space; alliances with nonprofits, community groups, and houses of worship; joint ventures with area realtors; distribution of print materials; and community presentations.

Funding Sources

OHBC is a for-profit corporation that provides the physical facilities in the community and associated leasehold improvements as well as ATMs, partnership agreements, and administrative support. Operation HOPE, Inc., the affiliated nonprofit corporation, provides the economic education and empowerment programs and all on-site programs, using a fee-for-services agreement with each OHBC office. Private sector contributions and foundation and government grants currently fund the education programs. Through membership, partnership, and strategic alliance agreements, the private and public sector partners provide all financial products and services available at the banking centers.

Wilmington Housing Partnership Corporation
Wilmington, Delaware

The Wilmington Housing Partnership Corporation (WHP) is a public/private partnership dedicated to promoting affordable housing and homeownership. The partnership, the first of its kind in the state of Delaware, was established as a nonprofit 501(c)(3) corporation in 1989.

WHP serves families earning less than 115 percent of the area median income. The partnership's goals are to

- Assist in increasing the city's homeownership rate to 60 percent by the year 2000;
- Promote affordable homeownership and rental opportunities;
- Encourage both new construction and rehabilitation of existing properties;
- Ensure high-quality design and construction standards;
- Encourage community involvement as well as participation and partnerships on the part of disadvantaged businesses, nonprofit organizations, and housing professionals;
- Intensify efforts to market the city as a desirable place to live;
- Complement initiatives undertaken by the city, the state, Wilmington 2000 (an organization formed to promote economic development in the downtown business district), local nonprofits, and other partners.

Participants

A board of directors, representing both the public and the private sectors, oversees WHP's operations. The mayor of Wilmington makes all appointments to the board, within guidelines established by WHP's bylaws. Public sector members include representatives from several city departments (real estate and housing; finance; and planning), the office of the mayor, the city council, and the Wilmington Housing Development Corporation. At least seven board members (out of a total of 15, as of 1998) are appointed from the private sector. Private sector members of the board currently include representative from lenders, a foundation, and a local nonprofit. The director of the Enterprise Community serves as an ex-officio member. A private sector developer also serves in an ex-officio capacity on the project review committee.

Program Description

A strategic planning process is used to set goals in three primary areas: support for predevelopment activities, construction subsidies, and downpayment and settlement assistance for first-time homebuyers. The following six programs are among those offered by the partnership.

Downpayment and Settlement Assistance. Through WHP, eligible first-time homebuyers can obtain deferred-payment loans to assist with downpayment and settlement costs. The program provides an incentive for working families who have sufficient income to pay their mortgage and other living expenses but little cash available for downpayment and settlement expenses. The loans (of up to $5,000) are interest free to qualified families who earn less than 80 percent of the area median income. Moderate-income families—those earning no more than 115 percent of the area median—are eligible for loans of up to $7,500 at 5 percent interest. The Downpayment and Settlement Assistance Program received an award of merit from the National Association of Housing and Redevelopment Officials.

Assistance with Predevelopment Costs. WHP provides support—in the form of deferred loans and grants—for market studies, environmental assessments, architectural plans, and engineering studies associated with affordable-housing projects. The WHP board approves the loans, which are typically made to a nonprofit organization, on a case-by-case basis. Assistance is granted primarily to projects in federal homeownership zones and projects for which the city has already demonstrated support. The program encourages community revitalization by lowering predevelopment funding needs.

Construction Subsidies. WHP provides financing (primarily to developers, though homeowners or rental-property owners may also apply) to subsidize the construction of new homes or the rehabilitation of existing dwellings to help revitalize declining neighborhoods. Specific neighborhoods are targeted for assistance, particularly those where vacancy rates for rental property are high and housing is generally of lower value. Because the partnership provides deferred loans or grants specific to the needs of each project, it is able to subsidize projects that will attract homebuyers from a wider range of incomes than those who are typically served by public programs. Subsidies range from $10,000 to $20,000 per unit, which helps keep the cost of housing affordable; many homes are priced between $50,000 and $80,000. Projects are selected on a case-by-case basis by WHP's board. Although multifamily rental projects have been approved, the emphasis is on the development or rehabilitation of owner-occupied housing. To date, the partnership has provided financial support for 200 new homes and the renovation of 250 others. Current projects include the construction of McCaulley Court, a development of 53 new townhomes in an historic eastside neighborhood just three blocks from Center City.

Marketing and Brokers' Fees. Marketing efforts and the payment of brokers' fees help "get the word out" to families who consider homeownership a dream beyond their reach. WHP will pay brokers' fees to real estate agents who actively market WHP-owned property to potential homebuyers. Marketing activities include advertising campaigns for partnership-sponsored housing; special events, such as open houses and housing fairs; and auctions of vacant properties.

Real Estate Transfer Tax Waivers. Each year, to promote city living and spur home sales, WHP—along with the city of Wilmington—sponsors a month-long waiver of the 1 percent real estate transfer tax. WHP initiated the idea and successfully lobbied the city to adopt the program in 1995. WHP manages the marketing and nonlegal administrative aspects of the program.

Statistics show that almost 70 percent of the family incomes of all purchasers were in the low- to moderate-income range. In addition, over half the homes sold during the waiver periods were purchased by first-time homebuyers. Wilmington has a related program targeted specifically to this group: for first-time homebuyers in Wilmington, the city offers a year-round waiver of the buyer's portion of the transfer tax. From the city's perspective, the short-term loss of revenue translates into an investment in the community: it expands the tax base, helps stabilize neighborhoods through the addition of new homeowners, and strengthens the image of the city as a desirable place to live.

Vacant Property Initiatives. To support the city's effort to decrease the number of abandoned, boarded-up homes, the partnership conducts periodic auctions of vacant housing. As properties come into the city's inventory, they are auctioned off to owner occupants and investors who will provide the improvements needed to make the homes livable. Renovations must be completed and a certificate of occupancy obtained within one year of purchase. Since the fall of 1996, 50 homes have been sold at five auctions.

A new, six-month pilot project—the Vacant Property Strike Force—combines the expertise and jurisdictions of three city departments (real estate and housing, licenses and inspections, and law enforcement) in an effort to reduce the number of "worst-case" vacant properties. The strike force's current efforts are focused on 140 properties classified as worst-case.

Revolving Construction-Loan Pool. The revolving construction-loan pool, a new program, is designed to assist with projects sponsored by community development corporations and to support homeownership, the development of affordable rental housing, and the rehabilitation of vacant properties. Construction financing is provided by participating lenders in the form of low- or no-interest loans. WHP will administer the fund.

Currently, the loan pool is targeted for two development projects. In developing the idea for the loan pool, WHP refined its overall fundraising strategy, allowing contributors to earmark funds for specific programs. WHP feels that this approach strengthens the relationship between contributors and the neighborhood improvements they support.

Financial Management and Homeownership Counseling. WHP's new financial management and homeownership counseling program links community-based organizations with local financial institutions, focusing attention on asset-building strategies to promote homeownership in targeted neighborhoods. Local housing counseling agencies will contract with the partnership to educate first-time homebuyers on topics such as how to build equity and how to prepare for buying and maintaining their first home. The partnership plans to assist about 250 clients per year at a cost of $625 per client.

Funding Sources

More than $5 million in private and public funds was raised from 38 contributors: $2.5 million came from government sources and over $700,000 from foundations. Contributions provide for staff salaries and other administrative expenses, and the city provides office space and other in-kind support.

Accomplishments

Since 1994, WHP has provided downpayment and settlement assistance loans to about 300 families. The predevelopment and construction subsidies have supported 200 new and 250 renovated homes, and a 53-townhome project is underway.

> **Contact**
> Wilmington Housing Partnership Corporation
> Bob Weir, Executive Director
> 800 North French Street, Seventh Floor
> Wilmington, Delaware 19801
> Telephone: (302) 571-4057
> Fax: (302) 573-5588

Jacksonville Housing Partnership, Inc.
Jacksonville, Florida

Founded in 1992, the Jacksonville Housing Partnership (JHP) is a community-based organization committed to promoting, developing, and financing affordable housing by creating links between the public and private sectors.

Participants

JHP brings together a large number of nonprofits, lenders, builders, and government agencies to provide a comprehensive array of housing services. Initially staffed by volunteers, the partnership hired full-time staff in October of 1993.

Program Description

JHP's focus encompasses more than homeownership: its programs address safe housing, community improvement, the prevention of homelessness, and coalition building. JHP's activities include the following:

- Home renovation and repair programs for low-income and elderly homeowners;
- Homebuyer training (which is combined with two affordable-mortgage programs);
- A HUD-funded supportive housing program for the homeless;
- Emergency assistance to prevent homelessness;

- Joint venture redevelopment, management, and provision of support services for two apartment complexes;
- Coordination of local housing organizations through a housing roundtable.

JHP provides a number of services in-house and sponsors the following seven programs.

Neighborhood Housing Rehab Program. JHP provides on-call, emergency repair services for several hundred low-income or elderly homeowners each year; services include weatherization, roof repair, plumbing and electrical repair, safety and sanitary upgrades, and wheelchair accessibility. JHP uses its own construction staff, private contractors, and trained volunteers to do repairs. Funding for the Neighborhood Housing Rehab Program comes from state and local grants. Repairs range from $5,000 to $10,000 per house and may be provided free or through a no-interest loan.

Paint-The-Town During Rehab Week. Paint-The-Town is an annual, week-long repair and rehabilitation program focused on a selected neighborhood and organized by JHP in conjunction with the local neighborhood association. Professional contractors join forces with large crews of volunteers to paint and repair homes. In addition to serving an important public relations function for JHP, the program also strengthens connections between JHP, low-income neighborhoods and institutions, and the larger community.

Homebuyers' Club. Through a consortium of JHP member banks, the partnership offers budget and credit counseling, a six-hour homeownership training course, and special financing for low- and moderate-income homebuyers. Participants who complete the curriculum are eligible for low-interest first mortgage loans. After the home is purchased, JHP maintains contact with the homebuyers through postpurchase counseling and a newsletter. (JHP also tracks delinquent payments.) Because the Duval County Housing Authority provides downpayment assistance for participants in the Homebuyers' Club, participating families have to pay only $500 in closing costs.

Value Homes Program. A consortium made up of several local banks and the Duval County Housing Finance Agency provides 100 percent financing for low- and moderate-income homebuyers. Prospective homebuyers must earn less than 100 percent of the median area income and have good credit; they must also provide $500 for the downpayment and the buyer's portion of the closing costs. Blended financing for the loans keeps rates at below-market levels. Interest is based on the time at which the application for financing is made: the county housing finance authority provides 15 percent of the loan at 2 percent interest; the remaining 85 percent is lent at current market rates by the participating lenders. The home must be within the county, with a maximum sale price of $92,490. Both new construction and existing homes qualify. The program assists about 100 families each year.

JHP recently affiliated with the National Reinvestment Corporation (NRC); as a Neighbor-Works program, JHP will now be able to offer Neighborhood Housing Services (NHS) loans, and consortium lenders will be able to sell mortgages through the secondary market program of Neighborhood Housing Services of America, Inc.

Supportive Housing Program. JHP administers a $2.3 million grant under HUD's Supportive Housing Program. The grant allows two local agencies to provide case management and employment services and to acquire and rehabilitate housing units for use as transitional housing for the homeless.

Forbearance Fund. To prevent homelessness or loss of essential services, JHP assists low-income renters on an emergency basis to pay rent or utilities. JHP administers the program, and a network of local social service organizations and agencies provide case management.

Jacksonville Housing Roundtable. JHP has organized a coalition of 85 groups—including nonprofits, neighborhood organizations, government agencies, and corporations active in the housing arena—to work together to plan, implement, and finance affordable-housing programs.

Multifamily Joint Ventures. JHP has established joint ventures with other organizations to purchase, renovate, and operate two apartment complexes with a total of 376 units. The properties, which were purchased from HUD and Resolution Trust Corporation, have many units targeted to low- and very low-income residents; they also offer community services, youth services, and economic development programs.

Funding Sources

The bulk of JHP's funding comes from Florida's State Housing Initiatives Partnership (SHIP) program, which receives proceeds from the state's documentary stamp tax. JHP also receives funding from a number of other sources, including the city, Community Development Block Grant funds, the Northeast Florida Area Agency on Aging, NRC, and private donations.

Accomplishments

In 1997, JHP assisted 75 homebuyers through the Homebuyers' Club and 95 homebuyers through the Value Homes Program.

Contact
Jacksonville Housing Partnership, Inc.
Carolyn Ettlinger, Executive Director
First Union National Bank
4401 Emerson Street
Jacksonville, Florida 32207
Telephone: (904) 398-4424
Fax: (904) 398-0828
Web site: www@jaxhousing.com

Fort Wayne Neighborhood Housing Partnership
Fort Wayne, Indiana

The Fort Wayne Neighborhood Housing Partnership (FWNHP) is a nonprofit organization that develops housing, fosters homeownership, and helps fund housing rehabilitation. It was created in 1991 as the result of recommendations from an Urban Land Institute panel that had studied housing needs in south central Fort Wayne. FWNHP's goals include the following:

- Providing affordable loans for home purchase and repair through an innovative loan pool;
- Fostering development and redevelopment to increase the stock of decent affordable housing in targeted city neighborhoods;
- Providing homebuyer education for prospective purchasers.

Participants

Members of FWNHP include lenders; real estate professionals; residents; representatives from social service agencies; and representatives from city government and law enforcement. The partnership's 18-member board of directors consists of six lender representatives, six neighborhood residents, and six community leaders appointed by the mayor. The partnership's growing professional staff includes a development and marketing specialist, a loan processor, rehabilitation specialists, a broker, a real estate agent, and a property manager.

Program Description

To achieve its goals, FWNHP sponsors six different programs and loan products, described in the sections that follow.

Housing Production. To ensure a steady supply of decent affordable housing, FWNHP acquires and renovates existing homes and constructs new homes on vacant lots in targeted neighborhoods. Many of these homes are produced in partnership with local organizations and institutions, including faith-based organizations, homebuilders, realtors, the Urban Enterprise Association, and neighborhood improvement associations.

FWNHP created two affiliate organizations to carry out development activity: the Neighborhood Housing Partnership (NHP) Land Holding Company and the NHP Realty Company. The first acquires and develops vacant parcels of land contributed by Allen County from its tax foreclosure inventory; over 100 properties have been acquired under this program. The NHP Realty Company manages the sale of properties owned by the partnership, listing all partnership properties at no cost and working closely with low-income buyers who require extra assistance in navigating the homeownership process.

Responsible Community Investment Program. The Responsible Community Investment Program (ReCIP) allows individuals or corporations to invest their reserve funds in rehabilitation or new-construction projects. Investors receive tax benefits from the investment and are guaranteed the return of their original investment with virtually no risk. FWNHP manages the construction phase and the sale of the project, as well as providing financing for the completed homes. If the project generates a profit, FWNHP and the investor divide the gain equally.

Home Purchase Program. The Home Purchase Program provides special financing for low-income homebuyers who are "unbankable" because of credit problems or very low incomes. Pooling below-market loan funds from five area lenders, FWNHP provides loans to homebuyers for the purchase price, rehabilitation costs, and closing costs. Loan-to-value ratios may be as high as 125 percent (including closing costs), with a first mortgage of as much as 100 percent of the value of the home and a grant, loan, or shared equity position for the remainder. These soft funds come from HOME, Community Development Block Grant (CDBG) funds, the Federal Home Loan Bank Affordable Housing Program, the Indiana Housing Finance Agency, and foundation grants. In addition to making possible higher loan-to-value ratios, soft funds are blended with lender funds to produce lower interest rates for buyers. The Suelzer Memorial Fund, named for a longtime board member, is a no-interest revolving loan fund used in combination with lender mortgages to bring down interest costs for low- and very low-income borrowers.

The participating banks lend funds to FWNHP at 6.25 percent, and FWNHP uses the funds to make fixed-rate, first mortgage loans to home purchasers at 6.75 percent, amortized over 20 years with a five-year term. Half of the spread between the bank interest rate and the partnership rate (.25 percent) covers loan servicing; the other half is used to fund a loan-loss reserve. The partnership is responsible for all application, underwriting, and loan-approval activities, and each lender contributes a pro rata portion of each loan. Below-market funds allow FWNHP to "blend down" the rate to around 5.5 percent, which allows the partnership to reach its target market of families with incomes in the $18,000 to $20,000 range. At the end of the five-year term, borrowers refinance with a conventional first mortgage; buyers who are unable to refinance conventionally may refinance for another five years through the partnership.

All homebuyers must complete a 20-hour homeownership training course that covers personal finances and budgeting, credit management, borrowing, homebuying, and home maintenance and repair. A cooperative venture on the part of FWNHP, Project Renew, and the Fort Wayne Urban League, the course relies on real estate professionals as volunteer instructors.

Although bank funds will be "recycled" as buyers refinance their five-year loans, the total volume of lending is currently limited by the extent to which participating lenders are willing to expand their portfolios of FWNHP loans. Because demand outstrips the available money each year, the partnership is exploring secondary-market options for the loans to expand future lending capacity.

Lease-Purchase Program. Under FWNHP's Lease-Purchase Program, would-be homebuyers with especially severe credit or other problems work with FWNHP's social service committee to develop a plan to resolve the barriers to homeownership. After completing the homeownership training program, the client establishes a home purchase budget and signs a lease-purchase agreement for a home in FWNHP's inventory. As soon as the client is on a firm financial footing, the lease is converted to a mortgage loan from either the partnership or a private lender.

Home Improvement Program. For current homeowners with repair or renovation needs, FWNHP offers home improvement loans to fund cosmetic improvements or repairs required for compliance with building codes. The maximum loan amount is equal to the difference between the home's appraised value and the balance owed on all mortgages and other liens. To qualify for a home improvement loan, homes must be—or be brought into—full compliance with building codes. Renovation work must be competitively bid and completed by licensed contractors.

Home Ownership for Police Program. To improve the safety of neighborhoods targeted by the partnership, FWNHP created a special program for police officers. Through this program, the home improvement, home purchase, and lease-purchase products are all available to police officers, who are also provided with marked police cars to drive home and park on the street as visible signs of neighborhood security. Participating officers must become active members of the neighborhood association, and FWNHP pays the officers' first-year membership dues.

Funding Sources

While FWNHP receives operating support from CDBG funds, most of its operating budget comes from development fees, which run between $3,000 and $4,000 per home. The organization also receives operating grants and donations from corporations, foundations, government agencies, community associations, and individuals.

Accomplishments

In 1997, FWNHP assisted 100 families to meet their housing needs, a 69 percent increase over the previous year. The dollar value of loans closed in 1997 was more than $4.7 million, and 84 percent of those funds were provided through the partnership's loan pools. According to the partnership's 1997 annual report, the FWNHP had become "the largest not-for-profit developer in Indiana of single-family, scattered-site, affordable housing."

The spirit of partnership is evident in virtually every FWNHP project. In addition to forging relationships with lenders, housing professionals, nonprofit organizations, and the community, FWNHP also provides technical assistance—for example, helping the East Wayne Street Center form a housing corporation. The first two technical assistance meetings are free, and additional assistance is on a fee basis. Finally, FWNHP developed—and now owns—a neighborhood resource center, which provides free office space to the Southeast Neighborhood Partnership, a consortium of neighborhood associations, and leases space to small businesses.

Neighborhood Finance Corporation
Des Moines, Iowa

The Neighborhood Finance Corporation (NFC) of Des Moines, Iowa, was created in 1990 as a nonprofit organization and licensed state mortgage banker to ensure a continuous stream of residential real estate funding for neighborhood improvement and revitalization. NFC serves as a conduit for funds to assist both developers and homebuyers. The addition of the Greater Des Moines Housing Trust Fund to NFC, in 1994, expanded NFC's role to include operational support and capacity building for affordable-housing organizations and support services for residents of housing programs.

Participants

NFC relies on a number of partners, including the Des Moines Development Corporation, a coalition of 80 area businesses; the city's corporate community; the city, county, and federal governments; and private investors.

Program Description

NFC offers a variety of products and services through its homeownership assistance programs and housing trust fund.

Homeownership Assistance. NFC funnels public and private funds for neighborhood revitalization to private homeowners, prospective purchasers, and project developers. Because NFC's goal is to stabilize and revitalize targeted neighborhoods, anyone who wants to buy a home in those neighborhoods is eligible for assistance. Nevertheless, the incomes of most prospective homeowners tend to fall below the area median. NFC loan officers work to combine programs to make homeownership affordable.

NFC can provide forgivable loans for downpayment and closing costs; finance the first mortgage; then finance a second mortgage for rehabilitation (a portion of the second mortgage may also be forgivable). Maximum loan amounts are $75,000. Applicants whose incomes are at or below 100 percent of the area median pay a $50 application fee; those whose incomes are higher pay $250. Downpayment requirements vary from 3 to 5 percent, depending on the buyer's household income. Applicants with incomes below a certain level are eligible to receive a forgivable loan equal to 2 percent of the purchase price so that they can make a 5 percent downpayment. The purchaser must live in the home for at least five years for the rehabilitation loans to be forgiven.

The city and county designate the participating neighborhoods, and each neighborhood establishes its own revitalization goals. Once these goals are met, NFC ceases lending in that neighborhood in order to direct funding to other areas. To date, five designated neighborhoods have met their housing goals and have "graduated" from NFC funding eligibility. Additional neighborhoods have developed revitalization plans and have been approved by the Des Moines City Council and the Polk County Board of Supervisors for participation in NFC programs.

Housing Trust Fund. NFC administers a Housing Trust Fund (HTF) targeted to households earning 80 percent or less than the area median income. The mission of the trust fund, which allocates affordable-housing funds through directives recommended by the Greater Des Moines Housing Partnership, is

> to expand housing opportunities to families and individuals whose needs for affordable housing are not met by the conventional housing market; to encourage and support revitalization of neighborhoods that need investment in housing to make and keep them viable and attractive choices for housing consumers; and to meet the housing needs of the residents.

The trust fund pools monies not only for the creation of affordable housing units but also for the support of a variety of other activities, such as provision of support services to stabilize families and help them become self-sufficient. The HTF also funds operating expenses and capacity-building efforts for nonprofit agencies that provide housing services. Six nonprofit organizations—Anawim Housing, Inc.; Des Moines Coalition for the Homeless; Des Moines Habitat for Humanity, Inc.; Good Samaritan Urban Ministries; HOME, Inc.; and Neighborhood Housing Services of Des Moines—have committed to apply for funds through the HTF and to refrain for three years from seeking contributions from corporations that give to the HTF.

The Greater Des Moines Housing Partnership Board, which is appointed by the Polk County Board of Supervisors, oversees the HTF. NFC administers development and predevelopment funds. The human services coordinating board administers the operational, support services, and capacity-building grants.

Funding Sources

Public funds are used to subsidize rehabilitation, downpayments, and closing costs. All subsidies take the form of a junior lien, which is forgiven over a five-year period of owner occupancy. Private sector participation is critical to the NFC's first-mortgage program. NFC assets (funds) are subject in many cases to donor-imposed restrictions. NFC has entered into agreements with 14 area financial institutions to leverage these restricted funds. These investors have agreed to buy an interest in loans made by NFC; however, NFC continues to administer the loans, making principal and interest payments to the investors on a monthly basis. As of 1997, over $7 million in loans had also been sold to Fannie Mae, and an additional $23 million had been sold to private investors. Investors are partially protected from losses associated with participation in loans originated through the NFC loan origination program: protection is provided through mortgage insurance and through an NFC guarantee/first-loss reserve fund. As of March 1997, NFC had foreclosed only 13 loans, with a total estimated net loss to investors of $53,210 (an average of $4,093 per foreclosure).

Startup funds for the HTF include $1 million from the proceeds of a tax-exempt general bond obligation issued by the county; $2 million from HUD; and private sector support of over $1 million.

The Des Moines Development Corporation has contributed $100,000 to NFC's operating budget, and the corporate community has contributed another $600,000. Public sector support has come from the city, the county, and the federal government; a significant portion of private sector financial support is from investors who purchase private placement offerings of loan participation interests.

Accomplishments

NFC has raised more than $43 million in private funds and $10 million in bond funds for use in designated neighborhoods in the city of Des Moines and surrounding Polk County. Over 1,000 families have been assisted through both loans and grants, and minority applicants have received 26 percent of NFC loans.

Through the HTF, a 1994 demonstration project funded by Polk County and the United Way created 50 units of low-income housing, including owner-occupied infill housing, lease-purchase housing, rental units, and single-room occupancy units.

> **Contact**
> Neighborhood Finance Corporation
> Gary Dodge, Executive Director
> 1912 Sixth Avenue
> Des Moines, Iowa 50314
> Telephone: (515) 246-0010
> Fax: (515) 246-0112

The Housing Partnership, Inc.
Louisville, Kentucky

The Housing Partnership, Inc. (HPI), of Louisville, Kentucky, was created to facilitate cooperation among government, the private sector, and not-for-profit organizations; its goal is to ensure safe, decent, and affordable housing for every citizen in Louisville and the surrounding counties by the year 2000.

HPI is a homeownership counseling agency, a development consultant, and a "developer of last resort," taking on the community's most difficult housing development projects.

An outgrowth of the Louisville Housing Development Corporation (LHDC), the partnership was incorporated in 1990. LHDC was a quasi-private nonprofit organization created by Louisville's department of housing to develop affordable housing. When LHDC's activities expanded beyond city boundaries, HPI was created. In 1995, another existing organization —Home Ownership Partners (HOP)—was brought under the HPI umbrella. The Louisville Housing Authority created HOP to provide comprehensive homeownership and financial counseling for Section 8 recipients. Combining the organizations brought development expertise and homeownership counseling services to Louisville and the surrounding counties.

Participants

HPI members include ten of the 11 banks active in the Louisville market, the home builders association, the local board of realtors, the city and county governments, the Association of Professional Women, and the Kentucky Housing Authority.

Program Description

HPI administers eight programs, described briefly in the subsections that follow.

Development. As a developer of last resort, HPI uses its development capacity to catalyze risky or complicated projects that the private sector is unwilling or unable to undertake alone. HPI works closely with nonprofit and for-profit developers and builders, involving them at the earliest possible stage of a project.

For example, in the RiverGreen project, HPI purchased land from Jefferson County for $1, completed land development (including lot subdivision and infrastructure construction), and sold lots to private builders at below-market prices. The builders constructed homes that met HPI's affordability restrictions, and the homes were then sold to low- and moderate-income buyers who received assistance under HPI's housing counseling program. By bearing the risk of market analysis and land development, HPI was able to attract private sector builders to complete the project.

In another innovative project, Nichols Meadow, HPI moved homes slated for demolition because of airport expansion, relocating them to county-owned land. To do so, HPI worked with the state and with local governments to obtain a waiver of a state law that prohibited houses from being transported on state highways. Once again, HPI succeeded in drawing private sector involvement: private developers built the foundations, completed the homes, and sold them.

Consulting. HPI provides development consulting services for local nonprofit and for-profit developers, specializing in projects that are eligible for tax credits. For projects that move forward, HPI receives a consulting fee based on a sliding scale; the fee begins at 3 percent of development costs for projects of $1 million or less and decreases as the project size increases.

Collaborative Financing. HPI's finance committee structures collaborative financing for projects that are too big or too risky for any one lender to undertake. Typically, one bank will act as lead lender and each bank will contribute a portion of the funds required, effectively sharing the risks and rewards of each project. As an example, the infrastructure loan for the RiverGreen project was a $600,000 collaborative project, with each bank contributing $60,000. The Kentucky Housing Corporation often participates in these collaborative projects, taking the role of "gap financier"—that is, committing the first funds to the project, the last to be paid off, or both.

Second Mortgage Program. The spirit of cooperation fostered by the HPI finance committee led the ten member lenders to submit a joint application to the Federal Home Loan Bank Affordable Housing Program (AHP), providing funds for 20 soft second mortgages. The AHP grant, matched by funds from the city and the state housing finance agency, provided $5,000 second mortgages for families whose incomes were 70 percent of the area median. The loans may be used to purchase homes developed by five local nonprofit organizations, and the balance on the principal will be forgiven after ten years of owner occupancy.

Equity Pool. HPI created and administers a $10 million housing equity pool: funds were raised from ten financial institutions and invested in local developments that are eligible for tax credits. The Kentucky Housing Finance Agency gives preference to small projects, which had historically had difficulty obtaining equity investments from private syndicators. While the fund has invested in projects with as many as 660 units, its current market niche is smaller projects with between five and 24 units.

Home Ownership Partners. HOP continues as the homeownership counseling and education arm of HPI, using a network of 75 professional volunteers and links with realtors, lenders, homebuilders, and local government agencies. HOP provides comprehensive, one-on-one counseling for homebuyers and conducts seminars throughout the metropolitan area. HOP's realtor referral network trains realtors to work with newly qualified low-income homebuyers, creating a pool of real estate professionals that clients can draw on.

HOP continues to work closely with local public housing authorities, including those of Jefferson County and the city of Louisville, to provide homeownership training for public housing residents. HOP clients depend upon local lenders for home mortgages, and a number of lenders have their own affordable-mortgage products geared to low- and moderate-income buyers. HPI provides buyers with information about available mortgage products but does not have any in-house loan products or downpayment assistance programs. HPI also works with local lenders to create custom loan products for specific projects.

Loan Default Insurance Pool. HPI is creating a default insurance pool that would guarantee up to three loan payments in the first five years of a mortgage. Since most client defaults occur within the first five years, it is hoped that the default insurance will induce lenders to make home loans to borderline buyers.

Lease/Purchase Pilot Program. HOP has started a pilot program to create affordable homeownership opportunities through lease-purchase arrangements. The housing is created through a partnership with local developers who use low-income housing tax credits (LIHTCs) to help lower the costs of development. Because LIHTCs extend for 15 years and are intended to be used to create rental units, the houses may not be purchased until the end of the 15 years. HOP manages the program and provides financial counseling, home-buyer education, and maintenance education to participating families, who are primarily Section 8 recipients enrolled in self-sufficiency programs.

The first projects were 19 scattered-site, single-family homes rented to Section 8 self-sufficiency participants. When occupants' incomes increase, rent increases correspondingly. Under this program, however, the additional rent money is placed in an account to be used for a downpayment at the end of the 15-year period specified by the LITHC program. Generally, the purchase price of the home is agreed upon when the lease is signed, and the participant benefits from the increase in valuation over the 15-year period. If a tenant chooses to move during the 15-year lease period, subsequent tenants can enter into the same agreement. Tenants must participate in a home-maintenance education program; they must also assume typical homeowner responsibilities and are charged for minor repairs if they call for service. The program also provides financial assistance for the purchase of items such as lawnmowers. About 150 properties are currently involved in lease-purchase arrangements under the LIHTC program.

Funding Sources

The HPI finance committee provides innovative and collaborative loans to meet a wide variety of affordable-housing needs. By investing funds from local financial institutions in local developments that are eligible for tax credits, HPI has created a $10 million equity pool.

Although the partnership receives annual funding from the city of Louisville, the housing authorities of Louisville and Jefferson Counties, and HUD, its staff of 14 is funded largely through fees. Local lenders pay HPI $175 for each client referred by HOP. As noted previously, consulting fees begin at 3 percent of development costs for projects of $1 million or less, with the fee percentage decreasing as the size of the project increases. Finally, clients in the homeownership training programs pay fees on a sliding scale: for clients with incomes below $10,000 the services are free; fees gradually increase to as much as $304, depending on income and the services received.

Accomplishments

The success of HPI's projects has encouraged private sector builders to become more active in affordable-housing production: for example, since HPI has demonstrated market viability, several homebuilders are now active in the $80,000 to $90,000 segment of the new home market. Through its consulting services, the partnership has assisted with the development of more than 50 projects comprising over 2,000 units.

Future Plans

HPI is part of the HOPE VI development team, which is redeveloping the Park DuValle public housing complex in Louisville. The for-sale housing component of the project is the partnership's responsibility: over a period of years, HPI will build 250 homes to be sold to mixed-income buyers, including former residents of public housing.

HOP is developing an employer assisted housing initiative (called HOPE), enlisting major Louisville employers—such as United Parcel Service, Jefferson County Public Schools, and PNC Bank—for the purpose of creating homeownership opportunities for established employees who still find homeownership out of their reach. HOP is conducting a strong outreach effort to begin the program, under which various forms of housing assistance would be offered as fringe benefits to eligible employees.

Contact

The Housing Partnership, Inc.
Maria I. Gerwing, President
333 Guthrie Green, Suite 404
Louisville, Kentucky 40202
Telephone: (502) 585-5451
Fax: (502) 585-5568

New Opportunities for Homeownership in Milwaukee
Milwaukee, Wisconsin

The mission of New Opportunities for Homeownership in Milwaukee (NOHIM) is to increase homeownership for low- and moderate-income families through innovative partnerships. NOHIM does not serve as a direct lender, nor does it sponsor an investment pool. The focus instead is on collaboration: helping member lenders, homebuyer counseling agencies (HBCs), and local government increase their productivity and effectiveness by working together. In addition to improving communication among participating institutions, NOHIM's efforts have yielded performance standards and standardized guidelines and underwriting criteria for organizations with a role in the provision of affordable housing.

Under the arrangements fostered by NOHIM, benefits accrue to homebuyers, lenders, and HBCs alike. Clients benefit from a well-organized process in which they can move smoothly from counseling through the loan application process. (If clients are not yet ready to apply for financing, the HBC helps them to develop a corrective action plan.) Because the participating HBCs gather the detailed information required for loan applications, lenders not only save time but also have the assurance that HBC-referred clients have a complete portfolio of information.

Membership in NOHIM affords the six participating HBCs a number of advantages: regular, structured communication with lenders; continuing education, which keeps the HBCs abreast of changes in the market and in loan products; and improved cash flow: the HBCs receive $350 for each successful loan application, a valuable source of revenue.

Participants

NOHIM is a collaborative effort on the part of 46 representatives from the city of Milwaukee and from participating banks, thrifts, credit unions, and HBCs. Staff and administrative support are provided by Select Milwaukee, a communitywide information clearinghouse that works with nonprofit organizations, the private sector, and the city.

NOHIM asks each of its member lenders to meet clearly stated eligibility standards that provide the framework for the partnership. When they join the partnership, lenders make a one-time financial contribution to administrative costs (on the basis of size) and agree to certain lending, follow-up, and administrative practices. Lenders also pay an annual administrative fee of $95. Participating lenders are the exclusive lenders for the downpayment and closing-cost assistance program of the Milwaukee Joint Central City Housing Cost Reduction Initiative.

HBC members must have nonprofit status and at least one year of experience; they must also meet certain standards with respect to recordkeeping, staff training, and professional knowledge. Finally, member HBCs also agree to abide by NOHIM's accountability requirements.

Program Description

Though NOHIM's focus is on collaboration rather than on programs, NOHIM plans, develops, and implements a number of training programs for realtors. These include bimonthly breakfast workshops, tours, and an annual community lending conference. In addition, Select Milwaukee, the city, and NOHIM sponsor a professional education program. Realtors who participate in the program are designated as "Milwaukee Value Real Estate Professionals"—a designation that helps the public identify real estate professionals who are particularly knowledgeable about city neighborhoods and the full range of programs and services available to homebuyers. So far, over 60 realtors have earned the special designation.

Accomplishments

Since the creation of NOHIM in 1991, both participating members and the low-income homebuyers have enjoyed substantial benefits. By 1994, the number of mortgages closed for families assisted by community-based counseling agencies had more than doubled, from 103 to 254. During the same period, the value of mortgages closed for families assisted by community-based counseling agencies rose from $3.9 to $10 million. The number of families receiving prepurchase counseling increased by 64 percent, and the percentage of loans originated to minority homebuyers increased as well.

Contact
Select Milwaukee
Raymond Schmidt, Executive Director
2209 North Dr. Martin Luther King Jr. Drive
Milwaukee, Wisconsin 53212
Telephone: (414) 562-5070
Fax: (414) 562-5072

State and Local Homeownership Programs

HouseHartford
Hartford, Connecticut

Since 1995, the city of Hartford has successfully used HOME funds to create homeownership opportunities. The foundation of the program is similar to that of homeownership assistance efforts in other communities: interest-free downpayment and closing-cost loans to qualified buyers that may be forgiven after the participant lives in the home for a required number of years. However, by negotiating with HUD to waive certain regulations, Hartford was able to tailor its program and make it more responsive to local homeownership needs.

Program Administration

The city of Hartford administers HouseHartford, working in partnership with Fannie Mae and 14 private sector lenders.

Program Description

HouseHartford has two components: single-family homeownership assistance and multifamily homeownership assistance.

Single-Family Homeownership Assistance. To be eligible for the single-family homeownership assistance program, applicants must have incomes no higher than 80 percent of the area median. Eligible homebuyers must make a downpayment of at least 3 percent of the sales price from their own funds; for the remainder of the downpayment, the city provides an interest-free loan of up to 7 percent of the purchase price, depending on the borrower's income. The city also offers eligible buyers interest-free loans of up to $3,000 to assist with closing costs. The loans are forgiven if the borrower maintains the property as his or her principal residence for a specified period of time: five years if the total loan amount is less than $15,000; ten years if the total is greater than $15,000.

Multifamily Homeownership Assistance. When HouseHartford began, HUD allowed HOME program funds to be used for first-time homebuyers of multifamily homes only if all units subsidized by HOME funds were occupied by families who met the HOME income and rent limits. Because the city recognized that households whose incomes were just above the HOME income thresholds often needed assistance to become homeowners, House-Hartford negotiated with HUD to obtain a relaxation of the regulations: the result is a program that addresses a wider range of buyers and supports small (up to four-family) mixed-income units.

Under the modified HUD regulations, applicants whose incomes exceed 80 percent of the area median are eligible for assistance in purchasing two-, three-, or four-family homes, and only one of the units must meet HOME income and rent guidelines. Purchasers must maintain the property as their principal residence and must rent at least one unit to a family whose income is 60 percent or less of the area median; the term of the lease must be at least one year, and the maximum rent is established by HUD. If the purchaser meets the low-income requirements, there are no income or rent restrictions for tenants. The waiver enables moderate-income families to become homeowners and supports the conversion of duplex and triplex rental units into owner-occupied rental units.

Financial assistance provided by HouseHartford for two-family homes is the same as that provided for single-family homes. For three- and four-family homes, the city requires the buyer to make a downpayment of up to 10 percent of the purchase price, depending on income.

All properties purchased through the multifamily homeownership assistance program must have an initial purchase price (or a postrehabilitation appraised value) that does not exceed 95 percent of the median purchase price for that category of housing. Although the majority of applicants have incomes near the area median, purchases of multifamily homes are evaluated on a case-by-case basis to ensure that the goals of affordable homeownership are met.

Funding Sources

In addition to HOME funding from HUD, HouseHartford has received a pledge from Fannie Mae of $75 million in mortgage financing for HouseHartford and other Hartford housing programs. Private lenders have also committed to participating in the program.

Accomplishments

Since 1995, HouseHartford has used nearly $1.3 million in HOME funds to leverage almost $10.10 million in private lending.

> **Contact**
> Hartford Department of Housing and Community Development
> Mark A. Ronaldes, Senior Project Manager
> 10 Prospect Street, Third Floor
> Hartford, Connecticut 06103-2814
> Telephone: (860) 522-4888
> Fax: (860) 722-6630

Affordable Home Ownership Program
Boise City, Idaho

Initiated in 1991, Boise City's Affordable Home Ownership Program supports homeownership by providing low-interest loans to qualified buyers for the purchase of vacant residential lots and the construction of new affordable homes.

Program Administration

Boise City runs the Affordable Home Ownership Program in partnership with U.S. Bank.

Program Description

To qualify for Boise City's Affordable Home Ownership Program applicants must meet credit
standards and have incomes that are less than 80 percent of the area median. Participants
receive low-interest loans from both the city and U.S. Bank: the bank issues a first mortgage
for construction, and the city issues a second mortgage for the purchase of the land.

U.S. Bank provides 30-year financing for takeout loans with no loan origination fee or
discount points. Applicants must be able to make a minimum downpayment (based on a
sliding scale) and pay all customary closing costs. The realtor, lot, and design of the house
are all selected by the applicant.

A new component of the homeownership program uses the same funding sources and
two-mortgage strategy to assist disabled residents to purchase existing homes. Recipients
of Social Security disability payments are eligible, and the interest on the loans is deferred
for at least five years. So far, five disabled individuals have purchased homes through the
program.

Funding Sources

The bank uses participation in the Affordable Home Ownership Program to meet Community Reinvestment Act requirements, charging only enough interest to make a small profit.
Boise City relies primarily on HOME and Community Development Block Grant funds for
its portion of the program. The city's investment of $4.75 million during the span of the pro-
gram has leveraged over $13 million in private investment from U.S. Bank.

Accomplishments

Two hundred and ten new homes have been constructed in Boise City since the program
began. The homes average 1,161 square feet, with average PITI (principal, interest, tax, and
insurance) payments of about $500. The average downpayment is under $2,500. There have
been no foreclosures, and as of June 1998, no households were in arrears. Participants average 61.8 percent of the area median income. Eighty-five are single mothers; 39 are recent
immigrants from Bosnia.

FIX ME Home Repair Loans
State of Maine

The FIX ME program provides very low-interest loans to help low- and very low-income homeowners afford basic home repairs. The need for a program to repair substandard homes was identified in the state's consolidated plan. An estimated 85,000 Maine home-owners have incomes that are below 50 percent of the state median income, including about 30,000 with annual incomes of $10,000 or less.

Program Administration

The energy and housing services division of the Maine State Housing Authority (MSHA) administers the FIX ME program in partnership with the state's Community Action Program (CAP) agencies.

Program Description

The FIX ME program provides low-interest loans for basic improvements such as repairs to home systems (electrical, plumbing, heating), roof repairs, energy conservation, septic systems, and accessibility improvements. Applicants must be low- or very low-income. The loans carry an interest rate of either 2 or 4 percent, depending on the type and scope of the repairs needed. The maximum loan amount is $15,000, and the term of the loan is 15 years. A home replacement option for homes that are beyond repair allows borrowers access to up to $25,000 with up to 20 years to repay.

Homeowners apply for a FIX ME loan at their regional CAP agency. The CAP agency may leverage the FIX ME loan with other program resources, including the Department of Energy and Health and Human Services Weatherization programs and Rural Housing Services Housing Preservation Grants; MSHA expects to leverage about one-third of the loans with funds from other sources. Loan funds are held in escrow while repairs are being made, and payments are made in the form of a two-party check. The CAP agency is responsible for inspecting the structure three times—before, during, and after repairs are completed. MSHA contracts with a loan servicing agency, and the homeowner makes loan payments directly to this agency.

Funding Sources

In 1998, MSHA planned to invest $12 million to finance repairs to 1,200 homes. Funding for the FIX ME program comes from four sources: MSHA tax-exempt bonds, MSHA state HOME funds, MSHA federal housing block grant funds, and the Maine Municipal Bond Bank.

Accomplishments

From 1995 through 1997, FIX ME financed repairs for more than 2,700 homes.

Contact
Maine State Housing Authority
Energy and Housing Services Division
John Guimond
353 Water Street
Augusta, Maine 04330-4633
Telephone: (207) 624-5707 or (800) 452-4668 (voice)
Fax: (207) 626-4678

Boston Community Capital's
One- to Four-Family Homeownership Program
Boston, Massachusetts

Boston Community Capital (BCC) provides capital for sustainable investments that create affordable housing and jobs and provides services for low-income or otherwise disadvantaged residents of communities in Boston and eastern Massachusetts. BCC's priorities include affordable housing, special-needs housing, child care facilities, and business loans.

Participants

BCC consists of three entities: the Boston Community Loan Fund (BCLF), the Boston Community Venture Fund, and Boston Community Managed Assets. BCLF works in partnership with the Local Initiatives Support Corporation (LISC), the state of Massachusetts, the cities of Boston and Cambridge, and nonprofit community development corporations (CDCs). The Boston Community Venture Fund invests equity in neighborhood businesses. Boston Community Managed Assets provides financial management services to community-based organizations—primarily the Boston Homeowner Service Collaborative, Inc., a consortium of seven Boston-area CDCs that provide home-improvement loans.

Program Description

Initially, BCLF focused exclusively on affordable housing, but the fund now makes loans for diverse community development needs such as the development of daycare centers and small businesses. Most BCLF funds, however, are still dedicated to housing.

BCLF offers a unique one- to four-family program that targets a difficult niche in the Boston and Cambridge housing markets: severely dilapidated properties that are too expensive for a single household to rehabilitate and too small to interest developers. The program provides construction financing for CDCs and permanent loans to first-time homebuyers.

CDCs purchase and renovate the homes and qualify the buyers. The completed homes are sold to low- and moderate-income homebuyers who occupy one unit in the property and rent out the additional units, subject to affordability restrictions. According to senior loan officer Mike Nilles, a typical project would be a three-unit home with total development costs of $250,000. The property would be sold for the maximum price that can be supported by the buyer and rental income—roughly $140,000—and the gap would be filled by city and state soft second mortgages.

Funding Sources

BCLF and LISC provide revolving lines of credit to participating CDCs. The line-of-credit funds cover up to 90 percent of the appraised "as completed" value of the properties, and BCLF provides loans for the remaining 10 percent of development costs to bridge city and state financing. City and state agencies use federal HOME funds to provide buyers with soft second mortgages, filling substantial affordability gaps.

Accomplishments

During its 12 years of existence, BCLF has financed affordable apartments, cooperatives, and single-family homes for 1,050 households, as well as 850 special-needs units for people with AIDS, battered women, homeless people, and elderly people. As of May 1998, 46 properties comprising 85 units had been completed under the One- to Four-Family Program.

> **Contact**
> Boston Community Capital
> DeWitt Jones, Executive Director
> Eva Clarke, Loan Fund Manager
> 30 Germania Street
> Jamaica Plain, Massachusetts 02130
> Telephone: (617) 522-6768
> Fax: (617) 522-7786

One Percent Downpayment Loan Program
State of Michigan and PMI Mortgage Insurance Company

The One Percent Downpayment Loan Program is a $10 million pilot program to expand homeownership for lower-income Michigan households by broadening the reach of Federal Housing Administration (FHA) financing. The Michigan State Housing Development Authority (MSHDA), which initiated the program, designed it to make FHA financing primarily serving central cities more attractive to traditional lenders, thus broadening the geographic scope. In particular, the program promises to increase homeownership among minorities and single mothers in cities.

Program Administration

MSHDA operates the downpayment loan program in partnership with PMI Mortgage Insurance Company, a national private mortgage insurance company. Homebuyer counseling organizations and private lenders also participate in the administration of the program.

Program Description

The downpayment loan program modifies the requirements for PMI's existing 3 percent downpayment program, allowing lower-income applicants to purchase a home with a conventionally insured first mortgage and a total cash requirement of 1 percent of the price of the house. The first mortgage has a 97 percent loan-to-value ratio, with 28 percent debt coverage required. The second mortgage, funded by the federal HOME program, is a zero-interest, nonamortizing loan that will fund closing costs, prepaid expenses, and the balance of the required downpayment. The maximum second mortgage amount is $5,000, due on sale or if the first mortgage is refinanced. If the home is sold at a loss during the term of the second mortgage, either the full amount of the second mortgage or the amount of the loss—whichever is less—will be forgiven.

To qualify, the borrower's household income cannot exceed 60 percent of the median (in Standard Metropolitan Statistical Areas—SMSAs) or 80 percent of the lowest rural-county median (in non-SMSAs). Debt-to-income ratios of 30 percent for housing payments and 35 percent for total debt are allowed; more liberal ratios can be applied to borrowers who have good credit, a history of stable income, and savings equal to two months of mortgage payments. Participants must receive homebuyer counseling either through approved nonprofit counseling organizations or through the Michigan State University Cooperative Extension Service. Homes must be valued at $60,000 or less and may be single-family homes, townhouses, or condominiums.

The downpayment loan program benefits lenders by helping them meet Community Reinvestment Act lending requirements. In addition, MSHDA pays lenders a fee to provide the low downpayment loans. A standard 1 percent origination fee is allowed on all loans, but for downpayment assistance loans, MSHDA pays an additional 1 percent loan origination fee. The agency also permits lenders to service the loans, which increases their profits. Because the program is designed to reach underserved populations, default rates are expected to be higher than normal; however, the insurance provided by PMI makes the loans more acceptable to lenders.

Funding Sources

Program loans are made by traditional lenders and, as noted, HOME funds provide second mortgage financing.

Contact

Boston Community Capital
DeWitt Jones, Executive Director
Eva Clarke, Loan Fund Manager
30 Germania Street
Jamaica Plain, Massachusetts 02130
Telephone: (617) 522-6768
Fax: (617) 522-7786

Minneapolis/St. Paul HOME Program
Minneapolis and St. Paul, Minnesota

The HOME program helps families who live in St. Paul or Minneapolis public housing or who receive Section 8 rental assistance become homeowners.

Program Participants

The St. Paul Housing Agency and the Family Housing Fund of Minneapolis developed the HOME program in the early 1990s, and the Minneapolis Housing Authority adopted the program several years later. Thompson Associates, Inc., a local real estate consulting firm, administers the program and provides all counseling, education, and support services to program participants.

Program Description

The Minneapolis/St. Paul HOME program offers a combination of intensive, one-on-one counseling and special financing assistance.

Homeownership Counseling. Several times each year, all families living in public housing or receiving Section 8 rental assistance are invited to attend outreach sessions held at various locations throughout the cities of St. Paul and Minneapolis. Attendees are encouraged to sign up for individual counseling at no charge. Participating families work with a counselor who educates them about the opportunities and responsibilities of homeownership and examines the family's income, employment, and credit history. Families who qualify immediately are referred to a real estate agent, who helps them find a home and negotiate a purchase agreement. Families who are unable to qualify during the initial counseling process are assisted in putting together a "work plan" to help resolve barriers to homeownership. Counselors continue to work with families until these barriers are overcome and a home is selected; a follow-up visit to the family's new home is made within six months of closing. Thompson Associates, Inc., provides homeownership education, preliminary loan counseling, and ongoing support and assistance.

Special Financing. The HOME program's special financing includes closing cost loans, equity participation, and downpayment grants. Interest-free closing cost loans of up to $3,000 are payable when the property is sold or the mortgage is paid off. Equity participation is in the form of a deferred loan at 3 percent interest; the loan amount can be up to 10 percent of the acquisition cost, and payment is deferred until the property is sold or the mortgage is paid off. (The interest on the loan does accrue during the deferral period.) Downpayment grants are made for the difference between the FHA minimum downpayment requirement and a $500 cash contribution. This grant is "repaid" by the borrower through various forms of community service credited at $25 per hour. Each participating family contributes approximately $1,200 toward the downpayment, loan application fees, homeowners' insurance, and escrow and prepaid items.

Funding Sources

Funding for the HOME program comes from a partnership formed by the Family Housing Fund of Minneapolis and St. Paul, a locally based private foundation; the cities of St. Paul and Minneapolis; and the St. Paul and Minneapolis public housing agencies. Financial assistance for downpayments and closing costs comes from a pool of funds created by the Family Housing Fund of Minneapolis and St. Paul. Both cities originate the mortgage loans for HOME program families through their mortgage revenue-bond programs, although many buyers choose to use private lenders who sponsor special mortgage programs for first-time borrowers.

Accomplishments

The HOME program is in its ninth year in St. Paul and in its sixth in Minneapolis. Over 210 families have purchased and moved into their first homes. The foreclosure rates are less than 2 percent, and over 50 percent of the families assisted are first-generation homebuyers.

> **Contact**
> Thompson Associates, Inc.
> Missy Staples Thompson, President
> Iris Park Place
> 1885 University Avenue
> Saint Paul, Minnesota 55104
> Telephone: (612) 644-2710
> Fax: (612) 644-3282

Richfield Rediscovered
Richfield, Minnesota

A first-tier suburb of Minneapolis, the city of Richfield has adopted a successful revitalization strategy to address problems created by an aging housing stock. Richfield's housing efforts are targeted differently than most other programs described in this book: instead of focusing on increasing homeownership, Richfield has chosen to stabilize and improve its neighborhoods by creating incentives to increase property values over time. By helping homeowners build new homes to replace substandard structures and remodel to improve aging housing, the city hopes to keep families in the community.

Program Administration

Richfield Rediscovered is administered by Richfield's housing and redevelopment authority.

Program Description

Through Richfield Rediscovered, the city's housing and redevelopment authority buys and demolishes substandard housing to free lots for new construction; conducts a marketing and technical assistance program; and offers deferred loans to encourage homeowners to remodel homes.

The vacant lots are sold to the future homeowners or to developers. New residential construction on these lots must be owner occupied and meet minimum standards for size and amenities. A development agreement between the city and the developer or home-owner details these conditions and stipulates a recommended market value for the finished property. The tax increment on the improved property is used to support the city's new-construction program or in some cases to help fund specific redevelopment projects.

Complementing the new construction is a strategy that encourages homeowners to improve the existing housing stock, most of which was built after World War II. The city provides remodeling advice and offers a deferred, no-interest second mortgage loan for up to 10 percent of remodeling costs (when the remodeling contract is between $30,000 and $50,000), and up to 15 percent (when the costs exceed $50,000). The deferred loan is for-given after 30 years but is payable if the house is sold. The 30-year deferral period is an incentive designed to encourage families to remain in the community.

The technical assistance provided by the city goes beyond remodeling advice. Advisors assist with general cost estimates, provide a remodeling manual, help homeowners under-stand how improvements affect a home's future market value, and provide guidance to secure financing. Mortgage products available to assist homebuyers and remodelers range from tra-ditional FHA loans to transition grants to assist families that must relocate temporarily dur-ing remodeling. Additionally, remodelers may qualify for the "This Old House" program, which defers property tax increases on improvements to the home. (This program, which is described more fully in another section of this volume, was established by the state leg-islature and is implemented at the local level. Central cities and first-tier suburbs are the primary users.) To assist homeowners to locate competent professionals, the housing and redevelopment authority maintains a list of contractors that have been recommended by other Richfield residents. This list and other similar information are available on the city's Web site.

In 1998, under "This Old Apartment" legislation, Richfield initiated a pilot program offering tax incentives for the remodeling of apartment buildings. In an arrangement that parallels the "This Old House" program, owners who remodel apartment buildings that are at least 30 years old are permitted to exclude from their tax calculations for five years the increase in assessed value created by the improvements. The increased valuation is phased in over a second five-year period, for a total of ten years of tax benefits. To qualify, improvements must exceed $5,000 per unit. The pilot program is set to expire in 1999, but the city is asking the state legislature to extend the life of the program to give more apartment owners the chance to participate.

Funding Sources

To launch Richfield Rediscovered, the Richfield housing and redevelopment authority borrowed $1.5 million from reserves in the city's long-term capital improvements fund, then used the monies to finance the acquisition and clearance of deteriorated properties. Local funds are obtained through tax increment financing, which the housing and redevelopment authority sees as one of the "best local tools available."

Accomplishments

The results of Richfield Rediscovered have been impressive: over 100 substandard homes have been demolished to make room for new construction, and nearly 1,000 homes have participated in the remodeling program (out of a total single-family housing stock of less than 12,000). Between 1991 and 1996, the average sale price of a single-family home in Richfield rose from $82,000 to $100,000.

> **Contact**
> Richfield Redevelopment and Housing Authority
> Bruce Nordquist, Manager
> 6700 Portland Avenue South
> Richfield, Minnesota 55423
> Telephone: (612) 861-9777
> Fax: (612) 861-8974
> Web site: www.ci.richfield.mn.us

Blanket Mortgages for Limited Equity Cooperatives
New York, New York

New York City's program for the financing of blanket mortgages for limited equity cooperatives is one of the few initiatives of its kind in the nation. First implemented in the early 1990s, the program provides homeownership opportunities for moderate-income families. In a city of mostly renters, the program works to revitalize and stabilize working-class neighborhoods by providing below-market-rate financing from tax-exempt mortgage revenue bonds for the underlying (or "blanket") mortgages of limited equity cooperatives on city-owned sites.

Program Administration

The New York City Housing Development Corporation (HDC) operates the blanket mortgage program, working in cooperation with the city's department of housing preservation and development (HPD); the State of New York Mortgage Agency; Chase Manhattan Bank, N.A.; and Fannie Mae.

Program Description and Funding Sources

HDC provides a 30-year, permanent, first blanket mortgage at below-market rates from the proceeds of tax-exempt bond issues privately placed with Fannie Mae. All bonds to date have received an AA rating from Moody's Investors Services, and none have defaulted. HPD provides an interest-free construction loan, which converts to a subordinate permanent loan. The city has also sold land for development, then taken back a subordinate purchase money mortgage that represented the difference between the cash price and the appraised value of the land. HPD loans are repaid only from the appreciation on the sale of a unit; 50 percent of the profit is returned to HPD. Projects may also qualify for a 25-year real estate tax exemption provided by the city.

The State of New York Mortgage Agency provides credit enhancement by fully insuring the HDC permanent mortgage. Chase Manhattan Bank, N.A., has served as the lead construction lender for these projects.

Purchasers must meet income limits for respective household size. Price limits on an initial purchase equal 110 percent of the average area purchase price for new construction in a targeted area; if the purchaser decides to sell in the future, the subsequent purchase price must be no more than 110 percent of the average area purchase price for existing projects in target areas. The unit must be the primary residence of the purchaser and may not be sublet. HDC mortgages cannot be used to fund commercial or other nonresidential space.

Accomplishments

The first projects financed were five low-rise cooperatives in Brooklyn and the South Bronx. In 1994, HDC funded Maple Court, a 135-unit mid-rise cooperative in East Harlem. North General Hospital, a not-for-profit health care provider and the area's largest employer, sponsored the project. Because of the success of Maple Court, a second project—Maple Plaza, also sponsored by North General—is underway. Modeled after the first mid-rise, the cooperative will have 154 units with from one to three bedrooms. The developers of the Maple Court and Maple Plaza projects have a successful track record creating affordable-housing projects.

Families purchasing units in these cooperatives receive significant benefits. The average upfront cash requirement at Maple Plaza is $6,657. Since the cooperative is financed by a blanket mortgage, closing costs (such as lenders' points and attorneys' fees) are eliminated. The average monthly maintenance charges are affordable for families with moderate incomes. On the basis of common affordability ratios, HDC estimates that the apartments are affordable to families earning less than 90 percent of the city's median income.

Contact

New York City Housing Development Corporation
Charles Brass, Vice President of Development
75 Maiden Lane, Eighth Floor
New York, New York 10038
Telephone: (212) 344-8080
Fax: (212) 269-6121

Housing Occupancy Initiative
Rochester, New York

Rochester, New York's Housing Occupancy Initiative (HOI) coordinates the activities of multiple housing assistance providers and packages a variety of federal, state, and local resources to support citywide housing and community development goals. HOI has created a structure for organizing a variety of funding streams and "mixing and matching" them so that they make sense to the consumer. Under HOI's multiprogram approach, the city's vacant housing is the focal point for the creation of affordable-housing opportunities.

In 1993, Rochester began a total quality management effort to respond more effectively to affordable-housing needs and reduce the number of vacant residential structures. A 30-day work group—the Housing Occupancy Team—helped the city craft its first official housing policy, which established a commitment to (1) creating homeownership and affordable-housing opportunities for low- and moderate-income households and (2) opening suburban housing markets to low-income households. With these goals in mind, the team developed HOI.

Program Administration

The Housing Occupancy Team consisted of representatives from nonprofit developers, the Rochester Housing Authority, city government, and the Greater Rochester Housing Partnership; though the team is no longer officially in force, its members bring significant resources to the table to help meet the initiative's goals. The city of Rochester administers HOI.

Program Description

HOI has five programs, each of which is described briefly in the subsections that follow.

Vacant Building Information System. A key HOI information management innovation is the Vacant Building Information System, a comprehensive, computerized inventory that tracks the status of all vacant properties in the city. Water-meter readers use handheld computerized devices to collect the data. A centralized reporting system also tracks HOI properties in various stages of redevelopment, measuring progress on the basis of housing characteristics, development and sales status, buyer profiles, and geographic area.

Home Rochester. Under the Home Rochester program, long-term vacant properties are acquired, rehabilitated, and resold to low- and moderate-income homebuyers by one for-profit and 14 nonprofit developers. Thirteen of the nonprofit developers are HUD-designated community housing development organizations. The program targets single-family homes (predominantly HUD foreclosures) and generally operates within the Rochester Enterprise Community Zone. Development costs typically fall between $70,000 and $85,000, with development subsidies averaging $30,000 to $35,000.

Home Replacement. HOI aggressively targets the demolition of vacant homes when rehabilitation is not feasible. New infill homes are then constructed by new homeowners through private financing, with soft second mortgages of up to $22,500 available to income-eligible homebuyers from state housing authority funds, Urban Development Action Grant (UDAG) repayments, and local bonds. Since the vast majority of the dilapidated housing stock is privately owned, the city has refined its demolition code and procedures to encourage owners to rehabilitate or demolish these structures. Owners are also encouraged to donate deteriorated properties to avoid demolition costs, which would otherwise be added to their property tax bills. By encouraging donations, the city avoids lengthy legal proceedings and speeds up the conversion of derelict properties into new, safe, and affordable homes.

Subdivision Redevelopment. To meet broad community development and neighborhood revitalization goals, HOI encourages subdivision redevelopment. Target blocks or neighborhoods are chosen to act as catalysts for the surrounding area. The city or other partners acquire the land for redevelopment and demolish any dilapidated structures. The city then puts into place the necessary physical infrastructure and resubdivides the lots into usable parcels. During the construction phase, jobs are created for area minority contractors. In addition, a youth job-training program is put into place to give at-risk city high school students the opportunity to gain experience in a building trade by working in the field with contractors.

Development costs for new single-family homes are typically between $80,000 and $90,000. Subsidies of $22,500 (in the form of a soft second mortgage from state housing authority funds and UDAG repayments) are available to income-eligible homebuyers in the subdivision redevelopment program.

Home Owner Occupancy Program. The Home Owner Occupancy Program (HOOP) evolved from a home reoccupation program operated by HOI. Having determined that most of the formerly vacant houses whose new owners were receiving assistance from HOI had come from HUD's FHA-foreclosed inventory, the city intervened directly with HUD to market properties suitable for owner occupancy. The city, in turn, would purchase the homes at a 30 percent discount, which would be passed along to the buyer, minus the real estate commission. (With the commission factored in, the buyer purchases the home at a 23 per-cent discount).

Each week, HUD reviews its new foreclosed inventory with the city. The city then inspects eligible houses, determines the rehabilitation costs, and provides financing pack-ages for interested buyers. The city advertises these selected properties and has enlisted the participation of area realtors to market the homes. At the closing, the city acquires each house from HUD (in order to place an owner-occupancy clause on the deed), then transfers it to the new owner, who must agree to live in the property for a minimum of three years.

Funding Sources

Rochester combines resources from HOME, HOPE-3, local funding, the state housing authority, and UDAG repayments to finance its programs.

Accomplishments

First Place of Rochester was HOI's first subdivision redevelopment project, and another is underway. The partners in the First Place project included First Federal Saving and Loan Association, the North East Block Club Alliance, the City of Rochester School District, the New York State Affordable Housing Corporation (NYSAHC), and the Federal Home Loan Bank (FHLB) of New York. The average subsidy per housing unit from NYSAHC and FHLB was about $33,800; all the 52 new homeowners earn less than 80 percent of the area median income, and nine earn less than 50 percent of the area median. Spin-off investments include new infill construction on adjoining blocks, revitalization of a nearby retail plaza, and 17 new units of affordable rental housing. As an added benefit, the area has experienced a sig-nificant decrease in crime. In partnership with First Federal Bank, the city of Buffalo is work-ing to replicate the subdivision redevelopment program.

HOI has received national recognition from Public Technology, Inc., the National Affordable Housing Training Institute, the National Association of Housing and Redevelop-ment Officials, the National Social Compact of Banks and Lending Institutions, the U.S. Conference of Mayors, and HUD.

In HOOP's first year of operation, 65 homes were sold. The program has won a John J. Guenther Blue Ribbon Practices in Community Development Award from HUD and a Best Practices Award from the U.S. Conference of Mayors.

Contact

Rochester Department of Community Development
Bureau of Housing
Linda Luxenberg, Director
30 Church Street
Rochester, New York 14614
Telephone: (716) 428-6814
Fax: (716) 428-6229

North Carolina State Employees' Credit Union Programs for Homebuyers
State of North Carolina

According to the bylaws of the North Carolina State Employees' Credit Union (SECU), the organization is chartered, in part, to provide an opportunity for members to improve their lives, both economically and socially. Because SECU recognizes that many people face obstacles when they consider buying their first home, the credit union operates two programs to finance members' home purchases: the First-Time Homebuyers Program and the Homestead Mortgage Program.

Program Administration

SECU operates and funds the First-Time Homebuyers Program and the Homestead Mortgage Program.

Program Description

Both of SECU's financing packages provide first-time homebuyers with 100 percent financing for the purchase of a new home. A first-time homebuyer is defined as one who has not owned any interest in a home (other than a mobile home) in the previous three years.

First-Time Homebuyers Program. The First-Time Homebuyers Program makes loans for the purchase of a primary residence that must be located within reasonable distance of the borrower's place of work. The property to be financed must be a freestanding, traditionally built home: factory-built homes; condominiums and townhouses; and duplexes and triplexes are not acceptable collateral for a first-time homebuyers loan. Financed homes must be located on lots that front a publicly maintained road, although easements and privately maintained roads may be considered acceptable.

The First-Time Homebuyers Program requires an appraisal performed specifically for SECU. The SECU loan is limited to 100 percent of the appraisal amount or the home's purchase price, whichever is less. The maximum allowable loan is $125,000 and must be in the form of either a two-year or five-year adjustable rate mortgage (ARM). Closing costs must come from members' savings and may not be obtained through a gift. (SECU estimates that the closing costs for a $50,000 loan are approximately $1,500.) Qualifying ratios are 30 percent of gross income for the mortgage payment and 40 percent for total obligations. Private mortgage insurance is not required.

Interest on the two-year ARM is 4 percent above the most recent one-year Treasury Bill auction average. After three years, a borrower who has not been delinquent on this or any other SECU loan may request a new appraisal. Depending on the loan-to-value ratio with the new appraisal, the margin may be reduced to 3.5 percent or 2.5 percent.

Potential borrowers are required to have worked for their current employer for at least 12 months and must have good credit, as established by a 12-month credit report.

Nonspousal income used to qualify for the loan will be considered only if the coapplicant will also be a co-owner and -occupant. During the first three years of the loan, borrowers are not eligible for any unsecured borrowing (including credit cards) from the credit union. Loans must be repaid by payroll deduction—or, if payroll deduction is not available, by the transfer of funds from a SECU account. SECU first-time homebuyer loans are not assumable under any circumstances.

Homestead Mortgage Program. Designed to provide 100 percent financing to credit union members who are unable to qualify for a first-time homebuyers loan, the Homestead Mortgage Program has somewhat less restrictive guidelines than the First-Time Home-buyers Program. Like the First-Time Homebuyers Program, the Homestead Mortgage Program requires that borrowers use their loan only for the first-time purchase of a traditionally built, single-family home to be used as their primary residence. Any major repairs required must be made prior to closing. In addition to being creditworthy members of SECU, bor-rowers must be current on all existing obligations and able to explain adequately any aber-rations in their credit records.

The maximum loan amount under the Homestead Mortgage Program is $75,000, with an additional $1,500 available to assist with closing costs, bringing the total loan amount available to $76,500. Qualifying ratios are 35 percent of gross income for the mortgage pay-ment and 40 percent for total obligations. Private mortgage insurance is not required under the Homestead Mortgage Program.

Because the homestead program is more flexible—and therefore higher risk—than the First-Time Homebuyers Program, financing terms are somewhat less favorable. The margin on the homestead mortgage loan is 4.5 percent above the most recent one-year Treasury Bill auction average and is not subject to future reduction. The interest rate is subject to adjustment every two years, with a maximum biannual adjustment of 1 percent. The adjust-ment cap on the life of the loan is 8 percent, and the floor rate is 6.5 percent. Like the first-time homebuyers loan, the homestead mortgage loan must be repaid by payroll deduction or fund transfer, and accounts from which funds are transferred must be held with the credit union.

Funding Sources

SECU's board of directors has approved commitments of $125 million to the First-Time Homebuyers Program and $15 million to the Homestead Mortgage Program. SECU has close to 600,000 members and total assets (as of July 1998) of approximately $5.4 billion.

Accomplishments

As of April 1998, there were 1,213 active first-time homebuyer loans, with a total worth of $88.5 million, and 113 active homestead mortgage loans, with a total value of $6.6 million.

Contact
First-Time Homebuyers Program and Homestead
Mortgage Program
State Employees' Credit Union
P.O. Box 25279
Raleigh, North Carolina 27611
Telephone: (919) 839-5018
Fax: (919) 839-5289

Neighborhood Improvement Program
Akron, Ohio

The city of Akron's Neighborhood Improvement Program is a comprehensive housing strategy to strengthen neighborhoods and maintain housing affordability.

Participants

Akron's department of planning and urban development is the lead agency for the Neighborhood Improvement Program. So that homes can qualify for low-interest repair loans, the city health department supports the program through property inspections and identification of code violations prior to purchase. Participating lenders include Bank One, Fifth-Third Bank, First Federal Savings, First National Bank of Ohio, National City Bank, and Society Bank.

Program Description

Instead of offering assistance for individual properties scattered around the city, Akron's Neighborhood Improvement Program combines mandatory housing code enforcement; technical and financial assistance for rehabilitation; public improvements; and demolition and new construction in selected neighborhoods.

Participating neighborhoods are selected on the basis of physical decline, high levels of owner occupancy, and resident incomes sufficient to make some—but not necessarily all—local investments. Each neighborhood must have definable boundaries and between 400 and 700 structures. Smaller neighborhoods, with between 20 and 80 structures, may participate if 60 percent of the property owners sign a petition to do so.

The program makes a number of resources available to homeowners: for example, homeowners may receive grants and loans to help pay for major repairs, and owners of rental housing may receive matching grants to correct housing code violations (grant amounts are based on the number of rental units in the structure).

The health department inspects all structures being considered for grant assistance, and all violations noted must be corrected. After the health department inspection, a city rehabilitation specialist reinspects the property, writes detailed cost estimates for repairs, and provides assistance with the selection of a contractor—all at no charge. The city improves streets, sidewalks, curbs, sewers, and lighting in the neighborhood where necessary.

The city has two additional means of promoting homeownership in targeted neighborhoods: through new construction and through the Home Purchase Incentive Program. New construction is undertaken in cooperation with the Urban Neighborhood Development Corporation, which contracts with local builders to construct well-built homes on infill lots. Homes are currently priced below $60,00 and are designed to blend in with the existing neighborhood architecture. Each home has three bedrooms, one and one-half baths, a full basement, a two-car garage, landscaping, and a concrete driveway.

The Home Purchase Incentive Program provides several forms of assistance for buyers in targeted neighborhoods, including $5,000 grants that can be applied toward a downpayment or toward rehabilitation. The downpayment grant must be matched by the homebuyer, dollar for dollar, up to a limit of $2,000. The remaining amount, up to $3,000, must be applied to rehabilitation costs. Homebuyers can obtain low-interest loans of about 6 percent for repair costs that exceed the initial $3,000 grant or for general improvements. Low-income buyers may also be eligible for a deferred payment, no-interest loan of up to $3,000 for home rehabilitation needs identified during the inspection process. Special mortgage financing packages available from participating lending institutions feature downpayment requirements as low as 5 percent, reduced mortgage-interest rates, and reduced closing costs.

To participate in the purchase incentive program, a buyer must select a home in a targeted neighborhood. After the property is inspected by the health department, the buyer meets with a counselor to discuss program requirements. The sales agreement and a list of housing code violations are taken to a participating lending institution for mortgage financing. After the loan is approved, the buyer signs a promissory note and mortgage deed committing to occupancy within three months and completion of repairs within 18 months. The city provides the downpayment grant at the closing. The city then reinspects the property and writes a detailed cost estimate for repairs. Rehabilitation grant funds are then released and, if necessary, a low-interest loan is processed. To avoid repaying the rehabilitation grant, the buyer must reside in the property for at least five years after the repair work is completed.

Akron also administers several citywide programs that can be used within the targeted neighborhoods. Through the city's Waiver Demolition Program, structures that are beyond repair may be torn down without charge. The Minor Home Repair Program assists very low income elderly people and people with disabilities through $2,000 grants to repair serious housing problems. The Emergency Shelter Grant Program funds transitional and residential programs for a variety of urgent needs.

Funding Sources

Akron's housing programs are funded by Community Development Block Grant funds, federal HOME funds, the Emergency Shelter Grant Program, and local lending institutions. Public improvement funds are supported by a local income tax.

Accomplishments

Over 28 neighborhoods have participated in the Neighborhood Improvement Program, encompassing more than 15,000 homes and apartments.

> **Contact**
> Akron Department of Planning and Urban Development
> Warren L. Woolford, Director
> 161 South High Street, Suite 201
> Akron, Ohio 44308
> Telephone: (330) 375-2980
> Fax: (330) 375-2434

Cleveland Housing Network, Inc.: Lease-Purchase of Low-Income Housing Tax Credit Homes Cleveland, Ohio

The scattered-site lease-purchase program of the Cleveland Housing Network (CHN), Inc., in existence since 1981, is the oldest and largest program of its kind in the country. The program not only offers very low-income families an opportunity to buy their own homes but also salvages single-family houses that are badly in need of fundamental repair. In addition, CHN's efforts strengthen inner-city real estate markets where the full cost of renovating aging housing stock cannot be supported within market constraints.

Participants

CHN is an umbrella organization for 17 community-based organizations whose purpose is to develop a continuum of affordable housing and homeownership options for low- and moderate-income families in vibrant and economically viable neighborhoods. Operating with a 55-person staff, CHN has grown into a multimillion-dollar real estate business whose operations are of major consequence to the continued economic health of the neighborhoods of Cleveland.

CHN works with a number of partners to finance lease-purchase projects: the city of Cleveland, the state of Ohio, the Federal Home Loan Bank, the Ohio Community Development Finance Fund, the Ohio Housing Finance Agency, the Enterprise Foundation, Charter One Savings Bank, and private corporations (through the National Equity Fund).

In addition to the lease-purchase program, CHN operates two rehabilitation programs for single-family homes, a transitional housing program, and weatherization and energy conservation programs; it also offers welfare-to-work and other family support services. CHN's member community development corporations are responsible for overseeing the housing programs in their respective neighborhoods and for developing program policies and procedures.

Program Description

Using federal low-income housing tax credits (LIHTCs), the lease-purchase program funds property acquisition and construction or rehabilitation of single-family homes, then enters into lease-purchase agreements with income-qualified households. The program emphasizes comprehensive, sustainable rehabilitation: for example, vinyl siding and replacement windows are required on all homes. In addition to handling the financing necessary for the acquisition, rehabilitation, and construction phases, CHN manages the financial resources for replacement and the capital reserves for major home system repairs for the 15-year life of each project.

In addition to meeting maximum income thresholds (determined by the criteria set for tenants of units qualifying for the tax credits), prospective homeowners must undergo an extensive screening process. Participants' responsibilities, detailed in an annual lease agreement, include provision of routine maintenance during the period of the lease (lease violations can result in eviction). Annual rent increases cover increased operating expenses.

Sometime between the first and seventh year of the lease, the tenant may enter into a right of first refusal agreement, which gives the tenant the option to purchase the home at the end of the 15-year period required to achieve compliance with the regulations governing the tax credits. Between the time the agreement is executed and the end of the compliance period, title to the home is held by a limited partnership controlled by a local nonprofit development corporation. At the end of the 15 years, the nonprofit assumes ownership of the house, a transaction that takes between six and 12 months, including negotiation of a reduction of the public debt. Once the nonprofit takes ownership, the tenant can exercise the right of first refusal; the sale price—"all the remaining debt plus exit taxes"—will be much lower than the original development costs for the home.

Few restrictions apply once the home is purchased. If a new home is sold within five years, owners are generally required to sell to another low- or moderate-income household. There are no restrictions for rehabilitated homes. Program participants can expect that the cost of operating the home (mortgage, utilities, and maintenance expenses) will be the same or slightly less than the rent payments they had been making.

Funding Sources

The lease-purchase program is financed through the syndication of LIHTCs, resulting in a 68 percent equity contribution that leverages 32 percent in private and public investment. Because the city of Cleveland and the state of Ohio contribute reduced first mortgage rates and funds for soft second mortgages, monthly payments are kept as low as possible.

Specifically, the city of Cleveland provides both interim and permanent debt through federal HOME and Community Development Block Grant funds. The state of Ohio allocates LIHTCs, energy conservation grants, and other grants for the lease-purchase program. Participating banks provide private construction financing and private permanent financing. The Federal Home Loan Bank and the Ohio Community Development Finance Fund have provided interest-rate subsidies, and the Enterprise Foundation has provided a flexible line of working capital. Equity investment for recent projects came predominantly from Cleveland-based corporations and was organized by the Enterprise Social Investment Corporations and the National Equity Fund, tax syndicators affiliated with the Enterprise Foundation and the Local Initiatives Support Corporation, respectively. A bridge loan covering multiyear equity pay-ins from corporate investors is provided by Charter One Saving Bank and the Ohio Housing Finance Agency.

CHN has an annual operating budget of $23 million. In addition to the program financing sources listed previously and other grants and contracts, CHN receives annual contributions from over 75 organizations.

Accomplishments

Since 1981, the lease-purchase program has generated over $77 million in direct capital investment in Cleveland's neighborhoods, allowing the construction of over 120 new houses and the rehabilitation of over 1,000 scattered-site homes.

In most lease-purchase markets, the pattern of private investment has followed CHN's lead; in a number of neighborhoods, markets have strengthened to the point where the lease-purchase model has been displaced altogether by conventional sales products.

Contact
Akron Department of Planning and Urban Development
Warren L. Woolford, Director
161 South High Street, Suite 201
Akron, Ohio 44308
Telephone: (330) 375-2980
Fax: (330) 375-2434

Downpayment Assistance Program
Memphis, Tennessee

Memphis's most important initiative to strengthen homeownership is its Downpayment Assistance program (DPA), which is targeted to low- and moderate-income buyers and to police officers who purchase in designated areas.

Program Administration

The city of Memphis administers the DPA program with the participation of local lenders.

Program Description

The DPA program offers low- and moderate-income homebuyers up to $3,500 in downpayment assistance (in the form of deferred payment, second mortgage loans) for new or existing homes anywhere within the city of Memphis. This amount increases to $10,000 for homes in targeted neighborhoods, such as those within the city's designated empowerment community, or those located in areas designated for revitalization. Residents of public housing who qualify to purchase a home may also receive up to $10,000 in downpayment assistance for a house anywhere in the city. Police officers may qualify for up to $15,000 in downpayment assistance for home purchases in targeted census tracts.

Funding Sources

The DPA program is funded by federal HOME and Community Development Block Grant funds and by the city of Memphis.

Accomplishments

Between 1992 and 1997, over 4,500 first-time homebuyers received assistance from the DPA program, and over $6 million in public funds leveraged over $140 million in private mortgage money. Strong private sector support for the program is evidenced by the participation of about 40 mortgage lenders. In 1996, Memphis received national recognition for the DPA program: the Association of Local Housing Finance Agencies designated it as the HOME project of the year.

> ### Contact
> City of Memphis
> Division of Housing and Community Development
> Harry Greene, Director
> 701 North Main Street, Suite 100
> Memphis, Tennessee 38107-2311
> Telephone: (901) 576-7300
> Fax: (901) 576-7318

Walk-to-Work Program
Milwaukee, Wisconsin

Select Milwaukee, a communitywide information clearinghouse that works with nonprofit organizations, the private sector, and the city, has developed partnerships with Milwaukee employers to create affordable homeownership through the Walk-to-Work Program: under this program, employers assist employees with the upfront costs of purchasing a home in a neighborhood within walking distance of their place of work.

Program Participants and Administration

As of March 1998, 14 employers had participated in the Walk-to-Work Program. Select Milwaukee handles all paperwork, prepares documentation, and coordinates the homeownership benefit at the loan closing.

Program Description

The employee must purchase a home within designated areas near the work location. Benefit amounts are determined by the employer and typically range up to $3,000. The benefit can be offered as a loan, a forgivable loan, a salary advance, or a grant.

Select Milwaukee tailors the program to each employer's needs, addressing issues such as employee eligibility, level and type of benefit, selection of targeted neighborhoods, promotional strategies, and tax and ERISA (Employee Retirement Income Security Act of 1974) implications. Employees work directly with Select Milwaukee and are offered comprehensive home-purchase services and referrals to realty professionals.

The benefits of the program are wide ranging, including neighborhood improvements, improved employee attraction and retention, shorter commutes, and reductions in air pollution.

Funding Sources

The Wisconsin Department of Transportation funds the administrative costs of the Walk-to-Work Program, and participating employers provide the employee benefits. Select Milwaukee may provide additional downpayment assistance to income-eligible employees.

Accomplishments

So far, more than 200 homes have been purchased with assistance from the Walk-to-Work Program. Select Milwaukee estimates that every dollar of an employer's investment in the program yields $22 in additional neighborhood investment.

Contact

Select Milwaukee
Raymond Schmidt, Executive Director
2209 North Dr. Martin Luther King Jr. Drive
Milwaukee, Wisconsin 53212
Telephone: (414) 562-5070
Fax: (414) 562-5072

Rural Community Assistance Corporation
Western United States

As part of a wide range of housing and environmental services offered throughout the western United States to improve the quality of life in rural communities, the Rural Community Assistance Corporation (RCAC), an independent nonprofit organization, provides funding for the development of affordable housing throughout the region. Using partnerships and technical assistance, RCAC provides access to resources to increase the availability of safe and affordable housing and to improve water quality and the management of wastewater and solid waste. RCAC has funded projects in California, Colorado, Oregon, Nevada, Washington, Arizona, and Hawaii.

Participants

In its efforts to help community-based organizations and rural governments increase their problem-solving capacity, RCAC has created strong partnerships with the federal government, local nonprofits, rural governments, corporations, and foundations.

Program Description

RCAC's four major programs are described in the subsections that follow.

Housing Development Loan Pool. RCAC maintains a low-interest loan pool for the development of affordable housing and community facilities in rural areas. Short-term financing for up to three years is available to nonprofit housing developers. Loans may be used for land purchase, site improvement, predevelopment costs, purchase of improved land, new construction, or rehabilitation. Long-term financing (up to 15 years) is available for acquisition, rehabilitation, and bridge financing for low-income housing tax credit projects. RCAC originates and services the long-term loans, which are sold to the Local Initiatives Managed Asset Corporation.

While the primary borrowers are nonprofit housing developers, the beneficiaries are low- and very low-income rural residents. The housing made possible by the loan fund often represents a family's first secure shelter.

Blended-Rate Mortgage Demonstration Program. Much of RCAC's lending is in conjunction with single-family-home loans offered under Rural Development Section 502. In response to reductions in that program, RCAC is conducting a "blended rate mortgage" demonstration program that combines RCAC dollars with Section 502 funds, Norwest Bank mortgages, and Federal Home Loan Bank Affordable Housing Program funds. Predevelopment loans carry an interest rate of 6.5 percent, with a two-point origination fee.

Technical Assistance. RCAC offers technical assistance to both private and public organizations, collaborating with the Neighborhood Reinvestment Corporation and other providers of technical assistance to sponsor training institutes in small markets throughout the West. RCAC also provides a number of housing-related publications to rural borrowers and funders.

Infrastructure Loans. Because the condition of such systems can be a major barrier to housing and community development in rural areas, RCAC provides short-term financing for improvements to small water or wastewater systems. The loans may be used for purchase of unimproved land, predevelopment expenses, and system improvement costs. RCAC has also initiated lending programs for child care facilities and environmental infrastructure.

Funding Sources

RCAC obtains capital from corporations, foundations, and government agencies. Major funders include the Ford Foundation, Bank of America, the Rural Development Intermediary

Relending Program of the U.S. Department of Agriculture, and Sisters of the Holy Cross. No individual investments are accepted.

Accomplishments

As of September 1995, RCAC's loan fund had closed 53 loans totaling $11.7 million and had leveraged funds to produce 1,820 units of affordable housing.

Future Plans

RCAC is exploring the possibility of lending for health care facilities and long-term care facilities.

Contact

Rural Community Assistance Corporation
2125 Nineteenth Street, Suite 203
Sacramento, California 95818
Telephone: (916) 447-9832
Fax: (916) 447-2878

Notes

1 Fannie Mae National Housing Survey, July 16, 1998. www.fanniemae.com/news/housing survey/1998_full_nhs.html

2 Joint Center for Housing Studies, Harvard University, *The State of the Nation's Housing 1997* (Cambridge, Mass.: Joint Center for Housing Studies, 1997), 18–19.

3 In this volume, the term *minority* refers to African Americans and Hispanics.

4 Denise DiPasquale and Edward L. Glaeser, *Incentives and Social Capital: Are Homeowners Better Citizens?* Working Paper W97-3 (Cambridge, Mass.: Joint Center for Housing Studies, Harvard University, December 1997), 1.

5 Cited in Kent W. Colton and David A. Crowe, "Is There Sufficient Research to Determine Housing Policy?" (paper presented at the midyear meeting of the American Real Estate and Economics Association, Washington, D.C., 1998), 12.

6 Joint Center for Housing Studies, Harvard University, "Towards a Targeted Homeownership Tax Credit" (paper prepared for the Center on Urban and Metropolitan Policy, The Brookings Institution, Washington, D.C., January 1999), 1.

7 Department of Housing and Urban Development, *Cuomo Welcomes Record Sales of New Homes*, press release, January 6, 1999.

8 Joint Center for Housing Studies, Harvard University, *The State of the Nation's Housing 1998* (Cambridge, Mass.: Joint Center for Housing Studies, 1998), 1.

9 The overall lending data are for the period 1993–1996. Joint Center for Housing Studies, *Nation's Housing 1998*, 1.

10 Department of Housing and Urban Development, *New Trends in American Homeownership* (Washington, D.C.: HUD, June 1996), 28.

11 The overall lending data are for the period 1993–1996. Joint Center for Housing Studies, *Nation's Housing 1998*, 8.

12 "Homeownership Partnership Grows into Solid Resource," *Affordable Housing Finance Special Report: Home Buyer Programs* (summer 1998): 1, 15.

13 HUD, *New Trends*, 28.

2

Increasing Homeownership by Helping Families Save

For nearly 150 years—through the Homestead Act, the home mortgage interest deduction, the GI Bill, capital gains legislation, and the creation of tax-saving individual retirement accounts (IRAs)—federal policies have encouraged the accumulation of individual assets.[1] Because most modern-day savings incentives such as IRAs and the home mortgage interest deduction operate through the tax system, they are either not effective in encouraging saving or investment among low-income groups, or they are not available at all because the marginal tax rates of low-income citizens are too low to enable them to take advantage of the programs.[2]

Overview

At least three efforts have been made in recent times to create special-purpose savings accounts to help low- and moderate-income households achieve homeownership. Under the Turnkey III public housing program of the late 1960s, aspiring tenant-buyers could earn credit toward a downpayment on a unit on the basis of the value of "sweat equity" they contributed toward maintaining their own unit. Turnkey III managed to produce just 263 projects with 6,010 units, only 18 percent of which were ever sold to tenant buyers; the rest became part of the low-rent public housing inventory for lack of qualified buyers. (The high interest rates of the 1970s made it very difficult for low-income families in public housing to get a mortgage, even with their equity credits.)[3]

The second effort, the Family Self-Sufficiency program (FSS), was developed in 1990 by HUD. Under HUD regulations, wage increases normally trigger rent increases. FSS puts varying portions of wage increases into special escrow accounts instead.[4] Participants can make partial withdrawals from the accounts for expenditures that will help them prepare for the future, such as paying college tuition or buying a car so they can get to work. Participants have full access to the funds in their accounts once they successfully complete the self-sufficiency program. The FSS program is important because it indicates that when properly motivated, low-income people respond positively to work and savings incentives. In 1998, the average balance in the escrow accounts for the 35,000 families that had been enrolled in the program for at least 14 months was $2,267.[5]

Finally, in 1996, the Federal Housing Finance Board (FHFB)—the safety and soundness regulator for the nation's savings and loan associations—amended the regulations for its Affordable Housing Program (AHP) to permit member banks to match up to 3:1 a first-time homebuyer's savings for a downpayment and closing costs. Participating households must have incomes at or below 80 percent of the median area income and must complete a counseling program for first-time homebuyers. If the property is sold within the first five years after purchase, a pro rated portion of the AHP funds must be repaid.[6]

The FHFB initiative represents a better way of helping potential homebuyers overcome one of the biggest hurdles to buying a home—the lack of cash for a downpayment. Instead of deferred-payment second mortgages or high-risk 100 percent first mortgages—both of which enable families to buy a home without placing any cash of their own at risk —the FHFB program prepares households for the responsibilities of homeownership by (1) encouraging them to reduce consumption in favor of saving and (2) enabling them to build some wealth right from the start.

Several regional home loan banks have established pilot programs for member thrifts; two of these programs can be used to illustrate the broad potential of savings incentives. The Federal Home Loan Bank of New York allocated $1 million in AHP funds for member banks to match households' savings on a 3:1 basis, up to a maximum bank contribution of $5,000. Each participating bank can enroll up to 25 households per funding cycle, and homebuyers must achieve their savings goals within 24 months.[7] The Home$tart Plus program of the Federal Home Loan Bank of Seattle targets working families who live in public housing and participate in HUD's FSS program. Participants must complete a counseling program in homeownership and money management and are then eligible for 2:1 matches of up to $10,000.[8]

Although previous welfare legislation discouraged savings, national welfare reforms and federal waivers granted to several states not only permit but encourage individuals receiving time-limited cash assistance to begin saving regularly for specific purposes—such as to buy a home, to pay for postsecondary or vocational education or training, or to cope with family emergencies. In California and Virginia, for example, families on public assistance may accumulate savings of up to $5,000 without jeopardizing their benefits. In addition to exempting the cash value of life insurance policies, South Carolina allows two-parent families to accumulate $2,500 in assets and to receive as much as $400 a year in interest and dividends. South Dakota and Minnesota, among other states, allow children whose parents receive public assistance to have up to $1,000 in individual savings accounts. The new rules incorporated in welfare reform protect the eligibility status of people *with* assets and also have the potential to help them *build* assets.

Savings incentive programs—generically referred to as individual development accounts (IDAs) and originally championed by social work professor Michael Sherraden[9]—offer a powerful vehicle for democratizing tax-driven incentives like IRAs by creating direct savings incentives that work for low-income, low-tax-bracket households. While these asset-building programs go by various names, all are integral to the community-building efforts of the grass-roots organizations that administer them, and all are carried out in partnership with participating financial institutions. A key feature of all IDAs is that every dollar an individual saves is matched by a community group, foundation, faith-based institution, or government.[10] Another distinguishing feature is that participants are required to enroll in an economic literacy program, the specifics of which vary from program to program. Because IDAs are designed to help low-income, low-wealth individuals build both financial and human capital, the programs typically limit withdrawals to three purposes: buying a house, getting an education, or starting a business. Permitted uses vary somewhat, however, from program to program.[11]

Welfare reform is encouraging the creation of even more IDA programs: federal legislation authorizes states to create community-based IDA programs with Temporary Assistance to Needy Family (TANF) block grant funds and to disregard all IDA savings in determining eligibility for means-tested government assistance.[12] To reinforce the traditional values of work and individual responsibility, the legislation provides that only earned income can be saved and matched in IDAs; it also designates nonprofit, community-based organizations as custodians of IDA accounts and restricts the use of IDA balances to education, homeownership, and business capitalization.[13] By mid-1998, less than two years after President Clinton signed the new welfare legislation, at least 25 states had already included IDAs in their welfare reform plans,[14] and several states are using portions of their TANF block grant surpluses to provide matching funds for local IDA programs.

In addition to the approximately 100 community organizations across the country that have initiated IDA programs, at least nine states have enacted IDA programs.[15] The Oklahoma Department of Human Services has announced a $400,000 IDA program for TANF recipients, and the Virginia legislature has allocated $500,000 for the same purpose.[16] Iowa expects to create 10,000 IDAs and provide $1 million in matching funds by 2000. In Massachusetts, Michigan, and Oregon, workfare programs combine IDAs with wage subsidies to employers hiring welfare recipients. Public benefits, such as food stamp payments under previous welfare guidelines, are used to provide the subsidies. Under these "full employment plans," after a welfare recipient has been on the job 30 days the employer is required to pay $1 for every hour worked into an IDA for the employee, who may use the money in the account to pursue further education or job training.[17]

Other states have begun IDA programs outside their welfare systems. The Tennessee Network for Community Economic Development administers an IDA pilot in 12 communities. In Pennsylvania, lawmakers allocated $1.2 million to an IDA initiative, administered by community-based organizations, that will match up to $600 over a two-year period for each account for about 1,900 families.

The Indiana legislature committed $6.5 million in general revenues over four years to match participant savings 3:1, and 22 community development corporations around the state have received grants to establish 800 IDAs.[18] The legislature also provided an additional $500,000 a year in tax credits to private contributors to the IDA program—an example that the National Governors' Association, a strong believer in IDAs—has urged its members to follow.[19] Several other states have recently taken actions in support of IDAs. In Maine, both recipients of Aid to Families with Dependent Children and the "working poor" (people who are employed but whose incomes fall below specified levels) may participate in the state IDA program. Missouri's program targets individuals and families at or below 200 percent of the federal poverty level; the program is funded by private contributors who receive 50 percent state tax credits—capped at $4 million annually—for their contributions.[20]

North Carolina is also enthusiastic about IDAs, with three new initiatives now underway. First, the state has appropriated $600,000 to fund a two-year pilot project of 600 IDA accounts. Second, $250,000 in Community Development Block Grant funds has been set aside for another two-year pilot program that will create 150 IDA accounts for homeownership. The program will be implemented by a local community development corporation or nonprofit partner and will provide 2:1 matches—up to a ceiling of $2,000—for working families in four rural and nonmetropolitan communities.[21] Finally, the Durham city council approved $50,000 in general revenues for a program similar to Seattle's Home$tart Plus, matching deposits 2:1 for up to 20 eligible families to cover downpayment and closing costs on the purchase of a home within the city. If the effort is successful, Durham will consider expanding it in the future.

The IDA movement has strong conceptual underpinnings and widespread grass-roots support, but there has been little evidence so far that it actually helps families get out—and stay out—of poverty. That may soon change. A national IDA demonstration project started in the fall of 1997[22] is the first systematic effort "designed to test the extent to which poor people can and will save if supported in appropriate ways; can use those leveraged savings to build businesses, homes and skills; and in so doing, generate jobs, profits, taxes and economic and social development."[23]

The American Dream Demonstration (ADD) as its sponsors are calling the project, will establish at least 2,000 IDAs in 13 low-income communities across the country.[24] The scope of the demonstration is grand not only in size but intention: it aims "to build the case for making available to low-income people asset-building incentives equivalent to those we currently offer the non-poor."[25] In addition, ADD will systematically test several propositions concerning the positive impacts of assets, including greater household stability; greater personal efficacy and self-esteem; increased effort to maintain and enhance assets; and increases in long-term planning, human capital development, risk taking, social status, community involvement, and political participation.[26]

The 13 nonprofit community organizations—competitively selected from 99 applicants—span the full range of community development missions. With the exception of Tulsa, Oklahoma, which will enroll 500 account holders and be subject to a rigorous impact evaluation, each organization will open between 50 and 150 IDA accounts.[27] While all will target low-income groups, several are focusing on youth; others on current or former welfare recipients; some on the working poor; and still others on single parents, low-income renters, or public housing residents. And while the broad parameters will be similar, specific program designs will vary. Matching rates will range from 1:1 to 7:1, and the matches at some sites will vary with the purpose for which the account is created. The Bay Area IDA Collaborative in northern California, for example, intends to match education or job training IDAs on a 1:1 basis, business development IDAs up to 2:1, and homeownership IDAs up to 4:1. Shorebank in Chicago will match homeownership IDAs 1:1 and education and business IDAs 2:1.[28]

Tulsa's program is particularly well targeted to the working poor because it links IDAs with the federal earned income tax credit (EITC),[29] and Tulsa's nonprofit IDA coordinator— the Community Action Project of Tulsa County (CAPTC)—also administers a large-scale volunteer income tax assistance program that helped more than 7,000 low-income working families prepare their federal tax returns in 1997 alone. CAPTC hopes to encourage EITC recipients to invest a portion of their tax credit in a savings account; CAPTC staff believe that the incentive of the IDA match will convince people who have never saved before to start saving. Though recruitment did not go into high gear until early 1998, more than 125 people had opened IDAs by August 1998, making CAPTC one of the largest IDA demonstration sites and ensuring that it is well on its way to enrolling 500 participants within two years.[30]

Despite the seemingly broad appeal of an antipoverty policy that "moves from subsistence handouts to investments, and from bureaucratically run income-security systems to direct community ties,"[31] the IDA movement has been slow to gain currency in Congress. Bipartisan IDA legislation, along with other asset-building measures, died in committee in the 104th Congress, and it was not until the waning days of a legislative session preoccupied by presidential scandal that the 105th Congress finally approved the bipartisan Assets for Independence Act (AFIA).

AFIA is a five-year, $125 million national pilot program similar to ADD, but conducted by the Department of Health and Human Services (HHS); $10 million has been appropriated for the first year. Indiana and Pennsylvania, the only states that had committed at least $1 million in state funds to IDA programs when AFIA was enacted, can apply directly to HHS for funding. All other states must collaborate with one or more nonprofit organizations, and grants will be made to nonprofit organizations on a competitive basis.

While it is much too early to draw any lessons from local IDA programs, in their early surveys of ADD participants, this is what Sheradden and his colleagues found: as of June 30, 1998, 533 people at the 13 ADD sites had opened an IDA; 440 participants had made at least one deposit, with a median deposit in the most recent month of $30.[32] At this early stage, 75 percent of the participants are female; almost 80 percent had at least a high school education; and about 70 percent were single, divorced, separated, or widowed. Participants' median income was $1,241 a month.

The programs described in this chapter span the range of shared savings and IDA initiatives.

Programs

Hawthorne HOPE Matching Grant Program
Los Angeles, California

The Hawthorne HOPE (Home Ownership Plus Empowerment) Matching Grant Program, initiated in 1996, seeks to assist qualified low- to moderate-income households to become homeowners through credit counseling and case management, and by matching savings designated for the purchase of a new home.

Participants

The Hawthorne HOPE Matching Grant Program is a partnership between Operation HOPE, Inc., America's first nonprofit investment banking organization, and Hawthorne Savings, a Los Angeles–area savings and loan institution that manages the savings accounts.

Program Description

The Hawthorne HOPE program is operated in conjunction with the Operation HOPE Home Loan Center, which provides participants with intensive homeownership assistance and access to participating lenders through a rotating lender pool. The program is primarily an internal mechanism for prospective homebuyers who come to Operation HOPE for assistance but are unable to secure financing.

Prospective homeowners who wish to participate in the Hawthorne HOPE program must meet low- to moderate-income (LMI) guidelines or agree to purchase a primary residence in LMI census tracts or other designated areas within Los Angeles County. Participants must have been employed in the same job or line of work for at least two years. The matched savings may be used as the downpayment for the purchase of single-family residences, up to four multifamily units, condominiums, townhomes, or units in planned unit developments (high-density, single-family cluster or townhouse developments that preserve open space). The maximum matching grant is $5,000.

Participants must meet a number of requirements to complete the program successfully and receive the matching grant. They must be enrolled in the Hawthorne HOPE/
Operation HOPE case management program (discussed in "Partnerships in Support of
Homeownership," in Chapter 1) for a minimum of six consecutive months and demonstrate
an "on time" payment history on their installment debt, revolving debt, and utility bill payments. They must complete a certified Operation HOPE Home Loan Center first-time
homebuyer's workshop. Downpayment savings must be deposited in a designated account
for a minimum of six months from the time of enrollment in case management. (Participants who had been enrolled in the Operation HOPE case management program for six to
12 months prior to the start date of the Hawthorne HOPE Matching Grant Program were
allowed to deposit their downpayment funds into the Hawthorne HOPE savings program
and have their savings matched at that time.)

A $50 minimum payment is required to open the account at Hawthorne Savings, which
will match deposits dollar for dollar, up to $5,000. There is no minimum monthly savings
requirement.

Once a participant reaches the end of the enrollment period, an Operation HOPE
Home Loan Center staff member reviews the file. If the participant meets the program guidelines, a residential loan application is completed. When the loan is conditionally approved
and a property found, a participating mortgage lender provides Hawthorne Savings with
escrow instructions, the loan application, a program checklist, and an estimated HUD state-
ment. Matching grants are made available once the first deed of trust loan has been
approved and is prepared for funding. The matching grant funds are dispersed directly to
escrow prior to funding.

Funding Sources

Hawthorne Savings provides the 1:1 matching funds for the program.

Accomplishments

Operation HOPE estimates that about 500 account holders are currently participating in the
Hawthorne HOPE matching grant program. In its first two years of operation, the program
helped 45 account holders become homeowners.

Contact
Operation HOPE Banking Center
Lester Gardner, Manager
3721 South La Brea Avenue
Los Angeles, California 90016
Telephone: (323) 290-2410
Fax: (323) 290-2415

Individual Development Account Program
State of Indiana

Indiana's individual development account (IDA) program, which became effective on July 1, 1997, is designed to help low-income individuals accumulate savings and personal finance skills. IDAs may be used for education, training, business development, or to purchase a primary residence.

Program Participants and Administration

The Indiana Department of Commerce provides overall administration of the IDA program; community development corporations (CDCs) manage the accounts locally.

Participating CDCs must be private, community-based, nonprofit 501(c)(3) organizations, in good standing with the Secretary of State, that provide housing, undertake community-based economic development projects, and offer social services that benefit low-income individuals.

Over 40 CDCs throughout the state are participating in the 1997–1998 IDA state matching program. The number of accounts managed by each varies greatly, from three accounts for the Southeast Neighborhood Development CDC, in Indianapolis, to 140 accounts for the Tradewinds Rehabilitation Center CDC, in Gary.

Program Description

The IDAs are deposited in a financial institution. Program participants may then receive matching funds for their IDAs from the state of Indiana and the administering CDC. The CDC reports the amount deposited in each IDA to the state department of commerce within the necessary time frame for the participant to receive the state match for a given fiscal year.

To qualify, a participant must receive—or be a member of a household that receives—public assistance and must have an annual household income that is less than 150 percent of the federal poverty level. Only one member of a qualifying individual's household may establish an account. Although there are no limits on the amounts that participants can deposit, the state will match no more than $900 per account.

The CDC determines the applicant's eligibility and acts as trustee for each account. It must approve participants' requests to make account withdrawals and provide (or arrange for each participant to receive) training in money management, budgeting, and related topics. The total number of IDA accounts funded by the state is limited to 800. However, the CDCs may also leverage matching funds for additional IDA accounts through income tax credits for private donations. (This portion of the IDA program is discussed in more detail in the next program description.)

Money withdrawn from an individual's account is not subject to state income tax if it is used for the allowed purposes; interest earned on an IDA account is also exempt from state income tax. IDA funds will not be considered assets in determining an individual's eligibility for public assistance.

The legislation establishing the IDA program requires the state department of commerce to evaluate the program to determine whether to extend it. Each CDC must also submit an annual evaluation of its program to the department of commerce. The overall evaluation of the program will begin by July 1, 2000, and must be completed by December 1, 2000.

Funding Sources

The IDA program is funded through two mechanisms: 800 accounts are supported directly through state funds, and CDCs offer tax credits to private sector contributors to finance additional accounts.

To fund the program, the state of Indiana earmarked $6.48 million from the general fund over a four-year period beginning in July 1997. The state will provide a 3:1 match for a maximum of 800 new IDAs each year. The maximum state contribution to each account is $900.

> **Contact**
> Indiana Department of Commerce
> Community Development Division
> Indu Vohra, IDA Project Manager
> One North Capitol, Suite 600
> Indianapolis, Indiana 46204-2288
> Telephone: (317) 233-0541
> Fax: (317) 233-3597

Tax Credits for Private Donations to Individual Development Account Programs State of Indiana

The state of Indiana can award up to $500,000 in state income tax credits per year to private contributors to the state individual development accounts (IDA) program.

On July 1, 1997, the state of Indiana initiated a program to support IDAs administered by community development corporations (CDCs). The program has two parts: one, discussed in the previous section, earmarked $6.48 million over a four-year period to help low-income individuals accumulate savings and improve their personal finance skills. The program described in this section provides an incentive—in the form of state income tax credits—for private donors to contribute matching funds for the creation of additional IDAs.

Program Administration

The Indiana Department of Commerce administers the tax credit program.

Program Description

Once each year, CDCs that administer IDA programs may submit requests to the state department of commerce to reserve IDA tax credits. To request the credits, the CDC must determine that it has secured enough investment to match the IDA funds on a 3:1 basis. If the CDC does not meet the anticipated investment goals, the department of commerce may reallocate the credits to another organization.

Contributions that receive IDA tax credits are subject to a number of restrictions: First, the contributions may be used to defray only Indiana tax liability. Second, in any given tax year, donors may claim credits for amounts of at least $1,000 and no more than $50,000; however, donors may claim no more than 50 percent of the actual contribution. Third, the credits must be claimed for the year in which the contribution was made.

Contact
Indiana Department of Commerce
Community Development Division
Indu Vohra, IDA Project Manager
One North Capitol, Suite 600
Indianapolis, Indiana 46204-2288
Telephone: (317) 233-0541
Fax: (317) 233-3597

Individual Development Account Demonstration Program State of North Carolina

In 1998, the North Carolina Small Cities Community Development Block Grant (CDBG) Program invested in the development of prototype programs at four rural sites. These programs are designed to foster homeownership through the creation of individual development accounts (IDAs) and the provision of ancillary homeownership support services.

Program Participants and Administration

The division of community assistance in the state department of commerce administers the IDA demonstration program. The demonstration is supported by the North Carolina Working Group on IDAs and Asset Building, a broad-based coalition of leading institutions in North Carolina's extensive community economic development network; major providers of human services; state agencies; policy makers; and private philanthropic and corporate groups. Partnership participants at individual sites vary.

Program Description

The pilot program will last two and one-half years: six months of planning time and two years of operation time. The sites were selected through an application process that evaluated organizational capacity, program design, project feasibility, and innovation. Selections were made by an eight-member committee of working group members.

Application was limited to local governments that were eligible for North Carolina's Small Cities CDBG Program. In addition, applicants had to demonstrate substantive partnerships with other community organizations involved in the provision of affordable housing. The sponsoring organizations at the sites are committed to homeownership and asset building and have strong links to other community groups that can provide outreach, training in economic literacy, counseling, account management, and postpurchase assistance.

The working group supports the sites through ongoing training, technical assistance, and peer exchanges; design of a common economic literacy curriculum, if needed; mobilization of a statewide funding pool for IDA matches and program costs; assistance with local fundraising; and vigorous policy advocacy and public education. The working group also plans to serve as a forum for all interested parties in North Carolina to promote asset building and build a high-performing network of community-based partnerships offering IDAs and support for other asset-building activities.

The target population for the pilot programs consists of families and individuals who are "on the cusp" of being able to own a home; participants must be employed, have a demonstrated interest in homeownership, and be willing to commit to the two-year process of savings and education. All participants must have family incomes equal to or below 80 percent of the area median. To qualify for a match, savings must come from household income (that is, funds to be matched may not include gifts from friends or family members or deposits from past savings).

The state department of commerce recommends that federally insured depository institutions hold the participants' savings accounts, pay interest, and issue monthly statements to the participants. The sponsoring organization must cosign or otherwise approve all withdrawals. Sponsoring organizations must also require comprehensive homeownership counseling; counseling may be provided by the sponsoring organization or through a partnership agreement with another organization.

Program implementation varies from site to site: for example, all sites have set criteria for the selection of participants, but Forsyth County plans a competitive selection process and Beaufort County plans to accept qualified applicants on a first-come, first-served basis. Minimum monthly savings criteria may vary, as well as the specifics of the economic literacy programs.

Most (if not all) sites will accept more applicants than their funding can accommodate (some participants are expected to drop out). Pilot-site managers are already looking for future program funding: some of the pilots have partnerships with other downpayment assistance programs to leverage additional homeownership opportunities. Buncombe County, for example, has joined with the Community Foundation, the local board of realtors, Mountain Housing Opportunities (which has access to federal HOME funds), and Neighborhood Housing Services to obtain additional downpayment assistance.

Funding Sources

The North Carolina Small Cities CDBG Program has invested $240,000 in the four sites. CDBG funds are used in conjunction with other contributions: for every $1 of CDBG matched savings, the saver must deposit $1 and local sources must contribute $1. Administrative funding from CDBG monies must also be matched 1:1 by a local source.

Accomplishments and Contacts, by Pilot Site

Caldwell County. Caldwell County received a $75,000 award to manage 75 IDA accounts. HOME funds will be used to match CDBG funds on a 5:1 basis, so participants will receive $6 for every $1 of savings. The Western Piedmont Council of Governments, a consortium of 27 member governments, will operate the program. The consortium has operated a down-payment assistance program for first-time homebuyers since 1996, and the IDA program will expand the pool of eligible families.

> **Contact**
> Western Piedmont Council of Governments
> Sherry Long
> 317 First Avenue, N.W.
> Hickory, North Carolina 28601
> Telephone: (704) 322-9191, ext. 151

Forsyth County. Forsyth County received a $50,000 award for 25 IDA accounts to be matched on a 1:1 basis by the county and local bank funds.

> **Contact**
> Forsyth County Planning Department
> Dan Kornelis
> 660 West Fifth Street
> Winston-Salem, North Carolina 27101
> Telephone: (336) 727-2540

Buncombe County. Buncombe County received a $50,000 award for 25 IDA accounts, which will be matched on a 1:1 basis by local funds. The Affordable Housing Coalition of Asheville, a strong network of area nonprofit and government entities with an interest in housing issues, will operate the program. The coalition also provides housing counseling programs.

> **Contact**
> The Affordable Housing Coalition
> Helen O'Connor
> 34 Wall Street, Suite 607
> Asheville, North Carolina 28801
> Telephone: (704) 259-9518

Beaufort County. Beaufort County received a $65,000 grant for 60 IDA accounts, to be matched on a 1:1 basis by local funds. The pilot program is operated by the Metropolitan

Low Income Housing CDC and Community Developers of Beaufort-Hyde. Matching funds have been raised from the Z. Smith Reynolds Foundation and the Rural Center.

Contact

Community Developers of Beaufort-Hyde, Inc.
Sam Thompson
P.O. Box 115
Belhaven, North Carolina 27810
Telephone: (252) 943-3058

General Contact

North Carolina Department of Commerce
Pam Wilson, Division of Community Assistance
1307 Glenwood Avenue, Suite 250
Raleigh, North Carolina 27605
Telephone: (919) 733-2850
Fax: (919) 733-5282

Individual Development Account Program: Community Action Project of Tulsa County Tulsa County, Oklahoma

Through its four-year matched savings program, the Community Action Project of Tulsa County (CAPTC) offers 630 participants the possibility of achieving homeownership, business, education, and retirement goals. One of the national individual development account (IDA) sites in the American Dream Demonstration sponsored by CfED, CAPTC is one of the largest IDA programs in the nation. The program expanded from an initial 1998 pilot study with 130 participants, adding 500 more participants who will be compared with a control group to estimate the impact of the IDA program.

Participants

CAPTC has secured a number of partners to operate the program, including local foundations and lenders and the city of Tulsa.

Program Description

Participants must be employed, and their gross household income must be no more than 150 percent of the federal poverty level. The IDAs are opened at the Bank of Oklahoma. Monthly deposits of at least $10 and no more than $50 are required, and participants may also deposit a portion of their earned income tax credit rebate every year. For every $1 deposited, up to $500 per year, CAPTC will provide either $1 or $2 in matching funds.

The savings and matching funds may be used for education (for participants or their children) for business startup or expansion, to fund a retirement account, for home repair or improvement, or for the downpayment and closing costs on a home purchase.

Participants have complete control over their accounts: they may withdraw funds at any time and may use savings and match money for more than one approved purchase. There are a few restrictions, however: the maximum savings period is four years—the duration of the program. If savings are withdrawn for an unapproved reason, no matching funds will be given, and the participant may become ineligible for further participation in the program. (Matching funds are held in a separate account until a withdrawal for an approved purchase is made.) Although participants may withdraw limited amounts for emergencies, they forfeit the match on those funds.

CAPTC markets the IDA program to potential participants through other programs it offers. To increase awareness of the program, CAPTC also networks with other nonprofit and government agencies that work with low-income families.

Funding Sources

CfED funding covers a portion of the operating costs and matching funds required for the program. CAPTC has leveraged those funds with support from the Bank of Oklahoma, the Zarrow Foundation, the Federal Home Loan Bank, and the city of Tulsa, which dedicated federal HOME and Community Development Block Grant funds for use in the pilot. The Bank of Oklahoma also acts as the repository for the accounts. The following table shows the breakdown of the IDA program's current funding sources:

Funding Source	Amount ($)	Time Frame	Restrictions
CfED/foundations	200,000	8/97–6/01	Matching savings
CfED/foundations	100,000	8/97–6/01	Operating expenses
Zarrow Foundation	140,000	Four years, exact dates flexible	Operating expenses and/or matching savings
Federal Home Loan Bank of Topeka	200,000	Two years, 1998–1999	Matching savings, home purchase only
CDBG funds	75,000	10/97–9/98	Operating expenses
City of Tulsa HOME funds	Currently unrestricted	Duration of program	Matching savings, home purchase only

Contact

Community Action Project of Tulsa County
Jennifer Robey, IDA Program Coordinator
125 North Greenwood, Third Floor
Tulsa, Oklahoma 74120
Telephone: (918) 582-6744
Fax: (918) 582-6794

Home Savings Program: Federal Home Loan Bank of Indianapolis
Regional

The Home Savings Program of the Federal Home Loan Bank (FHLB) of Indianapolis is designed for first-time homebuyers who earn 80 percent or less of the area median income.

Participants

The FHLB of Indianapolis initiated the Home Savings Program, in which about 40 member banks participate.

Program Description

The FHLB of Indianapolis matches participants' savings on a 2:1 basis, up to a maximum bank contribution of $5,000. Savings may be used for downpayment and closing costs. Housing counseling is required of all participants, but each member bank sets its own counseling criteria and establishes its own delivery mechanism. Some banks offer their own classes; others contract with local housing agencies. Member banks do their own marketing.

Funding Sources

To support the Home Savings Program, the FHLB of Indianapolis allocates about $1.5 million annually from the FHLB Affordable Housing Program (AHP). The AHP program is funded through a percentage of profits from home mortgage loans made by Federal Home Loan Banks: 10 percent of the profits go to AHP, and 20 percent of AHP funds go to the Home Savings Program.

Accomplishments

Since the program began in 1996, about 400 homebuyers have closed loans on homes using their matched savings.

Contact

Federal Home Loan Bank of Indianapolis
Frederick Hash, Vice President
P.O. Box 60 46206-0060
8250 Woodfield Crossing Boulevard
Indianapolis, Indiana 46240
Telephone: (317) 465-0371
Fax: (317) 465-0397
Web site: www.fhlbi.com

First Home Club: Federal Home Loan Bank of New York
Regional

The objective of the First Home Club is to prepare participants for homeownership by helping them establish a pattern of systematic saving.

Participants

The First Home Club was initiated by the Federal Home Loan Bank of New York (FHLBNY) and is operated in partnership with its member banks and nonprofit homeownership counseling organizations.

To participate, member banks must

- Establish a first-time homebuyer policy;
- Establish a homeownership counseling program;
- Offer dedicated savings accounts for the club;
- Develop a mechanism for recapturing funds in the event of resale or refinancing;
- Maintain appropriate documentation;
- Provide underwriting guidelines for club participants;
- Provide a list of closing requirements and a schedule of estimated closing costs;
- Provide additional incentives such as reduced points and below-market interest rates;
- Provide marketing materials.

Program Description

The First Home Club is targeted to first-time homebuyers who earn less than 80 percent of the area median income. Participants open a dedicated savings account at a participating bank and establish an equity goal, which they achieve by making regular deposits to the account during a ten- to 30-month period. Homeownership counseling is required and is typically provided by a nonprofit agency. Each participating institution makes its own homeownership counseling arrangements. Some participating banks pay counseling fees (if any) for clients; in other cases, nonprofit agencies have secured funding to cover the costs of homeownership counseling, and it is therefore free to the participants.

After a six-month qualifying period, families who have adhered to their savings and counseling plan have funds set aside for them. Through its member banks, the FHLBNY provides a 3:1 match of participants' funds, up to a maximum of $5,000 per family. These funds are committed for 24 months, and a family must achieve its equity goal and purchase a home within that period.

If within the first five years of ownership the homeowner resells the home to a buyer whose income is over 80 percent of the area median income or refinances the home at a profit, the matching contributions are subject to recapture. This provision ensures that the banks' funds are being used to secure homeownership opportunities, not as "free money" on which to make a profit. The recapture mechanism is typically a soft second mortgage for the matching dollars contributed by the bank, signed at the same time as the first mortgage. Twenty percent of the soft second mortgage is forgiven each year.

The program is marketed through the member banks, who agree to provide marketing materials when they sign up to participate.

Funding Sources

The FHLBNY has allocated $1 million annually to the First Home Club. The funding is derived from bank profits: 10 percent of bank profits go to an FHLB Affordable Housing Program (AHP) fund, and 15 percent of the AHP fund is dedicated to the First Home Club.

Accomplishments

As of February 1999, 125 families had closed loans. The program is limited each year by available funding.

> **Contact**
>
> Federal Home Loan Bank of New York
> Evelyn Tsugranis, Community Investment Analyst
> 7 World Trade Center, Floor 22
> New York, New York 10048-1185
> Telephone: (212) 441-6831
> Fax: (212) 608-4228
> Web site: www.fhlbanks.com/newyork/index.htm

Home$tart and Home$tart Plus:
Federal Home Loan Bank of Seattle
Regional

Home$tart and Home$tart Plus are typical of the matched savings programs that federal home loan banks (FHLBs) sponsor with Affordable Housing Program (AHP) funds. Rather than simply providing a grant or a loan to help cover downpayment and closing costs, matched savings programs encourage prospective buyers to establish a pattern of saving by requiring them to set up a savings account, then rewarding them for having done so by matching the clients' deposits.

Program Participants and Administration

The Home$tart and Home$tart Plus programs are administered by participating member banks, which apply for the matched savings funds, manage the funds, and provide the first mortgage for homebuyers. As of January 1999, 76 lenders had taken part in the Home$tart program. Lenders participating in the Home$tart Plus program include the Cascade Savings Bank; Key Bank, NA; U.S. Bancorp; and Washington Mutual, Inc.

Program Description

Under the Home$tart program, participating first-time homebuyers save in a dedicated savings account for at least six months. These deposits are matched on a 3:1 basis with Home$tart funds, up to a maximum grant of $5,000 per family. Participants receive home-buyer counseling during the saving period. Participants have up to two years from their enrollment date to purchase a home. To be eligible for Home$tart, families must earn no more than 80 percent of the area median income, adjusted for family size.

Home$tart Plus is a version of Home$tart designed to assist public housing residents to become homeowners. Six local public housing authorities (PHAs) and eight other organizations participate in this pilot program, which provides matching funds for downpayments for families who live in public housing or receive Section 8 assistance and who have signed a family self-sufficiency (FSS) contract with their local PHA. Under the FSS program, when a family's household income increases during its enrollment in the program, the rent increase that would ordinarily accompany the income increase is placed in an escrow account. In addition to entering into an FSS contract, the family must complete at least five hours of homeownership counseling.

The FHLB of Seattle provides $2 for every $1 accumulated in the family escrow account, up to a maximum of $10,000. The family's contribution comes from its PHA escrow account. These escrowed funds and the match provided by Home$tart Plus are applied toward downpayment and closing costs for the purchase of a home. Funds are available on a first-come, first-served basis.

The FHLB of Seattle prepares brochures describing the program benefits and eligibility requirements, which are distributed through a network of participating savings institutions and housing authorities. Participating savings institutions may also imprint their name and address on the brochures and promote the program on their own. In 1998, 63 savings institutions participated in Home$tart and Home$tart Plus programs.

Funding Sources

As of January 1999, the FHLB of Seattle had committed $4.1 million in AHP funds to the Home$tart program and an additional $250,000 to the Home$tart Plus program. (The AHP of the FHLB provides grants for the development, preservation, or purchase of housing for lower-income individuals and families. The AHP is funded annually with 10 percent of the FHLB's net income.)

Accomplishments

As of late 1998, 14 families had purchased homes through the Home$tart Plus program, with average FHLB assistance of $7,000. As of January 1999, Home$tart program funds had been committed for almost 1,000 families.

Contact
Federal Home Loan Bank of Seattle
Judith C. Dailey, Vice President
Community Investment Officer
1501 Fourth Avenue, Suite 1900
Seattle, Washington 98101-1693
Telephone: (206) 340-2300
Fax: (206) 340-2485
Web site: www.fhlbsea.com/

Notes

1 This essay draws from Chapter 6 of Michael A. Stegman, *Savings for the Poor: The Hidden Benefits of Electronic Banking* (Washington, D.C.: The Brookings Institution Press, 1999).

2 Karen Edwards, *Individual Development Accounts: Creative Savings for Families and Communities* (St. Louis, Mo.: Center for Social Development, Washington University in St. Louis, 1997), 14.

3 Michael A. Stegman, *More Housing, More Fairly: Report of the 20th Century Fund Task Force on Affordable Housing* (New York: 20th Century Fund Press, 1991), 46.

4 Robert W. Gray, Office of Policy Development and Research, U.S. Department of Housing and Urban Development, correspondence with author, August 25, 1998.

5 Ibid.

6 Edwards, *Individual Development Accounts*, 12.

7 Federal Home Loan Bank of New York, *First Home Club Program Guidelines*, May 1996.

8 Judy Dailey, Vice President and Community Investment Officer for the Federal Home Loan Bank of Seattle, telephone interview, November 1997.

9 Michael Sherraden, *Assets and the Poor: A New American Welfare Policy* (New York: M.E. Sharpe, 1991).

10 Neal R. Peirce, "Savings Incentives—For the Poor?" syndicated column, October 5, 1997.

11 *Starting Out: What Are Individual Development Accounts?* www.idanetwork.org/start.cfm.

12 *Personal Responsibility and Work Opportunity Reconciliation Act of 1996*, Section 404(h).

13 National Governors' Association, *Issue Brief: Building Assets and Economic Independence through Individual Development Accounts (IDAs)*, January 31, 1997, 1.

14 Karen Edwards, "Individual Development Accounts," *Bridges*, Federal Reserve Bank of St. Louis (summer 1998): 6.

15 Ibid., 6.

16 *Assets: A Quarterly Update for Innovators* (summer 1998): 13.

17 National Governors' Association, *Issue Brief*, 3.

18 "Indiana Supports Savings," *Shelterforce* 19, no. 3 (May/June 1998): 6.

19 National Governors' Association, "Innovative Missouri IDA Bill Utilizes Tax Credits for Funding," *Issue Brief*, 4.

20 *Assets: A Quarterly Update for Innovators* (winter 1997): 7.

21 "North Carolina IDA Working Group Secures Funding from State," *Assets: A Quarterly Update for Innovators* (spring 1997): 4.

22 See, for example, Peirce, "Savings Incentives."

23 Bob Friedman, "Down Payments on the American Dream: What's in a Name?" *Assets: A Quarterly Update for Innovators* (fall 1997): 2.

24 Gautam N. Yadama and Michael Sherraden, *Effects of Assets on Attitudes and Behaviors: Advance Test of a Social Policy Proposal* (St. Louis, Mo.: Center for Social Development, George Warren Brown School of Social Work, Washington University in St. Louis, 1995).

25 Ibid., 2.

26 Yadama and Sherraden, *Effects of Assets*.

27 "National IDA Demo Launched," *Assets: A Quarterly Update for Innovators* (fall 1997): 1.

28 "Down Payments on the American Dream Policy Demonstration Partners," *Assets: A Quarterly Update for Innovators* (fall 1997): 10.

29 Under the EITC, which provides a refundable tax credit for poor workers, a married worker who is raising one child and whose family income is less than $25,760 can receive up to $2,210, while a worker raising more than one child and whose family income is less than $29,290 can receive an EITC of up to $3,656. In fiscal year 1999, tax expenditures for the EITC are expected to exceed $28 billion. David Stoesz and David Saunders, *Welfare Capitalism: New Opportunities in Poverty Policy* (Richmond:

Virginia Commonwealth University, n.d.), 4–5.

30 Information about Tulsa's IDA program is from a telephone interview with Jennifer Robey, CAPTC IDA program coordinator, August 27, 1998, and from program materials.

31 Peirce, "Savings Incentives."

32 Evaluation data are from Michael Sherraden, Deborah Page-Adams, and Lissa Johnson, *Start-Up Evaluation Report, Downpayments on the American Dream Policy Demonstration: A National Demonstration of Individual Development Accounts* (St. Louis, Mo.: Center for Social Development, Washington University in St. Louis, January 1999), iv.

3

State Low-Income Housing Tax Credit Allocation Plans

T wo hallmarks of the federal low-income housing tax credit (LIHTC) program are its flexibility and decentralized character. As it has matured, the LIHTC has not only become the centerpiece of a sophisticated and increasingly efficient production system for low-income rental housing but has also provided critical financing for a broader segment of the multifamily market. In high-cost markets like Los Angeles and in places where tenant incomes are low in comparison with building costs (such as upper New York State), the LIHTC is what makes new construction economically feasible.[1] Since its creation in the Tax Reform Act of 1986, the tax credit has generated more than 700,000 affordable rental units and achieved steady production levels of between 50,000 and 60,000 units a year.

Overview

This chapter is designed for readers who have a working knowledge of the LIHTC and want to learn how the tax credit helps state and local governments meet their strategic housing goals. Each year, states prepare qualified allocation plans (QAPs) that describe how they will distribute tax credits—including the scoring system they will use to rank applications and any targeting criteria or setasides they will use to favor particular kinds of projects, market segments, or places. The program descriptions in this chapter show how states are using their QAPs to set broad priorities and establish a climate for local innovation. As competition for tax credits has intensified, it has become more important for all stakeholders to have a say in the development of the state QAPs, and the best way to do so is by participating in the public hearing and review process that accompanies the development of these strategic housing plans.

This essay begins with an overview of the performance of the LIHTC program during its first ten years; it relies heavily on the important work of Jean Cummings and Denise DiPasqaule, who have carried out the first empirical study of the tax credit that contains important financial data on project operations. The essay concludes with a brief discussion of how some states are fine-tuning their QAPs, which sets the stage for the more detailed descriptions of state strategic plans that follow.

The average rent of tax credit units ($436 in 1996 dollars) is just 9 percent lower than the national average; thus, while LIHTC projects are designed to serve low- and moderate-income households, rents are beyond the reach of many such households without additional subsidy.[2] A U.S. General Accounting Office study of the LIHTC showed that the average income of tenants assisted under the program was 37 percent of the area median, far less than the statutory minimum of 60 percent of the median but still well above the income range in which the most acute housing needs are concentrated—below 30 percent of the area median.

In analyzing the kinds of neighborhoods in which tax credit housing is located, Cummings and DiPasquale found distinctly different patterns in cities and suburbs:

> In major central cities the LIHTC program is much more often used to provide better housing in poor neighborhoods than to provide affordable housing in higher-income neighborhoods. Suburban projects are much more likely to be located in higher-income neighborhoods, providing affordable housing opportunities for low-income households. 37.8 percent of suburban LIHTC projects are located in neighborhoods with incomes at or above the area median; only 9.4 percent of central-city projects are located in these higher-income neighborhoods.[3]

The average total development cost (TDC) per tax credit unit is slightly more than $65,307, which includes lower-cost rural projects built with Farmers Home Administration (FmHA) funding.[4] Excluding FmHA-financed units, TDC rises to $70,226 per unit. On average, 46 percent of TDC is covered by the equity raised through the sale of tax credits, 38 percent is covered by first mortgages, and 16 percent by what is commonly called *gap financing*, which generally includes subsidies other than the tax credit. Cummings and DiPasquale found that private banks provide about 40 percent of all first mortgages, state governments 26 percent, local governments 19 percent, and nonprofit lenders 19 percent.

According to Cummings and DiPasquale, "suburban projects use virtually no soft loans or grants and have little concessionary financing";[5] however, in rural areas and in some lower-income communities (e.g., in upper New York State), it is difficult—even with the tax credit—to show a net operating income high enough to support a permanent mortgage. In such places, the tax credit must often be supplemented by gap financing that does not have to be serviced out of current income—a need that can often be addressed through HUD's HOME program. According to a June 1997 survey of 3,000 tax credit projects, 64 percent of tax credit projects used HOME funds for gap financing, proving "how critical the program has become since Congress made the program compatible with tax credits several years ago." According to the survey, developers also obtained gap financing from Community Development Block Grant funds (39 percent); Federal Home Loan Bank Affordable Housing Programs (34 percent); state subsidies or loans (32 percent); tax abatements (26 percent); historic tax credits (18 percent); tax increment financing (14 percent); and McKinney Act Homeless Programs (7 percent).[6]

As the tax credit has matured, the delivery system it spawned has become more efficient. As competition for tax credits has increased (in California's 1998 first-round allocation of 9 percent tax credits, for example, demand outstripped supply by about 4:1),[7] prices have risen. With the average price per tax credit dollar having increased from about $.47 in 1987 to $.62 in 1996 and $.70 to $.75 in 1998,[8] returns on investments have been driven down from the high twenties into the single digits. This shift means that a growing portion of every tax credit dollar goes into building costs rather than into syndication costs or investor returns.

"Spurred by the growing competition for new tax credit partnerships and continued escalation of equity prices," an active secondary market for tax credit projects has emerged, and established tax credit limited partnerships have become hotly traded investments.[9] One trade journal reports that corporations are tempted to buy on the secondary market because (1) doing so eliminates construction and lease-up risks, (2) projects have operating histories, which help determine pricing, and (3) investors can "see what the debt coverage has been, how well occupancy has been maintained, and whether reserves have been drawn on."[10]

Through four critical rulings in the past several years, the Internal Revenue Service (IRS) has played an important role in strengthening the tax credit delivery system:

- In September 1997, the IRS published a final rule to facilitate HUD's mixed-income, mixed-finance HOPE VI public housing transformation program. The rule confirmed that Section 8 rental assistance and public housing operating subsidies would not be treated as federal grants under the LIHTC—and will not, therefore, reduce the eligible basis of a tax credit project.[11] This rule makes it possible to use the LIHTC to leverage limited public housing funds to transform some of the worst public housing projects into mixed-income communities.

- Interpretive Letter 800, issued jointly by the IRS and federal bank regulators, "says that CRA [Community Reinvestment Act] regulations do not require that banks invest directly in low-income housing tax credits; investment in pooled funds will receive equal credit to those made by the institution directly."[12] Pooled equity funds reduce banks' exposure by enabling them to invest in a diverse portfolio of affordable rental housing developments without losing Community Reinvestment Act credit.

- IRS ruling 98-15, issued in March 1998, contains long-awaited guidelines for nonprofits on preserving their tax-exempt status when entering into joint venture partnerships with for-profit organizations. The essence of the ruling, which addresses health care partnerships, is that operating partnerships must be structured in such a way as to give the nonprofit a critical element of control, thus enabling it to carry out its charitable mission.[13] (In my view, the affordable-housing sector is strengthened whenever the IRS issues rules that facilitate greater collaboration between community-based organizations and for-profit developers.)

- A May 1998 private-letter ruling (PLR 9822026) by the IRS gave learning centers and other social service programs a boost by allowing the eligible basis of a tax credit project to include a community building used for daycare and Head Start classes "even if the services were available to nonresidents, as long as the size and scope of the building's services didn't exceed those necessary to meet the requirements of project residents and the services were commensurate with the project's character."[14]

Although most QAPs for calendar 1999 were still in process when this book went to press, several states had made important decisions that are worth noting. For example, there seems to be some intention to reduce preferences and setasides for applications from non-profit sponsors. A survey of 1999 plans by *Affordable Housing Finance* magazine found that only 15 percent of allocating agencies are planning to set aside more than the federally required 10 percent for nonprofits, which is an apparent reduction from previous years.[15] Among the states moving in this direction is Michigan, where the state housing development authority has reduced the number of points awarded to local nonprofit applicants and eliminated altogether the points formerly awarded to projects sponsored by statewide non-profits.[16] Nevada has also reduced preferences for joint venture partnerships between non-profit and for-profit developers because many for-profit developers had difficulty finding appropriate nonprofit partners.[17]

Many state agencies also seem likely to continue ramping up their use of tax credits as a tool to preserve older assisted housing, including both privately owned projects and public housing. In the last funding round of 1997, Massachusetts allocated virtually all its tax credits to the Boston Housing Authority for redevelopment of public housing into mixed-finance, mixed-income housing, and the state is likely to continue to emphasize preservation. Among other states, Illinois, Michigan, Connecticut, and Rhode Island are planning to do likewise.[18]

Some states, such as Florida, Maine, and Rhode Island, are beginning to favor the use of tax credits to help finance service-enriched housing for seniors. Florida's 1999 QAP notes that if assisted living facilities (ALFs) for seniors meet specified threshold criteria, they will face less competitive scoring requirements for the award of tax credits.[19] Rhode Island is planning an ALF pilot in 1999, and Maine is targeting bonus points to assisted living projects and setting aside $500,000 of its tax credits for projects that include a service commitment from the state department of human services.[20]

In the immediate future, states are likely to target the use of tax credits geographically—to locations that have the most acute housing needs. 1998 was the first year in which the bulk of California's tax credits were allocated proportionately to the 11 counties in which 80 percent of the state's rent-burdened households live.[21] In the 1996 competition, in contrast, the San Diego area received just over 4 percent of the credit allocation although the area included nearly 9.5 percent of the state's rent-burdened households. Ohio's 1999 QAP also creates geographic funding pools for the first time,[22] and geographic targeting is on the rise in North Carolina as well. No Tarheel county can receive more than $1.5 million of the state's $9.1 million allocation, and if a county has more than one project, it has to divide the $1.5 million among the projects. Missouri's QAP also caps the maximum credit allocations available in different areas of the state and assigns distributions on the basis of population: the St. Louis area receives 36 percent of the state's $6.7 million allocation, Kansas City 16 percent, the north-central area 16 percent, the southwest region 17 percent, and the southeast region 12 percent.[23]

More intense competition for tax credits is also leading to greater emphasis on performance: New Jersey and Massachusetts are among the first states to penalize developers who have submitted new applications but who have failed to deliver on promises for previous projects.[24] Under New Jersey's 1999 QAP, developers who have failed to correct problems in previous projects (in such areas as amenities and social services, for example) are docked ten points. Under Massachusetts' competitive scoring system, an application can be awarded up to 20 points on the basis of the development team's track record, with 12 points the minimum a developer must score in this category to be considered at all.

The program descriptions that follow provide a richer view of how states are using tax credits to steer rather than row.

Programs: Preserving Federally Supported Housing

Massachusetts: 60 Percent Preservation Setaside

In 1998, the Massachusetts Department of Housing and Community Development set aside 60 percent of available federal low-income housing tax credits (LIHTCs) for the preservation of existing housing, including projects whose use restrictions are set to expire and federal HOPE VI projects. The department will reconsider the need for the setasides during its yearly preparation of the state's qualified allocation plan (QAP).

Hundreds of existing housing units are at risk, some because they are located in properties whose use restrictions will soon expire, some because they are within extremely distressed federal public housing projects, and some because they are within properties that have been or are about to be foreclosed. In 1997, the greatest increases in demand for tax credits came from HOPE VI projects and projects with expiring use restrictions.

Plan Description

Applicants for the Massachusetts tax credit indicate whether they are competing in the "preservation" or "production" award categories. Applications in either category must meet a number of threshold criteria and are then awarded points under a detailed scoring system. Threshold requirements and scoring criteria differ by category.

Large projects are targeted in the preservation setaside: wording in the state's 1998 QAP allocates

> 60 percent of the [available tax] credit to large-scale projects with significant federal resources, such as the HOPE VI or expiring use restrictions projects, and other preservation projects. The minimum project size is eight units, although the Department expects that most or all applications in this category will represent fairly large-scale projects. There is no maximum project size in this category.

Though this setaside is designed to promote preservation of federally assisted housing, projects that propose the acquisition or rehabilitation of existing market-rate units are also eligible and currently represent about one-fourth of the tax credit awards in this category.

Because the state also recognizes a need for smaller-scale projects that will create new affordable-housing units, the remaining 40 percent of the tax credits allocated to the state are targeted to the creation of new units in projects with 50 or fewer units. Establishing separate setasides for preservation and new production allows smaller projects to be considered apart from large-scale preservation projects.

> **Contact**
> Massachusetts Department of Housing and Community Development
> 100 Cambridge Street
> Boston, Massachusetts 02202-0044
> Telephone: (617) 727-7824
> Fax: (617) 727-0532
> Web site: www.state.ma.us/dhcd

Virginia: Setasides for Public Housing Authorities

In 1998, the Virginia Housing Development Authority set aside 15 percent of the state's federal LIHTC allocations for public housing authorities (PHAs). The setaside is primarily intended to target HOPE VI projects, which had previously competed with other nonprofit projects and—at least in some areas—could not compete effectively against other affordable-housing projects. The setaside was continued in 1999 and will probably be maintained to meet the needs of PHAs administering HOPE VI projects.

Plan Description

Any project in which the controlling partner or the principal of the controlling partner is a PHA and/or receiving HOPE VI funds can apply to participate in this setaside. The maximum tax credit per project in this category is $650,000.

> **Contact**
> Virginia Housing Development Authority
> 601 South Belvidere Street
> Richmond, Virginia 23220-6500
> Telephone: (804) 782-1986
> Fax: (804) 783-6741
> Web site: www.vhda.com

Programs: Meeting State and Local Priorities in Housing Development

Maryland: Smart Growth Initiative Affects Tax Credit Allocations

In response to the governor-initiated "Smart Growth" initiative that became effective in October 1998, Maryland's department of housing and community development restricts the use of state funds and other resources to "priority funding areas," which include incorporated municipalities, areas inside the Baltimore and Washington beltways, neighborhood revitalization areas, empowerment zones, and certain other county-designated areas.

Plan Description

The Smart Growth initiative, designed to reduce the negative impact of uncontrolled growth, has three main goals: (1) to help existing communities by supporting development in areas where infrastructure already exists or is planned, (2) to protect natural resources from being lost to suburban sprawl, and (3) to protect taxpayers from paying for the development of unnecessary infrastructure.

Developers of new-construction projects who apply for tax credit allocations must include a letter from the local government certifying that the project is located in a priority funding area. (Acquisition and rehabilitation projects are exempt from the Smart Growth requirements.)

> **Contact**
> Maryland Department of Housing and Community Development
> Division of Development Finance
> Edward M. Hammond III, Deputy Director of Housing Development Programs
> 100 Community Place
> Crownsville, Maryland 21032
> Telephone: (410) 514-7400
> Fax: (410) 987-8763

New Jersey: Addressing Multiple Priorities through Setasides

Since 1995, New Jersey's housing and mortgage finance agency has allocated the state's federal LIHTCs through a complex system of funding cycles and setasides; the goal of these arrangements is to ensure that a variety of competing demands will receive a piece of the tax credit "action."

Plan Description

New Jersey has six funding cycles: urban, suburban/rural, HOPE VI, mixed-income, special needs, and a "final" cycle. Several of these cycles incorporate setasides for specific projects.

Urban cycle projects must be located in designated municipalities and may not include HOPE VI or "minimum rehabilitation" projects. Fifteen percent of the tax credits available in this cycle are set aside for projects in neighborhoods that are participating in the Strategic Neighborhood Assistance Program (SNAP) or that are designated as "targeted" neighborhoods. (SNAP, a program of the state department of community affairs, allows participating neighborhoods—those that have strategic plans approved by the department and that are located in cities designated by the governor's Urban Coordinating Council—to be targeted for revitalization. Another 15 percent is set aside for projects for seniors, and 15 percent is also set aside for projects sponsored by qualified nonprofit organizations.

Suburban/rural cycle projects are located in nonurban municipalities. There are two setasides in this cycle: 20 percent of the available tax credits are designated for family projects (those whose units are not restricted by age or special needs) and 15 percent for projects sponsored by qualified nonprofit organizations.

HOPE VI cycle projects must involve the use of HUD's HOPE VI funds, and sponsors may apply for tax credits only in this cycle or in the final cycle. There are no setasides.

Mixed-income cycle projects are those in which at least 50 percent of the units are for low-income households that meet tax credit eligibility requirements and at least 20 percent of the units are for market-rate tenants. The projects may be located anywhere in the state.

Special needs cycle projects are those in which at least 25 percent of the units are to be rented to special-needs clients (as defined by the LIHTC allocation plan) and at least three appropriate services are to be provided. (Special-needs clients are individuals and families who require certain types of home- or community-based support services in order to live independently.) There are two setaside categories: $300,000 in available credits has been set aside for projects providing housing for developmentally disabled people who are currently on the waiting list described in the Developmental Disabilities Waiting List Reduction and Human Services Facilities Construction Bond Act; $100,000 in credits has been set aside for projects providing housing for people who are (1) HIV-positive or have been diagnosed with AIDS and (2) homeless or at risk of homelessness. Projects may be located anywhere in the state.

Final cycle credit allocations occur only if there are unused credits or if the state is awarded an allocation from the national pool. All projects are eligible for the final cycle.

Oklahoma: Community Support Plays a Strong Role

Since 1996, the Oklahoma Housing Finance Agency has emphasized the role of community support in the administration of the state tax credit program.

Plan Description

The housing finance agency's scoring system awards 70 points if the "development provides needed housing in a community where there is tangible support for affordable housing." In comparison, the highest score any other individual criterion can obtain is 25 points. To earn the 70 points, a project must have a letter of support from the chief executive officer and governing body of the jurisdiction. If the proposed development is located outside any incorporated area, a letter of support from the chief executive officers and governing bodies of communities within two miles of the development must be submitted. The state's allocation plan devote several pages to (1) the manner in which the developer and the state housing financing agency must seek community input, (2) the time frame for notifying communities of proposed projects and obtaining their responses, and (3) procedures that local governing bodies are required to follow.

The plan also allows the community to veto the allocation of tax credits to a proposed development. If a local governing body follows the procedures outlined in the plan and determines, by binding resolution, that an allocation for a development proposed in its jurisdiction should be denied, the application must be denied a tax credit award.

Texas: Setasides for Prison Communities

Since 1996, the Texas Department of Housing and Community Affairs has set aside 15 percent of the state's federal LIHTC allocation annually for affordable housing in prison communities or rural areas.

Plan Description

A "prison community" is defined as a municipality or county that (1) is located outside a metropolitan statistical area or primary metropolitan statistical area and (2) was recently awarded a state prison. The department's decision to set aside credits for affordable housing in prison communities was based on the rapid growth in the number of state prisons in recent years: the concern was that the population growth created by new employment opportunities would outrun the available supply of housing, driving housing prices beyond the reach of lower-income families. Targeting rural prison communities has provided an incentive for developers to create additional units of affordable housing in these communities. According to the state department of housing and community affairs, about 36 municipalities and as many counties are designated as prison communities for the purpose of the tax credit program.

The application process for this setaside is similar to that for other setaside categories in Texas. Both nonprofit and for-profit developers may apply, and both new-construction and rehabilitation projects qualify. For the most part, the threshold criteria and competitive ranking factors are the same for the rural or prison community setaside, the nonprofit setaside (10 percent), and the general projects setaside (75 percent). Because applications are scored and ranked within each setaside category, rural and prison projects compete only with each other for credit allocations.

Contact
Texas Department of Housing and Community Affairs
507 Sabine, Suite 400
Austin, Texas 78701
Telephone: (512) 475-3340
Fax: (512) 476-0438
Web site: www.tdhca.state.tx.us

Programs: Innovations in Program Administration

Georgia: Preapplication Assistance

In 1998, the Georgia Department of Community Affairs implemented a preapplication review process for its tax credit program. The process gives the department to opportunity to review initial development proposals and to suggest changes that, if incorporated into the development plan, would strengthen the proposal's financial feasibility and long-term economic viability.

Plan Description

Submission of a preapplication is required for Georgia's LIHTC awards. The preapplication focuses on the underlying concepts of the proposed project, site information, and preliminary financing information. All information provided during the preapplication process is nonbinding.

Preapplications are reviewed and ranked into three tiers: first-tier applications are those that appear likely to compete successfully in the award process; second-tier applications are those that must address specific problems to compete successfully; and third-tier applications are those that are not likely to be competitive.

A written response from the department provides the applicant with specific information on the strengths and weaknesses of the proposal. Although the applicant's acceptance and incorporation of the department's recommendations do not guarantee funding, the applicant still benefits from having the proposal reviewed before beginning the site approval process and obtaining site control, both of which are necessary for consideration during the tax credit funding cycles.

The preapplication process has been received favorably by developers, some of whom have incorporated the process into their own decision making procedures: by submitting preapplications for several projects under consideration, developers can use the departmental review to identify those projects with the greatest potential to receive tax credits.

Contact
Georgia Department of Community Affairs
Office of Affordable Housing Development
60 Executive Park South, N.E., Second Floor
Atlanta, Georgia 30329-2231
Telephone: (404) 679-4740; LIHTC Infoline: (404) 679-0670
Fax: (404) 679-0667
Web site: www.dca.state.ga.us

Minnesota: Giving Local Government the Lead

In response to strong lobbying from local jurisdictions, the state of Minnesota—through the Minnesota Housing Finance Agency—authorizes certain cities and counties to directly administer the allocation of federal LIHTCs. The arrangement has been in place since 1987, when Minnesota began to administer LIHTC programs.

Plan Description

Minnesota's allocation of federal LIHTCs for local administration is based on a formula that applies indicators of need (such as the number of households paying more than 50 percent of their income in rent) proportionately to the population.

The tax credit "suballocators" are primarily public housing authorities. Each suballocator awards the credits, is responsible for the administration and compliance aspects of the program, and may modify the state's QAP to meet local priorities. Applicants not funded by a local suballocator may apply to the state in a final funding cycle if credits are still available. Although the state and the suballocators have similar application materials and deadlines, developers report some variation in approaches to administration and compliance.

In 1999, four of the seven suballocators agreed to participate in a demonstration project in which local jurisdictions will still have the authority to allocate credits but application and administrative processes will be streamlined and managed at the state level.

Contact

Minnesota Housing Finance Agency
400 Sibley Street, Suite 300
St. Paul, Minnesota 55101
Telephone: (651) 296-7608
Fax: (651) 296-9545
Web site: www.mhfa.state.mn.us

Nebraska: Using Available Technology

Since 1996, the Nebraska Investment Finance Authority has used the World Wide Web to make applications for LIHTCs and related administrative materials available to all interested parties.

Plan Description

In addition to a brief program description and notices of funding distribution, the investment finance authority maintains a dozen documents that LIHTC applicants and recipients can download. The allocation plan and information guide are available, as well as application forms; criteria for market feasibility studies; criteria for project management plans; and files on rent and income limits, carryover allocations, cost certification procedures, and land use restrictions.

Contact

Nebraska Investment Finance Authority
Randy Archuleta, LIHTC Administrator
1230 "O" Street, Suite 200
Lincoln, Nebraska 68508-1402
Telephone: (402) 434-3900
Fax: (402) 434-3921
Web site: www.nifa.org

Programs: Maximizing the Value of the Tax Credit

Arizona: Emphasizing Per-Unit Efficiency of Credit Use

In 1998, the Office of Housing and Infrastructure Development (HID) of the Arizona Department of Commerce revised its allocation competition to encourage the use of federal LIHTCs to fund a larger number of affordable units.

Plan Description

Before 1998, HID had emphasized efficiency in the use of tax credits by giving higher scores for (1) projects that required the fewest credits per square foot and (2) projects that provided the highest levels of conventional financing. This approach, however, can favor the creation of *larger* units instead of leveraging the use of tax credits to create *more* units.

The department now measures the efficiency of tax credit use on a per-unit basis, an approach that provides incentives for developers to limit labor and materials costs, reduce the size of units, and obtain more favorable financing terms.

> **Contact**
> Arizona Department of Commerce
> Office of Housing and Infrastructure Development
> 3800 Central Avenue
> Phoenix, Arizona 85012
> Telephone: (602) 280-1365
> Fax: (602) 280-1305

California: Balancing Efficiency Goals with Deep Income-Targeting

In 1996, in an effort to balance the goal of efficiency with the goal of serving those most in need, the California Tax Credit Allocation Committee created two allocation rounds for its LIHTCs: an affordability competition and a credit utilization competition.

Plan Description

Instead of awarding points for meeting or exceeding specific criteria in a variety of areas—typically the practice in other states—California relies on a unique method of ranking applications: the tax credit allocation committee sponsors two separate competitions, one that rewards projects for their affordability and another that rewards projects for making efficient use of tax credits. Once the scores have been determined in each competition, tax credit awards alternate between the two competitions according to setaside and geographic priorities.

Affordability. In the affordability competition, applicants gain points by committing to provide affordable housing for households whose incomes are even lower than those specified by federal LIHTC regulations (assuming that income and rent restrictions are applied for the term of the compliance period). For each type of housing unit (e.g., units for large families, for people at risk of homelessness, for people with special needs) the committee sets different threshold income targets (from 45 to 57 percent of the area median) that projects must meet or exceed. The greater the difference between the threshold income target and the applicant's proposed average income target, the higher the resulting score. Final scores are multiplied by a weighting factor that varies by type of housing.

To discourage applications in which the targeted income levels are so low that the project will not be financially feasible, the scoring system also contains "income floors" ranging from 35 percent to 40 percent of the area median income, depending on housing type. Applicants are free to offer affordable housing to households whose incomes are even lower than the income floor but will not receive additional points for doing so.

Credit Utilization. For the credit utilization competition, the tax credit allocation committee creates a "threshold basis limit" that reflects the development cost standard that applicants are expected to meet or exceed. Threshold basis limits for each funding cycle are based on development cost criteria established by HUD for its lending programs. The score an application receives depends on the difference between the threshold basis limit and the "unadjusted eligible basis" (a calculation of specified allowable development expenses) proposed for the project: the larger the difference, the higher the score. To ensure the quality of the housing, the difference between the threshold basis limit and the eligible basis requested for the project may be no more than 20 percent.

Contact

California Tax Credit Allocation Committee
Jeanne Peterson, Executive Director
915 Capitol Mall, Room 485
P.O. Box 942809
Sacramento, California 94209-0001
Telephone: (916) 654-6340
Fax: (916) 654-6033
Web site: www.treasurer.ca.gov

Minnesota: Adjusting Award Cycles to Reduce Construction Costs

In the expectation that extending the building season will lower construction costs, the Minnesota Housing Finance Agency has adjusted its funding cycle to give developers adequate lead time to begin construction in the spring.

Plan Description

In the late summer of 1998, the Minnesota Housing Finance Agency convened a focus group of prominent members of the construction and development industries. The agency learned from the focus group that the timing of its first funding round—held at the beginning of the calendar year—was pushing up construction costs: by the time tax credit award decisions were announced, developers had insufficient time to complete predevelopment activities and solicit construction bids. In the short building season of a northern climate, late construction starts raise the final cost. To enable developers to begin building in the spring, the agency plans to hold the first round of competitions for the year 2000 tax credits in the fall of 1999.

Contact

Minnesota Housing Finance Agency
400 Sibley Street, Suite 300
St. Paul, Minnesota 55101
Telephone: (651) 296-7608
Fax: (651) 296-9545
Web site: www.mhfa.state.mn.us

Nebraska: Increasing Efficiency through Credit Limits

In 1993, the Nebraska Investment Finance Authority placed maximum limits on the amount of federal LIHTCs that could be awarded to any single project. The purpose of these limits is to encourage greater dispersion in the award of LIHTCs, higher payments to tax credit projects by equity investors, and greater cost-efficiency in tax credit projects.

Plan Description

The maximum tax credit granted to any single project is $325,000, and no project may be divided into two or more projects to receive more credits within the same year. (Multiple applications in the same year that are determined to be a single project are returned to the sender, and all fees are forfeited.) No one developer, sponsor, or party with an identity of interest (excluding property management control) is eligible to receive tax credit reservations for more than an aggregate 25 percent of the authority's annual allocation, although exceptions to this limitation may be made to ensure maximum distribution of tax credits. The investment finance authority may also limit tax credits on the basis of measures deemed appropriate by the authority, such as per bedroom, per unit, or per occupant.

Contact

Nebraska Investment Finance Authority
Randy Archuleta, LIHTC Administrator
1230 "O" Street, Suite 200
Lincoln, Nebraska 68508-1402
Telephone: (402) 434-3900
Fax: (402) 434-3921
Web site: www.nifa.org

New Hampshire: Awarding Points for Equity Investment

In allocating the state's federal LIHTCs, the New Hampshire Housing Finance Agency favors projects with a high net equity investment.

Plan Description

In New Hampshire, applications demonstrating the ability to achieve a high net equity investment from the sale of LIHTCs can receive up to 20 points toward their final score. To receive points in this category, an application must include a letter of interest from an acceptable equity investor or syndicator stating the proposed equity rate (the cents on the tax credit dollar). Total equity must be calculated net of any bridge-loan fees, interest, and additional costs not included in the development budget. (For example, project reserve requirements in excess of authority requirements must be deducted from gross equity.) Projects with a net equity of 77 percent or more over ten years receive 20 points, those with 72 to 76.9 percent receive 15 points, and those with 67 to 71.9 percent receive ten points.

> **Contact**
> New Hampshire Housing Finance Authority
> 32 Constitution Drive
> Bedford, New Hampshire 03110
> Telephone: (603) 472-8623
> Fax: (603) 472-8729

Programs: Targeting Types of Housing Projects

Indiana: Targeting Mixed-Income Housing Projects

In 1998, the Indiana Housing Finance Authority modified its LIHTC program to give more weight to mixed-income developments that are located in large cities.

Plan Description

Indiana's large-city setaside represents 25 percent of available federal LIHTCs and includes the 25 largest cities in the state. Under the scoring criteria for this setaside, points are awarded to projects that will rent units to households whose incomes are at or below 40 percent of the area median: the number of points increases if at least 20 percent of the units are allocated to this income bracket. Points are also awarded to projects in which up to 50 percent of the units are reserved for market-rate tenants. To encourage the development of mixed-income housing projects, developments that can meet *both* criteria (20 percent low income and up to 50 percent market rate) can gain up to 30 points in this section of the rating criteria.

Contact

Indiana Housing Finance Authority
115 West Washington Street
Suite 1350, South Tower
Indianapolis, Indiana 46204-3413
Telephone: (317) 232-7777
Fax: (317) 232-7778

Kansas: Targeting Housing for Elderly People and People with Special Needs

Kansas's 1998 tax credit program emphasizes projects in rural areas that provide housing for elderly people and people with special needs.

Plan Description

To address the needs of elderly people and people with special needs in rural areas, Kansas requires all applications for tax credits to include an affidavit of compliance with accessibility requirements. Specifically, projects must meet (1) the requirements for public and common areas of the Americans with Disabilities Act and (2) the requirements of the American National Standards Institute for all first-level living units. In addition, owners must maintain on-site accessibility adaptive devices for those with disabilities for 10 percent of the units and adaptive devices for hearing- or vision-impaired residents for 5 percent of the units.

The scoring system rewards proximity to support services for targeted populations. Applicants can receive up to 20 points for locating affordable housing near retail facilities, schools, medical services, hospitals, daycare or support services, recreation facilities, and houses of worship. (Applications for projects that serve elderly people or people with special needs benefit from proximity to medical and other support services; large family projects benefit from proximity to schools and daycare services.)

Contact

Kansas Department of Commerce and Housing
Division of Housing
700 Southwest Harrison Street, Suite 1300
Topeka, Kansas 66603-3712
Telephone: (785) 296-5865
Fax: (785) 296-8985

Notes

1 *Affordable Housing Today* 1, no. 2 (fall 1997): 8.

2 Jean L. Cummings and Denise DiPasquale, "The Low-Income Housing Tax Credit: An Analysis of the First Ten Years," *Housing Policy Debate* (forthcoming October 1999): 3, 17.

3 Ibid., 17.

4   Ibid., 8.

5   Ibid., 33.

6   Andre Shashaty, "Tax Credits: Celebrating a Hollow Victory," *Affordable Housing Finance* 5, no. 4 (July/August 1997): 30.

7   "Big States Wrap Up Tax Credit Rounds: See High Bond Demand," *Affordable Housing Finance* 6, no. 6 (June/July 1998): 76.

8   The 1987 and 1996 data are from Cummings and DiPasquale, "Low-Income Housing Tax Credit," 8, and the 1998 data are from Andre Shashaty, "Beware the Ghost of Tax Credits Future," *Affordable Housing Finance* 5, no. 6 (November/December 1997): 4.

9   "Developers Capitalize on Resale Market for Tax Credits," *Affordable Housing Finance* 6, no. 6 (June/July 1998): 95.

10 Ibid.

11 Shashaty, "Beware the Ghosts," 1.

12 "Ruling Clarifies CRA Treatment of Tax Credit Investments," *Affordable Housing Finance* 6, no. 6 (June/July 1998): 56.

13 *Affordable Housing Finance* 6, no. 5 (May 1998): 1. Following are five structuring issues the IRS addresses in the ruling:

    1. Control: The composition of the governing board should give nonprofit members a numerical advantage. A board composed of an even number of members from both sides of the partnership cannot ensure the maintenance of the nonprofit's charitable mission.

    2. Fiduciary duty: The governing instruments should include a provision requiring the partnership to override any fiduciary duty to the owners when that duty conflicts with the nonprofit's charitable mission.

    3. Related officer: The key executive officers (chief executive officer and chief fi-
nancial officer) should not be transferred from the for-profit ownership entity because that would give the for-profit excessive control over the packaging of critical information for the board.

    4. Minimum distributions: Approval of distributions should be left to the governing board controlled by the nonprofit rather than formalized in the governing instruments.

    5. Large contracts: Governing instruments should require all contracts over a specified amount to be approved by the board. Provisions requiring board approval on the basis of vague language should be avoided.

14 "Learning Centers Improve Operations of Tax Credit, Bond-Financed Projects," *Housing Development Reporter: Current Developments* 26, no. 22 (October 5, 1998): 332.

15 "Tax Credit Allocation Priorities," *Affordable Housing Finance* 5, no. 6 (November/December 1997): 38.

16 "Tax Credit Allocation Updates," *Affordable Housing Finance* 7, no. 2 (February 1999): 1.

17 Brad Berton, "Multifamily Bonds Gain, Nonprofits Get Tax Credit Edge," *Affordable Housing Finance* 6, no. 4 (April 1998): 63.

18 "Tax Credit Allocation Priorities," 38.

19 *Affordable Housing Finance* 6, no. 7 (August/September 1998): 22.

20 "Tax Credit Allocation Priorities," 38.

21 Ibid., 58.

22 "Tax Credit Allocation Updates," 1.

23 "Allocation Limits Allow States to Stretch Tax Credits," *Housing Development Reporter: Current Developments* 26, no. 22 (October 5, 1998): 331.

24 *Housing Development Reporter: Current Developments* 26, no. 44 (March 8, 1999): 701.

4

Innovative Rental and Community Development Finance

With so much attention being paid to record home sales and to a homeownership rate that is at an all-time high, it is important to keep things in perspective: nearly universal homeownership is neither a feasible nor a particularly desirable national housing goal. One-third of all Americans are renters, and not all of them aspire to own a home or have the resources, temperament, or lifestyle best suited to homeownership. Therefore, it is in the national interest to foster a healthy "multifamily industry" that produces well-built rental housing that broadens choice, facilitates mobility, and expands the supply of affordable housing for people of modest means.

Overview

Because mortgages for multifamily housing are more risky than those for single-family homes, there is substantial policy interest in standardizing underwriting practices—and thereby helping to create a stronger secondary mortgage market for multifamily mortgages. The higher risks associated with loans for multifamily properties are caused by the risk of default and uncertainty about cash flow. According to William Segal and Edward Symonowski, evaluating the risk of default for multifamily loans or pools of loans (especially those backed by affordable units) is difficult for the following reasons:

- Loans are not homogeneous with regard to type of collateral, interest rate, amortization, covenants, subordinated financing layers, and so forth;
- Underwriting standards often differ among originators;

- Because loans are relatively large, a single defaulted loan can constitute a relatively large fraction of a mortgage pool;
- Information about the historical performance of similar loans is lacking;
- Financial information about borrowers is sometimes unaudited or not prepared carefully.[1]

Because cash flow and profitability are even more uncertain for the multifamily sector that serves low-income tenants than for the multifamily sector that serves tenants who pay market rates—and such properties may therefore be higher underwriting and investment risks—government has had to play an even more pronounced role in the production of affordable rental housing.[2] The provision of government support for affordable rental housing was the rationale for the creation of federal low-income housing tax credits (LIHTCs) and accounts for the significant level of state and local government involvement in tax credit housing. According to Jean Cummings and Denise DiPasquale, production subsidies of all kinds account for about 80 percent of total development costs for tax credit housing (a total that includes the implicit subsidies built into the 45 percent of all first mortgages for tax credit projects financed by state and local governments).[3]

This chapter focuses on innovative state and local government programs that stimulate the production of affordable rental housing either by increasing the effectiveness of LIHTCs or by other means.

States have developed a range of approaches to making federal LIHTCs work better. California and Missouri, for example, provide their own tax credits that work with and enrich the federal credit. Piggy-backing a state credit on top of the federal credit increases financial feasibility by requiring projects to carry less debt than would otherwise be necessary. California's low-income housing tax credit tracks federal tax credit rules while Missouri's is a stand-alone measure with eligibility requirements that differ from those that apply to the federal program.

An excellent example of a financing program designed to make the federal tax credit work better is the pioneering Community Investment Corporation of North Carolina, a voluntary statewide lending consortium for multifamily financing created by the North Carolina Bankers Association in 1990. This consortium of 103 financial institutions provides long-term, permanent financing for the development of low- and moderate-income housing and housing for elderly people, especially in conjunction with federal LIHTCs. To qualify for financing, a minimum of 51 percent of the units in a development must be affordable to renters earning no more than 60 percent of the area median income (80 percent of the median in nonmetropolitan counties).

Other programs, such as Texas's 501(c)(3) bond initiative for nonprofit sponsors, were created for the express purpose of helping to produce affordable rental housing outside of the increasingly competitive award processes for the increasingly scarce LIHTCs. 501(c)(3) bonds are growing in importance because they provide tax-exempt financing while remaining outside the state cap on private-activity bonds. Texas's program provides up to 100 percent financing for affordable mixed-income housing produced by nonprofit sponsors. To qualify for financing, developers must agree to reserve 60 percent of a development's units for low-income (61 to 80 percent of the area median) and very low-income (31 to 60 percent of the area median) households. Under the program, 100 percent of the families in the project cannot exceed 140 percent of the area median income.

Other programs discussed in this chapter reduce equity requirements by liberalizing mortgage-underwriting standards. In this regard, it is worth noting that Goldberg and Capone found that greater underwriting flexibility leads to increased default risk. Specifically, they show that extending standard conventional underwriting ratios—for example, allowing debt-coverage ratios below 130 percent or loan-to-value ratios above 70 percent— increases the probability of default. Goldberg and Capone also show that properties underwritten at conventional ratios can withstand a considerable amount of economic distress because they start with solid financial cushions.[4] Given such findings, local policies that reduce development costs and otherwise improve production efficiency may prove more effective in the long term than programs that simply increase underwriting ratios. Programs described in this chapter offer a number of other forms of development assistance that do not require any adjustment in underwriting standards. Examples include loans such as those provided by the Low-Income Housing Fund and the construction management assistance provided by the Reinvestment Fund.

Still other states, such as New Hampshire and California, provide tax credits for charitable donations for affordable housing and other community development initiatives, including capacity-building programs. Under Hennepin County's "This Old House" tax abatement program, enacted by the Minnesota legislature in 1993 to encourage rehabilitation of older, owner-occupied homes in Minneapolis, up to $50,000 of the increased value of renovated homes that are 70 or more years old is excluded from taxable value for ten years. North Carolina is also using tax credits to encourage the rehabilitation of older homes. Effective January 1, 1998, owners of historic homes who invest a minimum of $25,000 in rehabilitation costs over a two-year period are eligible to receive a 30 percent rehabilitation credit over five years.

Programs

Community Development Financial Institution Tax Program
State of California

In 1997, the state of California created the Community Development Financial Institution Tax Credit Program for the purpose of increasing private investment in community development financial institutions (CDFIs). CDFIs are independent, community-based organizations that make community and economic development loans and provide technical assistance and development services to their borrowers.

Program Administration

The California Organized Investment Network (COIN) administers the CFDI Tax Credit Program.

Program Description

The CFDI Tax Credit Program provides a state income-tax credit to individuals or corporations that make a non-interest-bearing deposit or equity investment of at least $50,000 in a CDFI for a minimum of 60 months. Any individual, partnership, or corporation with a valid tax identification number is eligible to make such a deposit and receive the one-year, 20 percent tax credit. The tax credit applies to a maximum of $10 million in investments annually, which means that a total of $2 million in tax credits is available annually.

The tax credit is available for tax years beginning on or after January 1, 1997, and before January 1, 2002. Urban, rural, and reservation-based community development banks, loan funds, credit unions, microenterprise funds, corporation-based lenders, and venture funds are all considered eligible CDFIs under the tax credit program. COIN certifies eligible CDFIs that wish to be qualified to receive deposits or equity investments and authorizes the tax credits for qualified deposits.

Accomplishments

As of August 1998, the tax credit program had generated approximately $350,000 worth of investment in eligible California CDFIs.

Contact
Community Development Financial Institution Tax Credit Program
California Organized Investment Network
300 Capitol Mall, Suite 1460
Sacramento, California 95814
Telephone: (916) 492-3527
Fax: (916) 323-1944

State Low-Income Housing Tax Credit Program
State of California

In 1987, the California state legislature created a "piggy-back" state income-tax credit to supplement the federal low-income housing tax credit (LIHTC). The state credit is not a stand-alone program: it is available only for projects that will receive an LIHTC allocation but that require additional assistance.

The program is designed to encourage the creation of affordable housing despite the high development costs that make the production of low-income housing in California particularly difficult.

Program Administration

The California Tax Credit Allocation Committee administers the state income-tax credit program.

Program Description

With a few exceptions, requirements for the state income-tax credit program are identical to those for the federal LIHTC program. Preference for the state credits is given to projects that are not eligible for the "130 percent basis adjustment" (an adjustment available to projects located in designated high-cost areas that increases the amount of federal tax credits awarded). Projects receiving federal HOME funding also receive preference. State income tax credits are not available for property acquisition unless the project is an assisted affordable-housing development at risk of conversion to market-rate rents. Projects receiving the state income-tax credit must remain affordable for 55 years. Twenty percent of the state credits are reserved for rural projects.

Projects approved for the state tax credit receive the credit over a four-year period. The amount of the credit is based on the same formula that is used to determine federal tax credit eligibility. As required by federal law, the maximum credit that may be allocated depends on the amount of the "qualified basis," which is determined using a formula that takes into account eligible project costs and adjustments to those costs. The total state credit available over the four years is equal to 30 percent of the qualified basis for new-construction or rehabilitation projects that are not receiving a federal subsidy (referred to as "9 percent LIHTC projects" for the amount of credits received), and 13 percent of the qualified basis for projects involving a federal subsidy (4 percent LIHTC projects). For the first three years, the actual annual credit for the state program is equal to the federal credit. In the fourth year, the state credit is calculated by subtracting the total credit percentages for the first three years from the maximum four-year percentage (i.e., either 30 percent for the 9 percent credit or 13 percent for the 4 percent credit).[5] The aggregate annual credit limit on the state program was raised from $35 million to $50 million for calendar years 1998 and 1999.

Contact

California Tax Credit Allocation Committee
Walter Liang, Executive Director
915 Capitol Mall, Room 485
Sacramento, California 95814
Telephone: (916) 654-6340
Fax: (916) 654-6033
Web site: www.treasurer.ca.gov/ctac.htm

Small Affordable Rental Transactions Program
State of Colorado

The Small Affordable Rental Transactions (SMART) Program provides funding for both non-profit and for-profit sponsors who wish to develop small rental-housing projects. The program is based on the view that the housing needs of people in certain markets (special-needs populations, people living in rural areas, and very low income populations) are often best served by rental developments that have 20 units or fewer.

Program Administration

The Colorado Housing and Finance Authority (CHFA) administers the program.

Program Description

The SMART Program makes permanent, long-term, fixed-rate, fully amortizing, nonrecourse first-mortgage loans of no more than $1 million. CHFA will take out construction loans upon the completion of a project.

The program offers two types of loan products: a taxable loan and a tax-exempt loan. The taxable loan has a 20-year term with 30-year amortization and allows developers to borrow up to 90 percent of the project cost or value, whichever is less. The tax-exempt loan has a 30-year term with 30-year amortization and allows developers to borrow up to 95 percent of the project cost or value, whichever is less.

Until the creation of the SMART Program, two CHFA resources had been reserved for nonprofit developers: (1) bond financing backed by CHFA's general obligation and (2) financing from the Housing Opportunity Fund (HOF), CHFA's trust fund. Both resources are now available to for-profit developers.

Bonds issued by CHFA and backed by CHFA's general obligation are the major source of capital for the SMART Program: tax-exempt 501(c)(3) bonds are available for nonprofit and public sponsors, and private-activity bonds and taxable bonds are available for for-profit sponsors. Loans are warehoused in the state general fund until the next available bond issue; CHFA takes the interest rate risk during this period. If necessary, and only where allowed, bond financing may be used jointly with very low interest rate HOF money; this arrangement yields a low-interest loan that can make a proposed project viable. Non-CHFA subsidies may also be used to help finance projects under the SMART Program.

HOF monies are also used under the SMART Program to target lower-income areas of the state, especially localities where the area median income is below the state median and areas designated as qualified census tracts under the federal LIHTC program. The inclusion of these criteria enables the SMART Program to serve both large rural counties and lower-income urban neighborhoods.

The creators of the SMART Program incorporated a number of techniques for reducing costs for rental-housing developers. When HOF monies are used under the SMART Program, CHFA combines the HOF loan and the bond loan into one first mortgage loan with just one set of documents and one monthly payment. The minimum debt service coverage is 1.05 with a 95 percent occupancy rate. The $500 application fee is applied toward the 1 percent origination fee. Appraisal and environmental requirements are less costly under the program, and processing and documentation are streamlined.

Because the rental income on small developments is often too small to cover expenses and debt service, the SMART Program allows for more lenient minimum occupancy requirements than those that apply to CHFA's other programs. The developer may choose between two options: either 20 percent (normally 25 percent) of the units must be affordable to households earning 50 percent of the area median income, or 40 percent (normally 45 percent) of the units must be affordable to households earning 60 percent of the area median income. An additional percentage—up to 75 percent of the units—must be affordable to tenants whose incomes are 100 percent or less of the area median.

Funding Sources

Funding for the SMART Program comes from the following CHFA sources: 501(c)(3) bonds backed by CHFA's general obligation; private-activity bonds and taxable bonds, also backed by CHFA's general obligation; and HOF. The SMART Program is expected to break even at best. CHFA's other rental-housing programs are used to subsidize some staff costs.

Accomplishments

Since its inception, the SMART Program has approved more than $60 million in loans. The program's monies have been used to fund 1,240 units for families, 53 units for elderly people, and 18 units for disabled people.

Contact
Small Affordable Rental Transactions Program
Colorado Housing and Finance Authority
Rental Housing Division
1981 Blake Street
Denver, Colorado 80202
Telephone: (303) 297-7351
Fax: (303) 297-0911

Tampa Bay Community Reinvestment Corporation
Tampa, Florida

The Tampa Bay Community Reinvestment Corporation (TBCRC) is a "nonprofit mortgage banking corporation whose member financial institutions pool resources and share risks to finance affordable housing."[7] The pool finances the development of rental housing and provides front-end financing for single-family homes developed by both nonprofit and for-profit organizations.

TBCRC resulted from a collaborative effort on the part of community leaders, bankers, and the mayor of St. Petersburg, Florida. Spurred in part by documented reports that area banks had poor records of lending to minorities, an initial meeting, in 1991, generated interest in the creation of a lending consortium that would provide underserved segments of Tampa Bay's housing market with access to capital. TBCRC opened for business in April 1993.

Participants

Members include large and small banks active in the Tampa Bay market. From a core group of 18 banks, membership had grown to include 37 financial institutions by 1999.

Program Description

Each member bank invests funds in a loan pool—initially funded at $50 million but now at $81 million—and the size of each investment is based on the size of the bank. The minimum required for participation is currently $250,000, and the largest contribution is capped at 15 percent of the total pool. The membership term is two years, and participating banks have the option to resign at the expiration of their term. New banks may join during an annual open-enrollment period.

Participation in the loan pool gives every lender a pro rata share in every loan, thereby distributing the risks and rewards of each loan. The loan pool allows member banks to make community development loans with relatively low administrative overhead, and small banks may engage in community lending without bearing the cost of maintaining a community lending staff.

TBCRC staff members review loan applications and make recommendations to a loan committee, made up of member bank representatives, which must give final approval on all loans. Member banks fund all approved loans according to their pro rata share of the loan pool, and each participating financial institution receives a participation certificate indicating its percentage interest in the loan. TBCRC engages one member bank to act as the agent bank for the corporation. Other member banks wire their funds into the agent bank, and the agent bank then disburses the loan funds. TBCRC services the loans. A critical component of the loan pool model employed by TBCRC is that loans are designed to be sold on the secondary market, which allows loan pool funds to revolve.

TBCRC administers three loan programs, described briefly in the subsections that follow.

Multifamily Permanent Loans. TBCRC's initial product was a permanent loan to fund multifamily rental projects. The maximum loan amount for any project or developer is $10 million. Fixed-rate loans carry terms of five, ten, or 15 years and may be used for new or renovated housing. The maximum loan-to-value ratio is 80 percent of total development costs, and debt-service coverage of 1.15 must be maintained on TBCRC debt.

All projects must be economically viable and affordable to targeted tenants and must retain their affordability for the term of the loan or longer. Rents are set at 30 percent of household income for targeted income ranges. Projects must meet one of the following income targets: 51 percent of units affordable at 80 percent of the area median income; 40 percent of units affordable at 60 percent of the area median income; or 20 percent of units affordable at 50 percent of the area median income.

Loans are priced at between 150 and 300 basis points above Treasuries of comparable maturities, with the lower spreads going to projects sponsored by nonprofit developers. Loan fees include an application fee of $3,000 for loans of $3 million or more, $1,500 for smaller loans, and an origination fee of 1 to 3 percent of the loan amount.

Community Development Financial Institution Revolving Loan Fund. Recognizing a need for below-market-rate loans, TBCRC applied for and received $2.5 million in federal community development financial institution (CDFI) funds. An innovative partnership among TBCRC, six counties, and two cities, the CDFI program is funded at $7.5 million dollars. Participating jurisdictions pledged matching contributions totaling $5 million from State Housing Initiatives Partnership (SHIP) funds. (Florida assesses a documentary tax on every real estate transaction, a portion of which funds SHIP and is used for affordable-housing programs.)

The revolving loan fund will allow TBCRC to make second mortgage loans to (1) developers who have first mortgages with TBCRC for multifamily developments and (2) other developers in need of gap financing. These mortgages carry interest rates of 1 to 5 percent, with repayment deferred for up to two years. Principal repayments will replenish the fund and provide capital for future loans.

TBCRC expected to make the first loans under the CDFI program in the summer of 1998. It had committed $4.2 million of its total available funds in less than one year.

Single-Family Loans. TBCRC's loan offerings include acquisition, construction, and rehabilitation financing for the development of single-family homes for sale to low- or moderate-income homebuyers. Rehabilitation and new-construction projects of five units or more are eligible, and acquisition and development loans are also offered for subdivisions. Loans are to be concentrated in designated areas, including low- or moderate-income census tracts and neighborhoods targeted by local jurisdictions.

Loans will range from $150,000 to $10 million, with interest rates, income targeting, and loan-to-value ratios comparable to those that apply to the multifamily program. Loan terms will vary, depending on the scope of a project, up to a maximum of five years.

Marketing is based on information from the agencies that operate housing subsidy programs. TBCRC learns who has applied for subsidies and sends information directly to applicants. It also markets to local governments and through participating banks. TBCRC staff also work with local nonprofit housing and community development organizations to identify and address lending needs.

Funding Sources

Up-front operating costs for TBCRC were capitalized by member contributions. As loan volume increases, the organization expects to support operations through loan fees.

Accomplishments

As of February 1999, TBCRC had funded 2,500 units of affordable housing and had committed to an additional 1,800 units. This represents $39 million in closed loans and $23 million in additional loan commitments.

Future Plans

TBCRC is developing a real estate–based community development loan product that would be used to finance commercial revitalization of properties in distressed neighborhoods.

By the end of February 1999, TBCRC will make its first sale on the secondary market by selling participations to the Federal Home Loan Bank of Atlanta; TBCRC will adopt the model created under the pilot Affordable Multi-Family Participation Program (see the profile in this chapter of the Community Investment Corporation of North Carolina).

Contact

Tampa Bay Community Reinvestment Corporation
Debra S. Reyes, President
2002 Lois North Avenue, Suite 150
Tampa, Florida 33607-4711
Telephone: (813) 879-4525
Fax: (813) 873-9767

Florida Affordable Housing Guarantee Program
State of Florida

The Florida Affordable Housing Guarantee Program encourages lending for affordable housing by issuing guarantees on obligations incurred in obtaining financing for affordable housing.

Created by the Florida legislature as part of the William E. Sadowski Affordable Housing Act of 1992, the program is intended to

- Stimulate creative private sector lending activities to increase the supply and lower the cost of financing or refinancing eligible housing;
- Create a security mechanism to allow lenders to sell affordable-housing loans in the secondary market;
- Encourage affordable-housing lending activities that would not have taken place or that serve persons who would not have been served but for the creation of this program.[6]

Program Administration

The Florida Affordable Housing Guarantee Program is administered by the Florida Housing Finance Corporation.

Program Description

The provision of a guarantee on a portion of a total obligation reduces the risk to the lender, which makes it possible for the lender to finance the project and may lower the interest rate.

Lower-interest, lower-risk loans are more attractive to buyers on the secondary market, and when a lender can sell all or part of a loan portfolio on the secondary market, the lender's resources are freed up to make new loans.

The loan guarantees offered by the Florida Affordable Housing Guarantee Program may be used for homeownership loans or for the development or acquisition and rehabilitation of multifamily rental projects by either for-profit or nonprofit developers. Given the nature of the program, the predominant use is for multifamily projects, although the guarantees have been used in four bond issues for the agency's pooled homeownership loan program.

Loan guarantees are issued on a noncompetitive, first-come, first-served basis. Developers and homeowners access the guarantee program through a "qualified lending institution" that has been approved by the guarantee program committee. These institutions submit an application for credit enhancement to the program. For each project, applicants must submit information on financing commitments, experience, and readiness to proceed (threshold check), as well as a loan underwriting package, an appraisal, a market study, income and expense schedules, and a rental unit absorption schedule. An application fee of ten basis points (0.1 percent) of the total mortgage amount is charged.

There is also an annual or one-time premium that varies with loan type, coverage, and coverage period. Each application is reviewed and assessed by a program-approved risk evaluator (currently Tibor Partners, Inc.). In addition to the application fee and guarantee premium, there are fees for the risk evaluation, architectural and engineering review, commitment, and legal services.

Eligible loans include those made to finance or refinance the purchase, construction, or rehabilitation of eligible housing by either for-profit or nonprofit developers. In each multifamily project, 20 percent of the units must be set aside for households earning less than 120 percent of the median annual adjusted gross income for the area (unless more stringent restrictions apply).

The intent of the loan guarantee is to make a project financially feasible: thus, the amount of the guarantee varies according to the needs of the project. The loan guarantees are often used in conjunction with other financing tools such as LIHTCs, HUD's risk-sharing program, and the state apartment incentive loan program (a soft second mortgage program targeted to the same audience).

Funding Sources

A one-time bond issuance was used to capitalize the guarantee program. Roughly $2 million per year is allocated from the state housing trust fund to pay off the bond. The program currently maintains a reserve fund of approximately $77 million, about $12 million of which is debt-service reserves.

Accomplishments

An analysis dated November 30, 1998, reports that the guarantee program has issued certificates guaranteeing loans to 38 developments: 28 multifamily bond projects financed by the Florida Housing Finance Corporation; six multifamily bond projects financed through a lending consortium; and two financed by a lending institution. Risk-sharing agreements have resulted in four bond issues for single-family housing. The program's guaranteed multifamily loans have produced 9,844 units of affordable housing.

> **Contact**
> Florida Housing Finance Corporation
> Finance and Guarantee Programs
> David Woodward
> 227 North Bronough Street, Suite 5000
> Tallahassee, Florida 32301-1329
> Telephone: (850) 488-4197
> Fax: (850) 414-5480

Minnesota Supportive Housing Demonstration Program
State of Minnesota

In 1996, the Minnesota state legislature created the Minnesota Supportive Housing Demonstration Program to develop more cost-effective long-term housing solutions for homeless people who cope with mental illness, chemical dependency, HIV-positive status, or AIDS. The program combines permanent housing with the provision of ongoing support services.

The aim of the demonstration program is "to determine whether supportive housing is a cost-effective, humane, long-term alternative to the cycle of institutions and street life that characterizes the lives of homeless people with chronic disabilities."[8]

Program Administration

The Minnesota Supportive Housing Demonstration Program was conceived, organized and coordinated by the Corporation for Supportive Housing (CSH), a New York–based nonprofit that helps local community groups develop housing for homeless and disabled people. The program is operated by nine community-based organizations in four Minnesota counties.

Program Description

The demonstration program offers residence in four housing types: scattered-site apartments (units in buildings located in different neighborhoods); clustered apartments (either in one large building or in several buildings in close proximity); mixed housing (an entire building with a mix of demonstration-program and low-income residents); and shared housing (a living arrangement in which all residents of a single-family home or apartment unit have special needs). Ownership and management for all housing types may be private nonprofit or for-profit.

The demonstration program is funded by a state entitlement program operated by the department of human services, which would ordinarily support the placement of homeless individuals in a regulated setting—a licensed group home, for example. Such settings have much higher costs.

The demonstration program provides a benefit that is similar to a Section 8 housing voucher. The four participating counties select service providers who are responsible for providing support services and for assisting program participants to obtain housing. Some of the service providers have their own housing units for participants, and some recruit other owners of rental housing to participate. (New housing is being developed in which some units will be set aside for this program, but other financing sources are being used.)

Tenants in the demonstration sites have to meet the state legislative definition for homelessness: they must (1) be "living on the street or in a shelter" or (2) have no fixed residence upon discharge from a treatment center, the psychiatric unit of a community hospital, a residential mental health facility, or a residential chemical dependency treatment program. Of the mentally ill tenants, over one-half were referred by the county social services department, and over one-fourth were referred by transitional housing programs. Of those tenants who are chemically dependent, close to two-thirds were referred by an alcohol or drug treatment program, while one in six was referred by a regional treatment center.

Examples of the services available through the demonstration program are support and self-help groups, benefits assistance, mental health services, budgeting assistance, and medication management. It is expected that costly visits to treatment centers will decrease if support services are made available to tenants. Use of available services is at each tenant's discretion.

Funding Sources

The Minnesota state legislature dedicated $2.2 million for operating support and service subsidies for 180 supportive housing units—funds that would normally have been spent on institutional care. Provider organizations can choose to collect rents from individual tenants or to receive checks directly from the state. Tenants occupying units with federal rent subsidies are eligible for the service component of the program but are not eligible for state rent payment.

Accomplishments

A study of the program's first year of operation concluded that supportive housing helps tenants reintegrate into the community and saves taxpayers money. The study found that tenants' attendance at support groups and contact with neighbors, friends, and coworkers more than doubled. Moreover, tenants' eviction rates dropped by more than two-thirds—from 21 percent (in the year before entering supportive housing) to 6 percent. The program reduced the average cost of caring for each participant by 36 percent, from $2,200 to $1,400 per person. It is estimated that when all 180 units are occupied year-round, the annual savings for taxpayers will come to $1.7 million.

Future Plans

A request to add 20 more people to the total number assisted was approved in 1998. The program is being restructured so that the rental assistance portion will work even more like the Section 8 vouchers. CSH is seeking legislation that would refine and strengthen the program.

Contact
Minnesota Supportive Housing Demonstration
Corporation for Supportive Housing
50 Broadway, 17th Floor
New York, New York 10004
Telephone: (212) 986-2966
Fax: (212) 986-6552
Web site: www.csh.org

Property Tax Classification
State of Minnesota

In Minnesota, a 1997 legislative reform created classification 4(d), which lowered property taxes to encourage the preservation and creation of affordable housing units. The new rate was first available in 1998 for taxes paid in 1999.

Program Administration

The legislation requires the Minnesota Housing Finance Agency (MHFA) to administer the application, certification, and monitoring processes for the 4(d) classification.

Program Description

For qualifying properties, the new tax classification rate is 1 percent of the market value of land and buildings.

To qualify for the 4(d) classification, a property must meet the following criteria:

- The rent charged for the unit must not exceed 30 percent of 60 percent of the area or statewide median income, whichever is higher;
- The unit must be occupied by a resident whose income does not exceed 60 percent of the area or statewide median income, whichever is higher;
- The unit must have been inspected within the past three years. When possible, MHFA uses local code standards and inspections. Otherwise, MHFA inspects the unit using standards established by HUD;
- Through a recorded deed restriction or a preexisting contract to provide federally subsidized housing, the property owner agrees to restrict rents on an agreed-upon number of units for a period of five years;

- For owners with deed restrictions, a percentage of the units must be made available for holders of Section 8 certificates or vouchers. (Within the seven-county Minneapolis–St. Paul metro area, 20 percent of the units in each project must be pledged as affordable housing; outside the metro area, 10 percent of the units in each project must be pledged as affordable housing.)

Owners are responsible for certifying that properties meet classification requirements and comply with the property tax statutes and must also instruct and train on-site agents and property managers on the requirements of the program. MHFA strongly recommends that the on-site agents and managers participate in MHFA continuing education programs each year to remain informed about regulatory and procedural changes in the program.

The owner must sign a five-year rent restriction agreement that is recorded with the county. (Properties participating in project-based Section 8 or in Section 42 low-income housing tax credit programs do not require a signed and recorded declaration.) The owner must obtain a written lease for each qualified unit rented and must notify the local housing and redevelopment authority of vacancies in the pledged units if the required percentages have not been met. Advertised vacancies must state that Section 8 certificates and vouchers are accepted.

Information and application materials for the 4(d) classification program are available on MHFA's Web site.

Contact

Minnesota Housing and Finance Agency
Cam Oyen, Housing Program Professional
400 Sibley Street, Suite 300
St. Paul, Minnesota 55101-1998
Telephone: (651) 296-8139
Fax: (651) 296-9545
Web site: www.mhfa.state.mn.us

"This Old House" Tax Abatement Program
Hennepin County, Minnesota

The Minnesota state legislature enacted the "This Old House" program to provide owners of older homes in Minneapolis and surrounding Hennepin County with incentives to repair and improve their property.

Program Administration

Hennepin County initiated the This Old House program in 1993 and has made several revisions since then. The program is administered through the county assessor's office.

Program Description

Through the This Old House program, owners who make home improvements can defer paying property taxes on the increased market value for up to ten years. At the end of ten years, the value that has been excluded is added back to the assessment in increments of 20 percent for each of the next five years.

For homes 70 years and older, the maximum deferral is $50,000 of increase in taxable value. Homes 35 to 70 years old may qualify for a deferral of 50 percent of the increase in taxable value. There are no income requirements, and—within the city of Minneapolis—no limit on property values; however, properties located in some areas of Hennepin County must be valued below specified limits to participate.

The community benefits from the improvement of older homes, which is why the incentives are greater for improvements to older dwellings and city neighborhoods. The financial burden to the local government is through the delay of new tax revenues.

To qualify for This Old House, the property owner must permit an appraiser to inspect the physical improvements, which must have a value of at least $1,000 to be eligible for exclusion. The property owner can select which among the home's projects will be used for the value exclusion. However, certain improvements—such as increasing square footage by a factor of more than two, constructing a third garage stall, or demolishing portions of an existing home—are not eligible. The owner must obtain the correct building permit, and work in excess of the amount proposed in the application will not qualify. Applications for exclusion of value must be made within three years of the date of the building permit.

The owner may apply for an exclusion of value up to three times for the same property. If the property is sold, the entire amount of value that has been excluded will be included in the assessment for the following year. However, the new owners will automatically be eligible to exclude three additional projects.

Accomplishments

As of June 1998, 5,225 parcels had qualified for deferred tax increases with a total value of $42.4 million.

> **Contact**
> City Assessor's Office
> Richard Stimmler, Director
> 309 Second Avenue South
> Minneapolis, Minnesota 55401
> Telephone: (612) 673-2387
> Fax: (612) 673-3538

Housing Assistance Tax Credit Program
State of Missouri

In 1990, the state of Missouri created a housing assistance tax credit program that provides state income-tax credits to businesses that make donations to nonprofit neighborhood development organizations for the development of affordable, income-restricted housing.

Program Administration

The Missouri Housing Development Commission (MHDC) administers the housing assistance tax credit program.

Program Description

The one-time tax credit is equal to 55 percent of the value of the contribution, which may take the form of cash, property, or professional services. To be eligible, a contribution must come from a business with Missouri tax liability and must support acquisition or construction of a specific housing development that is affordable to families whose incomes are at or below 50 percent of the area median. Both single-family and multifamily projects are eligible, but the income restriction applies to both. The housing project must remain affordable for ten years.

To apply for tax credits for a project, a nonprofit organization indicates the characteristics of the project and lists likely contributors. Local government officials are notified and given an opportunity to respond to the proposal. MHDC reviews the application and issues a tax credit reservation letter if it is approved. Once all financing is in place and the donation has been made, restrictive covenants are filed and the tax credit certification is issued to the project sponsor.

The annual funding availability for the Missouri tax credit program is $10 million in credits for the production of housing and $1 million in credits for the operating costs of participating nonprofits. Each donor is limited to a maximum of $1 million in credits. Donors may carry forward unused credits for up to ten years. Single-family homes may be sold only to income-eligible buyers during the affordability period, and appreciation is limited to no more than 5 percent per year.

In past years, all available credits were not used, in part because of the risk faced by the donor: if the housing project lost its "affordability" status during the required period, the donor could be asked to pay the tax credit amount to the state. The law was recently revised to limit the donor's liability, and the state expects the full credit allocation to be used in 1999.

Accomplishments

The tax credit program has encouraged a wide variety of donations that have assisted in the creation of affordable housing. In addition to cash, nonprofits have received donations of professional services: for example, electricians have rewired housing units, and telephone companies have installed phone lines. An accounting firm donated its services to a transitional housing shelter, and legal firms have donated services for property acquisition and rehabilitation projects. Some foreclosed properties have also been donated, as have goods such as carpeting.

Donations have varied in size as well, from a cash donation of $100 a month to a $1 million contribution from a large corporation. Habitat for Humanity is currently the only nonprofit organization that is creating homeownership opportunities through this program; all other participating nonprofits produce affordable rental housing in projects that range in size from a few units to hundreds of units.

Contact

Missouri Housing Development Commission
Jane Anderson, Tax Credit Administrator
3435 Broadway
Kansas City, Missouri 64111-2415
Telephone: (816) 759-6662
Fax: (816) 759-6828
Web site: www.mhdc.com

State Tax Credit for Community Development
State of New Hampshire

Through the New Hampshire Community Development Finance Authority (NHCDFA), the state of New Hampshire issues investment tax credits for charitable donations for affordable housing, economic development, and education and training. NHCDFA also administers a number of housing and economic development programs, including capacity grants for regional economic development; a community loan fund; an economic development ventures fund; the Housing Futures Fund; and a training and education fund. (Information about these programs and the text of the investment tax credit legislation are available at the NHCDFA Web site.)

Program Administration

NHCDFA administers the tax credit program.

Program Description

Donations may be in the form of cash or property. Income targeting generally parallels Community Development Block Grant limits, with a maximum of 80 percent of area median income.

Each donation is eligible for a state tax credit equal to 75 percent of the donation amount, and the remaining 25 percent may be deducted from state and federal income taxes under the standard criteria for charitable donations. Depending on the donor's tax bracket, the total write-off thus amounts to between 82 and 88 percent of the value of the gift. New

Hampshire does not have an income tax, but credits may be applied against the state business profits tax, the state enterprise (payroll) tax, and the state insurance franchise tax.

In the early years of the program (which was initiated in 1991), about 25 percent of the awarded credits were granted to lenders who had donated housing acquired through foreclosure: ownership was transferred to nonprofit organizations, creating additional affordable housing. During the same period, about 70 percent of the credits were for economic development, including some for large, mixed-use projects that also created housing.

Due to the unexpected popularity of the tax credit program, legislation was passed in 1994 and 1995 that repealed it, limited credits to projects approved prior to June 3, 1994, and established a $2 million cap on donations for the entire program, with credits issued on a first-come, first-served basis for contributions pledged to existing projects. Donors who did not receive credits in the year of the donation would be given priority the following year.

In June 1998, new legislation reestablished the program: effective July 1, 1999, new projects may be approved, and the annual donation cap is $5 million, yielding maximum annual credits of $3.75 million. No one donor may receive credits on contributions in excess of $1 million in any given year, but unused credit may be carried forward for up to five years. Donations are project specific, and if the project does not move forward, the funds are returned to the donor. If the donor does not wish the donation to be returned, it is forwarded to the state treasurer.

All projects that receive tax credit support must sign agreements granting NHCDFA right of first refusal and must agree to keep rents permanently affordable.

Funding Sources

NHCDFA charges the sponsoring nonprofit a fee of 10 to 20 percent of each donation, which is used for administrative expenses and for other program investments. Some of these funds go to the Housing Futures Fund, which awards capacity-building grants to housing organizations. For organizations that cannot afford the administrative fee, NHCDFA will issue a mortgage in the amount of the fee with repayments structured as a percentage of net operating income.

Accomplishments

In 1996, NHCDFA issued $1.5 million in tax credits on donations totaling $2 million, the maximum amount of credits available under the cap in place at the time.

The tax credit program has been particularly popular with lenders because it provides an opportunity to turn foreclosed properties into affordable housing while recapturing some of the value of those properties.[9] Lenders are also the largest cash donors, often dedicating additional resources to the rehabilitation of donated properties. Property donations benefit nonprofit organizations as well by enabling them to begin development projects with an equity stake equal to the value of the property: an equity stakes makes borrowing much easier and, in many cases, allows the nonprofit to maintain affordability without rent subsidies. Because the program was implemented when the state was experiencing a housing crisis, NHCDFA became one of the state's largest creators of affordable housing.

Contact

New Hampshire Community Development Finance Authority
Robert G. Nichols, Executive Director
14 Dixon Avenue, Suite 102
Concord, New Hampshire 03301
Telephone: (603) 226-2170
Fax: (603) 226-2816
Web site: www.nhcdfa.org

Community Investment Corporation of North Carolina
Voluntary Statewide Lending Consortium
State of North Carolina

The Community Investment Corporation of North Carolina (CICNC) is a voluntary statewide lending consortium created in 1990 by the North Carolina Bankers Association (NCBA). CICNC provides long-term, permanent financing for the development of housing for elderly people and for low- and moderate-income households, with emphasis on projects that use the federal low-income housing tax credit (LIHTC) program.

Participants

A subsidiary of NCBA, CICNC is a consortium of 109 financial institutions across the state. Any financial institution, regardless of whether it is a member of NCBA, may become a member of CICNC and participate in its voluntary loan pool.

Program Description

Both for-profit and nonprofit organizations may apply for CICNC financing, provided that a minimum of 51 percent of the units in a project are affordable to renters earning no more than 60 percent of the area median income (80 percent of the area median in nonmetropolitan counties).

CICNC staff members review loan applications, which must receive final approval from the board of directors. Once the project is approved, a description is circulated among member banks, which may subscribe to a portion of any CICNC loan. Participation is strictly voluntary, and the level of participation in a loan is up to the member. In addition to loan underwriting, CICNC staff provide technical assistance to applicants.

The chief advantage of a voluntary loan pool is flexibility. Each member bank has the opportunity to decline or invest in any project, in an amount that the bank deems appropriate. Minimum participation is $10,000 per project, and there is no maximum. The program's statewide scope permits some geographic diversification, allowing rural banks to invest in urban markets and vice versa. Each member is expected to participate in at least one loan per year, and the large size of the consortium facilitates the funding of loans without creating undue exposure for any one member.

The disadvantage of a voluntary system is that it requires an extra step between loan approval by the board and full subscription of the loan. According to Roger Earnhardt, CICNC's executive vice president, 30 days typically elapse between the time the board approves the loan and full funding. On occasion, Earnhardt has had to "dial for dollars" to fund larger loans, but all loans approved by the board have been funded. For oversubscribed loans, pro rata reductions in contributions may be made, or banks may be asked informally to change their contribution amounts. For small loans, large banks tend to step away, allowing smaller banks to participate. Overall, Earnhardt feels that the informal system has worked well.

CICNC currently offers two products: a multifamily permanent loan product and a pilot secondary loan program.

Multifamily Permanent Loans. CICNC's multifamily loan product is a conventional permanent mortgage secured by a nonrecourse first deed of trust. The maximum loan term is 30 years. Interest rates are fixed for the first 18 years, priced at 190 basis points above the monthly average for the ten-year Treasury Constant Maturity Index, and subject to a minimum interest rate of 7.5 percent (as of February 1999). The interest rate adjusts in year 19, with a lifetime cap of 4 percent. CICNC loan commitments are fixed for up to 18 months and may be extended for six months for a commitment extension fee. Fees include a 1 percent nonrefundable commitment fee and a 1 percent loan fee. The application and processing fee is $500. The minimum project size for a CICNC loan is 24 units.

Affordable Multifamily Participation Program. The success of the CICNC program during the first six years of operation led to a familiar problem: active CICNC lenders were reaching the limit of their intended involvement in the program, and growing portfolios presented an obstacle to future lending. In 1996, CICNC lenders who were also members of the Federal Home Loan Bank of Atlanta (FHLBA) worked with FHLBA to create a secondary market for CICNC loans.

These efforts resulted in an innovative pilot program, the Affordable Multifamily Participation Program (AMPP), which was approved by the Federal Housing Finance Board on September 8, 1997. FHLBA agreed to buy participation interests in loans originated by CICNC, recycling funds to allow CICNC members to make new loans. Under the program, FHLBA selects a loan for an existing project and solicits offers to sell from all CICNC members with a share in the project's mortgage. Members have the option of selling to FHLBA or retaining their share of the loan. According to program guidelines, FHLBA may purchase no less than 50 percent and no more than 80 percent of the outstanding principal of a loan. The pilot program has a limit of $50 million, with a minimum FHLBA participation of $50,000 and a maximum participation of $2 million in any given project.

Funding Sources

NCBA provided start-up funding for CICNC and still shares office space and overhead with the consortium. CICNC funds its staff of two from loan fees.

Accomplishments

Since 1990, CICNC has funded or committed to funding 75 projects totaling $62.8 million and providing 3,613 units of affordable housing. Annual lending commitments are fairly steady at $8 to $10 million per year.

The first two loan purchases under AMPP took place at the end of 1997, when FHLBA purchased 77 percent of the outstanding principal on the Graham Village Apartments and 79 percent of the $3.4 million loan on the Carillon Apartments. In the first full year of the program, FHLBA purchased participations in 15 loans, representing principal balances of $11.6 million.

Contact

Community Investment Corporation of North Carolina
Roger L. Earnhardt, Executive Vice President
P.O. Box 19999
Raleigh, North Carolina 27619-1999
Telephone: (919) 781-7979
Fax: (919) 881-9909

State Historic Rehabilitation Tax Credits
State of North Carolina

As of January 1, 1998, the state of North Carolina expanded its historic rehabilitation tax credit to encourage the preservation of historic properties. For income-producing properties, the state program is a "piggy-back" credit to be used in conjunction with the 20 percent federal tax credit for investment in historic preservation. The 1998 revision also created a state income tax credit that can be used by homeowners residing in historic buildings.

Program Administration

The North Carolina State Historic Preservation Office administers the tax credit program in conjunction with the National Park Service (NPS), although NPS does not directly administer the state tax credits. The state has adopted the standards of the National Register of Historic Places, and the rehabilitation of structures listed on the register must meet standards set by the U.S. Secretary of the Interior. NPS does the review primarily to ensure that federal program standards are met (and would be doing the review regardless) and to determine eligibility for federal tax credits. Meeting federal standards qualifies the structure for state tax credits as well. The homeowner portion of the program is overseen only by the state historic preservation office.

Program Description

Under the 1998 legislation, income-producing properties approved for federal income tax credits for the rehabilitation of historic structures are also eligible to receive state income tax credits. The total state tax credit is 20 percent of the expenditures that qualify for federal credits and is granted at an annual rate of 4 percent over five years. (Under previous legislation, only 5 percent of expenditures eligible for federal credits could receive state credits.) In addition to using the federal tax credit for investment in historic preservation, a number of projects also use the federal low-income housing tax credit.

To qualify, the minimum rehabilitation investment must exceed $5,000 or the "adjusted basis" (the formula to determine eligible costs) of the building, whichever is greater, within a 24-month period. Applications are reviewed by NPS and the North Carolina State Historic Preservation Office, with the park service making the final determination of eligibility.

Homeowners, who are not eligible for the federal historic investment tax credit, may receive a 30 percent rehabilitation credit over five years, subject to a minimum investment of $25,000 within a 24-month period. Applications are reviewed only by the state historic preservation office.

To qualify for the credit, a property (either owner occupied or income producing) must be listed in the National Register of Historic Places or located in a registered historic district. Costs for acquisition, new additions, site work, and personal property are not considered in the calculation for credits. Rehabilitation must meet the standards established by the Secretary of the Interior.

There is no cap on the total credits that may be approved in any given year. Initial estimates by the state fiscal research division projected that the program would cost the state $7.5 million in lost revenues and $892,223 in administrative costs through 2002.

Accomplishments

As of June 1998, the response to the program has been overwhelming. For income-producing properties, the state received as many applications in the first six months of 1998 as it had received in all of 1997. The state also received over 80 applications from homeowners, more than double the 34 applications that had been projected.

While not targeted specifically toward rental properties, the tax credit program has received a significant amount of use for affordable housing. Prior to the 1998 revisions to the legislation, nearly 40 projects that had been awarded tax credits were identified as affordable-housing projects by the state historic preservation office. These projects involved the adaptive use of historic buildings—primarily schools—as well as hotels, hospitals, and industrial buildings.

Contact

Restoration Branch, State Historic Preservation Office
North Carolina Division of Archives and History
Tim Simmons, AIA, Preservation Tax Credit Coordinator
109 East Jones Street
Raleigh, North Carolina 27601-2807
Telephone: (919) 733-6547
Fax: (919) 715-4801

Pennsylvania Community Development Bank
State of Pennsylvania

In 1998, as part of Governor Ridge's Project for Community Building, the state of Pennsylvania established the Pennsylvania Community Development Bank (PCD Bank) to make capital and technical assistance available for community development lending. PCD Bank is not chartered by the Pennsylvania Department of Banking or any federal regulatory agency.

Program Administration

An operational committee of the Pennsylvania Economic Development Financing Authority Board administers the PCD Bank.

Program Description

PCD Bank has four goals:

- The development of local community development financial institutions (CDFIs) that can leverage significant private sector funds for development initiatives;
- The creation of new businesses or the expansion of very small-scale businesses;
- The creation of comprehensive community development plans that link housing, access to employment opportunities, educational opportunities, and community service facilities;
- The provision of technical assistance and capacity-building services in partnership with community lending institutions.

PCD Bank achieves its goals by providing grants and loans.

To ensure that economically disadvantaged communities have access to the services of a community lending institution, PCD Bank provides grants and loans to state-accredited CDFIs, enabling them to make loans to local businesses and other community development borrowers. It will also make grants to organizations trying to become state-accredited CDFIs or to community-based organizations partnering with CDFIs.

Grants. PCD Bank is required by the state to allocate $7 million of state-appropriated funds for grants and technical assistance; $5 million of these funds came from the initial appropriation, and an additional $2 million was allocated in the state's 1998–1999 budget.

The three categories of grants for CDFIs are startup grants, expansion grants, and development services grants.

Emerging CDFIs (i.e., prior to accreditation) are eligible for three-year startup grants from PCD Bank. To receive this funding, a CDFI must demonstrate that it has identified a distressed community or population and that it is organized to work with this community or population. Startup grants provide $25,000 in the first year (to support operating costs) and $100,000 in the second and third years (on the basis of performance). These grants require a 1:1 match of nonstate dollars. The goal is to get CDFIs accredited so that they can make use of the CDFI loan fund.

State-accredited CDFIs are eligible to apply for expansion grants, which may be used to target new populations or to provide new financial products and services.

Development services grants are available to state-accredited or startup CDFIs and to nonprofit technical assistance providers working in partnership with either. The funds may be used to promote the creation of small businesses through financial training, technical assistance, or other support services.

Loans. Of the initial appropriation to the PCD Bank, $10 million has been set aside to leverage an anticipated $30 million in private sector capital. The state's $10 million will be the subordinate (junior) capital in this fund; however, if private sector investors choose to have their monies take a subordinate position, private sector capital above the $30 million can be raised. PCD Bank will maintain a senior-to-junior capital ratio of no more than 3:1.

The state and private sector funds will be used to finance the PCD Bank loan fund and will serve two purposes: first, because the state appropriation will be subordinate to the private sector capital, there will be a guarantee against potential financial losses; second, the funds will be used to subsidize the interest rates on private sector capital lent to CDFIs.

To enable funded CDFIs to make loans available to their borrowers at a rate that is profitable for the CDFI and advantageous for the CDFI's borrowers, loans made available to CDFIs through PCD Bank will have a number of characteristics. First, PCD Bank will seek to make loans to CDFIs at a favorable rate of interest. Second, at least initially, maximum loan terms are expected to be no more than five to seven years. Third, the minimum loan amount will be $250,000 over a five-year period (the maximum amount is still to be determined).

While loans are intended for use by microenterprises, business startups, small-business expansions, nonprofit community facilities, and business incubation, they may also be used to support housing initiatives—a result that will occur mainly as a byproduct of job creation efforts. For example, a mixed-use project may include businesses and housing in the same facility.

Funding Sources

PCD Bank is capitalized through a combination of public and private funds. A total of $17 million has been appropriated to the bank to date. The bank was originally established through a $15 million appropriation from the funds allotted to the Pennsylvania Economic Development Financing Authority in the state's 1997–1998 budget.

PCD Bank state allocation funds are held in a private sector trustee account managed by Chase Manhattan Bank, and the interest returns from this account are used to help cover PCD Bank's administrative costs. All loan repayments from CDFIs will be made into this account, and private investors and participating lenders will be repaid through this account.

Accomplishments

As of February 1999, nearly $18 million in private sector capital had been raised. Applications for CDFI accreditation are now under review. Grants have been awarded to ten startup CDFIs that will cover 60 of the state's 67 counties.

Contact
Pennsylvania Community Development Bank
Pennsylvania Department of Community and Economic Development
Kim Kaufman, Executive Director
466 Forum Building
Harrisburg, Pennsylvania 17120
Telephone: (717) 783-1108
Fax: (717) 234-4560

501(c)(3) Tax-Exempt Multifamily Bond Program
State of Texas

In a role defined in 1997 legislation, the Texas Department of Housing and Community Affairs uses 501(c)(3) tax-exempt bonds for the construction of mixed-income multifamily housing.

By adding specific 501(c)(3) language, the Texas legislature enabled the department of housing and community affairs to act as a conduit issuer of bonds to finance multifamily housing projects developed by nonprofit entities. The financing is a means of increasing the state's bond capacity without affecting competing uses for private-activity bonds, which are subject to a state cap and are in high demand because of their direct link to low-income housing tax credits.

Program Administration

The Texas Department of Housing and Community Affairs administers the tax-exempt multifamily bond program.

Program Description

Before the 1997 legislation, nonprofit organizations with 501(c)(3) status were unable to obtain tax-exempt bond financing. The new legislation not only enables them to do so but also offers several further advantages: first, because the bonds are funded completely by the private sector, they do not affect the state's credit rating; second, because no state program dollars are used, the department of housing and community affairs (which acts as a conduit issuer) can maximize the use of scarce funding by applying it to other programs.

By lowering the cost of financing, these bonds allow mixed-income housing developments to be assured of an income stream that is sufficient to cover operating costs. (If debt service is lower, less income is needed to cover costs.) Even when the bonds are used to purchase an existing property with affordable rents, bond financing ensures that lower-income tenants will be living in setaside units and that rents will remain affordable to lower-income residents regardless of fluctuations in the local economy.

Bonds can be used for 100 percent of a project's financing. For the purchase of an existing property to be converted to affordable housing, the savings yielded by tax-exempt financing may be sufficient to make the project viable. For new construction, bond financing may be combined with other sources of equity, such as HOME funds, to make the project feasible.

To qualify for 501(c)(3) financing, nonprofits must agree to reserve 60 percent of a development's housing units for low- (61 to 80 percent of the area median income) and very low-income (31 to 60 percent of the area median income) households. All units must be occupied by households whose income does not exceed 140 percent of the area median. Five percent of the units must be reserved for tenants with special needs. The rents must be set at affordable rates for the low-income tenants. The income and rent requirements are deed restricted for a term no less than the loan term, even if the loan is prepaid.

Each fiscal year, the department of housing and community affairs enters into a memorandum of understanding with the Texas Bond Review Board to set a limit on the amount of 501(c)(3) bonds to be issued during that fiscal year. The following guidelines ensure that projects financed with 501(c)(3) bonds are geographically dispersed throughout the state and are used primarily for the construction of new properties: (1) At least 50 percent of the annual issuance amount must be used for the purposes of new construction or the acquisition and substantial rehabilitation of existing properties; (2) no more than 25 percent of the annual issuance amount may be used in any one metropolitan area; (3) at least 15 percent of the annual issuance amount must be used for projects in rural areas.

Accomplishments

In 1996, nearly $62.8 million in bonds funded the acquisition and rehabilitation of 14 properties, mostly in the Dallas–Fort Worth area. Of the 3,380 units of housing involved, 1,876 were set aside as affordable.

Contact

Texas Department of Housing and Community Affairs
Housing Finance Division
Brent Stewart, Director of Multifamily Finance
507 Sabine, Suite 800
Austin, Texas 78701
Telephone: (512) 475-2213
Fax: (512) 475-3362
Web site: www.tdhca.state.tx.us

The Reinvestment Fund's Affordable Housing Group
Regional

Founded in 1986, The Reinvestment Fund (TRF)—formerly known as the Delaware Valley Community Reinvestment Fund (DVCRF)—is a community development financial institution that uses capital and technical expertise to build wealth and create economic opportunity for low-wealth communities and low- and moderate-income individuals in a 20-county region that includes southeastern Pennsylvania, southern Delaware, and Newcastle County in northern Delaware. The Affordable Housing Group (AHG), one of TRF's four departments, provides predevelopment loans, construction loans, and permanent financing to nonprofit and for-profit developers. AHG also provides specialized technical real estate services to key borrowers throughout the region. TRF's Commercial Loan Group and Economic Opportunity Group focus on lending and investment opportunities to build business, workforce, and community support services such as daycare, schools, and clinics to meet TRF's goals.

TRF has expanded its capabilities by creating subsidiaries: the Collaborative Lending Initiative provides loans for large projects, and DVCRF Ventures, a venture capital fund, provides subordinated debt and equity to growth businesses.

Program Description

AHG's goal, as stated in its 1998 annual report, is to "strategically position TRF as the primary lender, the key financial intermediary, and the nonprofit consultant/partner of choice in the affordable-housing market."

AHG's funding priorities include the following:

- Homes for sale to low- and moderate-income families;
- Housing with access to transportation and jobs;
- Low-income rental units with access to social and employment services;
- Urban projects with sufficient scale to affect market perceptions of the neighborhood (market tipping);
- Mixed-income projects;
- Low- and moderate-income housing in suburban locations.

Funding is targeted to developers of rental or homeownership housing. Community development corporations are the largest consumers of AHG loan products; other nonprofits rank second and for-profit developers third.

TRF does not actively market its programs, choosing instead to establish an institutional presence in the market by demonstrating that capital is available with few restrictions. Because the financing provided by AHG is for housing that has some "subsidy" relationship, what marketing TRF does is targeted more to the sources of housing subsidies (the public agencies) than to potential borrowers. These public agencies are likely to be aware of projects in need of financial and technical support, and most new deals and contacts come through them.

Loan Products. AHG currently offers the following loan products:

- Recoverable grants: AHG offers grants of $30,000 to $50,000 to nonprofit organizations to cover the costs associated with determining the feasibility of proposed projects. The grant need not be repaid if the project does not proceed. If the project goes forward, repayment of the grant may be written in as a line item within the project costs. No interest is charged.
- Predevelopment loans: Loans of up to $150,000 are available to help nonprofit developers meet predevelopment expenses. These loans tend to follow the recoverable grants once partial funding commitments have been secured. The term of the loan is one year at an interest rate of 4 percent or less.
- Property acquisition loans: Loans of up of $400,000 are available to cover between 80 and 100 percent of acquisition and holding costs. Interest rates are as low as 4 percent for nonprofits, higher for for-profit developers.
- Construction finance loans: AHG construction finance loans of up to $2 million can cover up to 100 percent of the value of construction. Although banks often permit developers to draw on construction loan accounts no more than once a month, TRF allows draws every two weeks, which enables developers to work with small subcontractors, who often lack lines of credit and need to be paid more frequently in order to meet payroll and other expenses. Loan terms are based on projected completion dates and the nature of the project; interest rates are 6 percent for nonprofits, higher for for-profits. Construction finance loans can also be used to augment funds from other sources.
- Minipermanent mortgages: For rental projects, AHG offers up to 100 percent financing in the form of "miniperms." Loans of up to $400,000 are available for terms of up to ten years, with interest rates as low as 6 percent. The loan can be fully amortized or structured as a balloon.
- Lease-purchase loans: AHG provides lease-purchase loans of up to $400,000 for up to 100 percent of the value of the property. Loans are for up to four years, with interest rates as low as 6 percent.
- Permanent mortgages: Permanent mortgages may be obtained from TRF's Long-Term Fund and from its Community Development Trust Fund. Loans from the Long-Term Fund may be up to $1 million at interest rates of less than 8 percent for terms of up to 25 years. These loans may be for up to 90 percent of a project's value. The Community Development Trust Fund offers loans of up to $3 million at market rates for terms of up to 18 years. These loans are for up to 95 percent of a project's value. Permanent mortgage loans can be used only used for rental projects.

Technical Assistance. For both nonprofit and for-profit developers whose projects and goals closely match the TRF mission, AHG provides a full range of technical assistance, beginning with the planning and feasibility stages and continuing through sales or lease-up. During the planning stage, assistance includes GIS analysis and data analysis. AHG also offers assistance with construction management, project management, and financial packaging. The fee that AHG charges for its services may be covered by a grant: the city of Philadelphia, for example, pays AHG to provide technical assistance to community development corporations that serve the city.

*Collaborative Lending Initiative.*The Collaborative Lending Initiative (CLI) is a $15 million fund created by TRF in 1994 in cooperation with 17 area banks. Member banks provide lines of credit, which TRF uses to finance construction projects that are too large for its loan pool. The "big loans" of up to $2 million are financed through CLI, the smaller loans through TRF's Loan Fund. TRF provides credit enhancement with a subordinate loan of $1 for every $4 of bank financing. CLI also originates loans that are sold to the Community Development Trust Fund.

Funding Sources

The TRF Loan Fund comprises $38 million in investments from more than 750 individuals and institutions. Investment terms range from one to 15 years, based on prospectuses issued by TRF. Large institutional investors (those investing $1 million or more) negotiate their own terms with TRF.

Operating funds for AHG come from net interest income, loan origination fees, and grants. The Housing Group projects that it will be self-sufficient by 2004.

Accomplishments

Between 1995 and 1998, TRF (then DVCRF) financed 30 percent of the units under New Jersey's Urban Home Ownership Recovery Program, 75 percent of the units under Philadelphia's Home Ownership Rehabilitation Program, and 29 percent of the low-income housing tax credit units in southeastern Pennsylvania. During 1997 and 1998, TRF financed more than 1,000 affordable housing units. Since the fund began in 1986, 564 loans valued at $108.3 million have been committed, and affordable-housing loans account for 65 percent of that amount.

Contact
The Reinvestment Fund
Jeremy Nowak, Executive Director
718 Arch Street, Suite 300 North
Philadelphia, Pennsylvania 19106
Telephone: (215) 925-1130
Fax: (215) 923-4764

Workforce Housing Preservation Programs
Northwestern United States

Workforce housing preservation programs are used to develop rental housing in tight markets where the private sector has been unable to meet demand. Two features are characteristic of these programs: the bond financing technique involved and a long-term strategy in which a project's cash flow is used to "endow" other affordable housing.

Local housing authorities have applied the workforce housing concept for the construction, acquisition, and rehabilitation of rental housing. Located primarily in the Northwest, these programs are targeted to working families who are being priced out of the local housing market. In addition, workforce housing preservation programs may be used to help stabilize neighborhoods and to preserve existing affordable housing in markets where demand is driving up prices.

Targeted income levels for workforce housing vary. Most programs set aside some portion of the units for families earning 80 percent or less than the area median income; some target even lower incomes. Other units are intended for moderate-income households.

Program Administration

Local housing authorities administer workforce housing programs. In some cases, for-profit developers may operate as turnkey developers; for the overall management of such projects, housing authorities typically engage the services of private management companies that are experienced in the management of nonsubsidized rental properties.

Program Description

A hallmark of workforce preservation housing programs is the use of two housing revenue bond issues—one senior and one subordinate—to fund project development. Traditional bond financing involves issuance of a single bond that has a 20- or 30-year term. Workforce preservation programs use the traditional, long-term bond (the "senior," or "A" bond) to finance the bulk of the project. A smaller portion of the project (the subordinate, or "B" bond) is financed through a bond with a shorter term (or in some cases with staggered maturity dates). The "accelerated" bond is subordinate to the term bond and is issued at a lower interest rate. When the accelerated bond is paid off, cash flow increases, and the housing authority can use the increase to reduce rents at that housing project or to fund other affordable-housing programs. Other forms of financing are used on a project-by-project basis. The Vancouver Housing Authority, for example, has several projects funded by tax credits, Community Development Block Grant (CDBG) funds, or HOME funds.

The financing for a workforce housing preservation project must be structured carefully: cash flow must be sufficient to ensure the repayment of the accelerated bond, while at the same time sufficient cash reserves must be maintained to cushion against the ups and downs of the local economy. Because workforce housing projects are designed to generate a healthy cash flow over the long term, the rents are typically only slightly below market rate. In some projects, a certain number of units are reserved for lower-income tenants and the remaining units rent at market rates.

Workforce housing preservation projects can be used in various ways. In the short term, such programs make affordable housing available for working families. Housing units developed through these programs may also be ideal for families using Section 8 vouchers who are otherwise unable to find suitable apartments. After the accelerated bonds are paid off, the housing authority can reduce rents within the project, making the units affordable to families with even lower incomes. Alternatively, the cash flow may be used for other affordable-housing programs and priorities. Housing authorities may also want to use workforce housing preservation bond financing techniques to purchase properties whose contracts for federal subsidies are due to expire.

The selection, management, and risks of workforce housing preservation programs are more characteristic of the private sector rental market than of the government-subsidized projects that most housing authorities are involved in. Before entering the workforce housing preservation arena, a public housing authority would do well to acquire or tap into private sector skills. In particular, in order to evaluate potential risks, the authority should determine which factors prevented the private sector from entering into this market.

Recent workforce housing projects by housing authorities in King County, Vancouver, Snohomish, and Portland have all received "A" ratings from Standard & Poor's. Although the evaluation process varies depending upon the nature of the project, factors typically evaluated include the quality of the project, debt repayment ability, the local economy and housing needs, and the experience and management history of the housing authority. Projects that are only partially affordable (i.e., income restricted) or that can convert to market-rate rents during the life of the bond issue are evaluated as market-rate commercial properties. One tool that may be used to develop the bond rating is the set of public housing authority evaluation criteria recently developed by Standard & Poor's.

Program Examples

The following three subsections describe examples of workforce preservation housing programs.

Kitsap County Consolidated Housing Authority. The Kitsap County (Washington) Consolidated Housing Authority (KCCHA) originated a workforce housing strategy in 1986 when the private sector was unable to meet the demand for rental housing. The housing authority, in partnership with the county, devised the workforce housing strategy to develop housing and generate cash flow.

Rental vacancy rates were at 1 percent, but developers could not obtain financing. Conventional lenders, including Fannie Mae, would not support housing activity in the area because of the high risks associated with the single-economy market. The economy of the Puget Sound region, where the county is located, is dominated by the military, and lenders feared that military downsizing could cause the entire housing market to collapse. In recent years, military downsizing has, in fact, driven vacancy rates to at least 9 percent, indicating the legitimacy of the perceived risks. However, the housing authority was careful to maintain significant cash reserves, and its projects remain viable.

KCCHA has used the workforce housing approach to finance five rental-housing projects that have recently been refinanced with a $26 million bond issue. Rental information is available on the Web. Little distinguishes these units from market-rate rentals.

One of KCCHA's more recent construction projects, Viking's Crest, is a 120-unit complex in which all units were available for sale to tenants as condominiums. At least 50 percent of the units are targeted to tenants with incomes at or below the low-income housing limits established by HUD, and rents for those units will be affordable. CDBG funds will be used to provide downpayment assistance to eligible buyers.

Having paid off some of the initial B bonds, KCCHA is now experiencing the financial benefits of its financing strategy. (Most workforce preservation projects are "younger" and have not yet paid off the accelerated bonds.) The cash flow from these projects now funds both staff and other affordable-housing programs; for example, a portion of the funds go into a revolving loan fund for ongoing support of affordable housing.

Contact

Kitsap County Consolidated Housing Authority
Norman McLoughlin, Executive Director
9264 Bayshore Drive, N.W.
Silverdale, Washington 98383
Telephone: (360) 692-5596
Fax: (360) 692-4374

Affordable Housing Preservation Program of Clackamas County. In 1996, Clackamas County, Oregon, adapted the workforce housing preservation program model to undertake the $14 million acquisition and rehabilitation of a 264-unit project. The county housing authority selected the project on the basis of the following criteria: ability to serve households earning between 50 and 80 percent of the area median income; good structural condition; location (i.e., the property is situated where such housing is needed); and compliance with the financial criteria for the bond financing. Until the accelerated bonds can be paid off, rents will not be much below market rates. After five to ten years, the authority's goal is to charge rents that are 10 to 20 percent below market rate and to generate cash flow (estimated to be between $400,000 and $500,000) to support other affordable-housing programs and priorities. Because of the large scale of this project, the housing authority does not plan to undertake another workforce project in the near future.

Contact

Housing Authority of Clackamas County
Gary DiCenzo, Executive Director
13930 South Gain Street
P.O. Box 1510
Oregon City, Oregon 97045
Telephone: (503) 655-8289
Fax: (503) 655-8676

Vancouver Housing Authority. The Vancouver (Washington) Housing Authority (VHA) undertook the development of workforce housing because despite strong economic growth, the gap between local housing costs and incomes has continued to widen. Since 1980, rents have increased 124 percent; in January 1996, the real average wage was about 1 percent lower than it had been in 1984. VHA works in partnership with county government, private developers, property management firms, builders, and realtors. The program provides mixed-income housing, renting 51 percent or more of the units to working people who earn 80 percent of the area median income or less.

Rather than set criteria for the selection of projects, VHA sets yearly goals for the number of workforce housing units it wishes to secure. However, each project must serve a public goal. Flexibility in identifying and structuring projects is a priority. The housing authority keeps close tabs on local housing markets, and factors such as new job creation and planned infrastructure and transit improvements play a role in decisions. The authority generally avoids selecting new projects that will compete with existing workforce housing projects.

Because VHA is now perceived as a "player" in the affordable-housing market, properties are now being shopped to the housing authority. VHA's ability to evaluate proposed projects and make board-approved decisions within weeks—rather than months—help the program succeed.

VHA is committed to workforce housing as an immediate answer to the needs of working people. Over time, the authority hopes to use workforce housing as a means of maintaining an inventory of housing stock and as an endowment source for homeless shelters and other housing initiatives for very low-income people. Since 1992, tax-exempt revenue mortgage bonds have financed the purchase of 766 units of workforce housing.

Contact

Vancouver Housing Authority
Kurt Creager, Executive Director
2500 Main Street
Vancouver, Washington 98660-7599
Telephone: (360) 694-2501
Fax: (360) 694-8369

Corporation for Supportive Housing: Rental Reserve Funds
National

Working with several states, the Corporation for Supportive Housing (CSH) is using a special strategy to ensure that supportive housing projects can meet their operating costs.

Program Description

Providing supportive housing for tenants with special needs creates challenges beyond those typically associated with the provision of affordable housing. Because special-needs and very low-income tenants living in supportive housing generally cannot pay sufficient rent to cover basic operating costs—and because meeting the needs of these populations tends to generate higher operating costs—some form of rental subsidy is required to keep such housing affordable and sustainable.

The CSH financing strategy uses proceeds from the sale of low-income housing tax credits (LIHTCs) to create a rental reserve fund. The reserve fund is capitalized for 15 years—the time required to comply with the restrictions governing the tax credits. The size of the fund is tailored to the project, taking into account the overall financial package and a number of local market conditions projected for a 15-year period (e.g., rental rates, expenses, vacancy rates, interest rates, and security coverage). Tailoring each project to local market conditions provides for the most efficient use of the reserve fund. Because the sale of the tax credits allows the reserve to be funded up front, the initial size of the fund can be reduced on the assumption of future interest earnings.

HUD housing programs do not permit the use of program funds to provide additional rental subsidies. Projects receiving government rent subsidies reduce the amount of money set aside for the reserve fund by the amount of the subsidy.

Because the structure of the rent subsidy in this CSH model differs from the Section 8 "norm," the program (1) reduces the disincentive for tenants to earn income and (2) eliminates overestimation of the cost of the rent contracts. As in Section 8 programs, tenants must earn less than 50 percent of the area median income to qualify for a rent subsidy. However, in the CSH model the tenant pays a fixed rent equal to 30 percent of the *average* monthly income of the targeted tenant population. Section 8 programs, in contrast, charge rent that is equal to 30 percent of the tenant's *actual* income, which can be a disincentive to earning more. The use of average income under the CSH model gives the tenant an incentive to do "better than average": even if the tenant earns more than the average income for the targeted population, his or her rent will not increase, as it would under Section 8.

Under current Section 8 programs, overestimation of the cost of rental contracts comes about as follows: contract rent rates vary on the basis of fair-market standards, but the subsidy calculation does not take into account tenants' rental payments or actual operating costs. The tailored assumptions used in the CSH model eliminate overestimation.

Unlike Section 8 programs, the CSH approach assumes that tenant rents and the rent subsidy cover only basic operating costs. Since the CSH programs use an up-front injection of cash from the sale of tax credits for the subsidy, they are not—unlike Section 8 programs—dependent on contract renewals. At the end of the 15-year period, however, unless a new source of subsidy funding is found, the project will have to convert to market-rate rentals.

Adequate oversight of the reserve fund is critical. CSH administers these funds for several projects under a detailed legal agreement that describes precisely how funds may flow in and out of the reserves.

Accomplishments

Currently, CSH has structured rental reserves for a nine-project demonstration program in Connecticut and has undertaken a similar program in Michigan. The city of New York has also implemented a similar model (although not with CSH). Typically, the projects receive a 1 percent soft first mortgage from HUD funds and obtain additional financial support from the state.

Contact

Corporation for Supportive Housing
Brigitt Jandreau-Smith
Director of Project Development and Finance
342 Madison Avenue, Suite 505
New York, New York 10173
Telephone: (212) 986-2966; in California, (510) 251-1580
Fax: (212) 986-6552

Low-Income Housing Fund
National

Established in 1984, the Low-Income Housing Fund (LIHF) is one of the oldest and most active community development financial institutions (CDFIs). In addition to making direct loans to nonprofit organizations from its revolving loan fund, LIHF plays a strong role as an intermediary and facilitator, packaging loans for conventional lenders and creating community lending pools.

Although loans are concentrated in California and New York, where LIHF has offices, the fund is national in scope. Recently, LIHF has been very active in Washington, D.C.

Program Description

LIHF's primary goals are to facilitate (1) affordable rental housing, particularly housing for people with special needs (over 40 percent of the total loan portfolio) and (2) homeownership (15 percent of lending activity). Over half of LIHF financing goes to critical acquisition (30 percent of loans, 7 percent of which is for land acquisition) and predevelopment (24 percent). LIHF is becoming increasingly involved in nonresidential lending for community facilities and mixed-use projects and is also exploring business lending.

LIHF offers interest writedown grants and loan guarantees to further facilitate affordable credit for nonprofit developers. In addition to loans, LIHF provides flexible lines of credit that may be used for acquisition, predevelopment, and working capital. LIHF also provides training and technical assistance.

Through LIHF, investors can invest in the revolving loan fund (RLF); purchase participations in RLF loans; allocate loan funds to LIHF (whereby LIHF packages and closes loans that are funded by an institution); participate in community lending pools; or make grants to LIHF.

Funding Sources

LIHF is funded by religious institutions, foundations, financial institutions, and individual donations and loans.

Accomplishments

According to its 1995–1996 annual report, LIHF has provided assistance in 19 states and "has made and/or packaged over $127 million in affordable loans to more than 400 projects [which] have yielded almost 13,000 units of highly diverse low-income housing."[10]

Future Plans

At the time of this writing, LIHF was exploring the possibility of issuing 501(c)(3) bonds to generate a source of long-term, fixed-rate financing for projects. LIHF's proposal for this innovative new program provides an overview:

> LIHF would originate loans by drawing against a line of credit and warehousing individual eligible loans until sufficient volume is available to cost-effectively issue 501(c)(3) tax-exempt bonds. Lenders would then purchase bonds that have specific eligible projects. Security for the bonds would be general recourse to LIHF, through both program phases.[11]

The Bay Area Community Loan Pool (BACLP)—a group of San Francisco banks established to work with LIHF—would provide the warehousing line of credit and purchase the 501(c)(3) bonds through private placement. A BACLP member bank would commit a dollar amount to the bond program and provide an equal amount to the line of credit. The total commitments of all BACLP members participating in the program would determine the ultimate bond amount. Using the line of credit, LIHF would make loans to eligible projects, then warehouse the loans for up to two years until the targeted bond amount is reached. When the warehousing is completed, bonds would be issued by the Association of Bay Area Governments, a membership organization of Bay Area government authorities, and purchased by BACLP members through private placement.

The program would provide both short- and long-term financing with targeted average loan maturities of seven to ten years and a maximum term of 30 years. Projects warehoused under the program must meet the requirements of the 501(c)(3) bond program. The projects must be owned by a nonprofit 501(c)(3) organization, and 20 percent of the units must be designated for households whose incomes are at or below 50 percent of the area median. Loans of $10,000 to $1 million would be available. A minimum loan pool size of $3 million would be necessary to make the bond issuance cost-effective.

The benefits of the program would include below-market interest rates for nonprofit borrowers and tax-exempt market returns for bond purchasers. The loan-warehousing component would benefit small projects, which would not ordinarily have access to this type of financing because of the costs of bond issuance.

Contact

Low-Income Housing Fund
Nancy Andrews, President and Executive Director
Main Office
74 New Montgomery Street, Suite 250
San Francisco, California 94105
Telephone: (415) 777-9804
Fax: (415) 777-9195
Web site: www.lihf.org

Notes

1 William Segal and Edward J. Szymanoski, "Fannie Mae, Freddie Mac, and the Multi-family Mortgage Market," *Cityscape: A Journal of Policy Development and Research* 4, no. 1 (1998): 61.

2 Amy S. Bogdon and David C. Ling, "The Effects of Property, Owner, Location, and Tenant Characteristics on Multifamily Profitability," *Journal of Housing Research* 9, no. 2 (1998): 315.

3 Jean L. Cummings and Denise DiPasquale, "The Low-Income Housing Tax Credit: An Analysis of the First Ten Years," *Housing Policy Debate* (forthcoming October 1999).

4 Edward J. Szymanoski, "Guest Editor's Introduction: The Evolution of Multifamily Financing," *Cityscape: A Journal of Policy Development and Research* 4, no. 1 (1998): 3.

5 "California State Credit Limit Raised to $50 Million in 1998–99," *Housing and Development Reporter: Current Developments* (May 18, 1998): 10.

6 Florida Affordable Housing Finance Corporation, "Florida Affordable Housing Guarantee Program Historical Analysis" (unpublished in-house document, Tallahassee, Fla.: Florida Affordable Housing Finance Corporation, November 30, 1998), 1.

7 Tampa Bay Community Reinvestment Corporation, "Tampa Bay Community Reinvestment Corporation: Status and Prospects" (informational document, Tampa, Fla.: Tampa Bay Community Reinvestment Corporation, August 1992), 2.

8 *Minnesota Supportive Housing Demonstration Program: One-Year Evaluation Report*, prepared by Terry Tilson for the Wilder Research Center (New York: Corporation for Supportive Housing, June 1998), iii.

9 When the program first began, New Hampshire was experiencing a housing crisis, which led banks to donate foreclosed homes. It is too early to predict the pattern of awards for the reestablished program, although changes in the housing market make it unlikely that donations of foreclosed properties will continue to be as significant.

10 Low-Income Housing Fund, *Financing a Future of Hope: 1995–96 Annual Report* (San Francisco, Calif.: LIHF, 1996), 2.

11 Low-Income Housing Fund, *Proposal for a Low-Income Housing Fund 501(c)(3) Bond Program* (San Francisco, Calif.: LIHF, 1997), 1.

5

Preserving Affordable Housing Stock: Not Just a Federal Issue

For sixty years, Congress has recognized that meeting America's housing needs requires a partnership between the federal government, the private housing industry, and state and local governments.[1] Today, a debate rages over the future of that partnership, the people it serves, and the millions of units of housing it has produced.

Overview

Preservation of Federally Assisted Projects

From 1965 to 1983, the federal government—through the Department of Housing and Urban Development (HUD) and the Internal Revenue Code—subsidized the development of nearly 1.5 million units of privately owned, multifamily apartments by providing low-interest loans; insuring mortgages made by private lenders; furnishing project-based rent subsidies; and providing tax incentives by allowing rapid depreciation on properties financed with nonrecourse debt. This system of assistance produced plenty of housing but has suffered serious and growing problems in recent years: because of automatic annual rent increases, 75 percent of the portfolio has subsidized rents that are above—often well above—market rates. Above-market rents drain scarce federal housing resources (an additional $150 million in fiscal year 1997 alone) and weaken public support for affordable-housing programs across the board.

By 2006, subsidy contracts will expire on more than 700,000 apartments housing more than 1 million households across the country. Their expiration offers an important opportunity to end excessive subsidies and to deal with the thousands of physically deteriorated properties in substandard condition.

HUD and Congress have responded to the challenge of preserving federally assisted housing in two ways. First, Congress has committed to renewing the expiring project-based rental assistance contracts of all property owners who comply with HUD's minimum property standards and who wish to remain in the Section 8 program. Second, through a program called "mark-to-market," HUD will put an end to excessive subsidies while improving the condition of thousands of physically deteriorated properties. Congress laid the foundation for the mark-to-market program in the Multifamily Assisted Housing Reform and Affordability Act of 1998 (MAHRAA), which becomes effective in fiscal 1999. MAHRAA's purpose is to bring down rental subsidy renewal costs by requiring owners of high-cost, Federal Housing Administration (FHA)–insured Section 8 projects to restructure their mortgages and accept lower rent subsidies in exchange for continued federal assistance.

This solution to excessive subsidies appears straightforward but will be extraordinarily difficult to execute. First, above-market rents must be reduced to market levels; at the same time, the mortgage amount must be reduced to a level that can be supported by the lower rent. And all this needs to be done in such a way that it does not trigger adverse tax consequences for project owners or make participation so onerous that owners choose not to renew their subsidy contracts with HUD.

Because HUD does not have enough expert staff to restructure financing for 8,500 properties, Congress has provided for that task to be delegated to third parties: competitively selected teams of state housing finance agencies and other public and private sector entities, both for-profit and nonprofit. These restructuring teams—referred to as participating administrative entities (PAEs) in the mark-to-market law—would be monitored by HUD and governed by public-purpose obligations laid out in the statute; these obligations include the protection of existing residents and communities and respect for the contractual obligations of owners and lenders. Of the initial 52 PAEs approved by HUD, 39 are state housing finance agencies and 13 are state and local housing agencies.

Although the mark-to-market program is still in its infancy, PAEs will soon have much to do. By 2002, contracts will expire on more than 3,100 low-income projects whose subsidized rents are much higher than HUD is able to pay. The owners of these projects will have two choices: they can elect to renew their HUD contracts, albeit at lower subsidies, so that their rents will remain affordable to their existing low-income tenants; or they can choose to opt out (not to renew), in which case they give up their rent subsidies and allow their properties to compete in the unsubsidized market, where there is no ceiling on the rents they can charge. States with the largest number of projects whose owners must make these choices are Ohio (274 projects), California (232), New York (232), Pennsylvania (143), Kentucky (138), Indiana (122), Illinois (118), Missouri (112), North Carolina (109), and Texas (104).[2]

Many property owners contend that they would be unable to operate profitably with the lower subsidies that HUD would impose on them. Fearing the loss of much-needed affordable housing that would result if owners were to opt out of the mark-to-market program, states and localities have begun to create "piggy-back" programs to make it more financially attractive for owners to stay in. Some states—such as Massachusetts, Wisconsin, West Virginia, Louisiana, and Illinois—are setting aside low-income housing tax credits (LIHTCs) for projects that preserve federally assisted low-income housing. Washington State gives preference points as a way of steering tax credits to preservation projects. In recent years, Massachusetts has set aside as much as 60 percent of its tax credit allocation for preservation, and in 1998, the West Virginia Housing Development Fund allocated all of its tax credits to a preservation setaside.[3]

In just the first eight months of 1998, the combination of large inventories of HUD-assisted housing in healthy real estate markets with strong demand for rental housing caused California communities to lose about 8,000 Section 8 units through owner opt-outs.[4] Fears of dramatically greater losses in the near future led the California legislature to create a mirror image of HUD's mark-to-market program. Under the new legislation, the California Housing Finance Agency (CHFA) initiated a taxable bond program that would provide up to $750 million over five years to help preserve 112,000 Section 8 units whose contracts will expire during that period. For fiscal 1999, up to $100 million will be made available to non-profit groups for refinancing and acquisition of these projects. Funding will increase by $25 million each year through fiscal 2003. At the time this book went to press, CHFA had been unable to offer sufficiently attractive loan terms to persuade owners to keep their properties affordable over the longer term. CHFA hopes that a new, $75 million, five-year preservation subsidy loan program will make the taxable bond option more attractive to owners. This new program will provide funds to bridge the gap created when Section 8 contracts are maintained under a refinanced loan with higher debt service costs. Loans will be structured as second mortgages for terms of up to ten years. Matching funds will be sought from other sources, including state or local government.

Highly specialized financing products are being used to help owners of formerly assisted properties to reposition their properties in the private market or to adjust to HUD's lower subsidy levels without having to subject themselves to the uncertainties of mark-to-market. "Owners of high-cost Section 8 projects concerned about the tax consequences and cash requirements of restructuring under HUD's mark-to-market process may find a safe haven in a real estate investment trust (REIT) being formed to acquire these projects and assist them in restructuring."[5] The sponsor of this REIT is New York City–based U.S. Select Management. The REIT can offer two benefits to owners who are reluctant to participate in restructuring: (1) a vehicle for avoiding the tax consequences that can arise from bifurcation of the project's FHA-insured debt into two new mortgages and (2) a source of capital for meeting the requirement that owners contribute 25 percent of the cost of rehabilitating the restructured project.

Preservation of Privately Owned Unsubsidized Housing

In the words of the Rouse-Maxwell National Housing Task Force, a "quieter housing preservation issue that could be even more damaging in the long run if not addressed soon [is] how to maintain the millions of privately owned, unsubsidized dwellings that the vast majority of poor people call home."[6] While the task force's alarm was sounded over a decade ago, if it continues to go unheeded the effects on the poor could be devastating. Because three out of four poor families receive no federal housing aid, even a successful resolution of the HUD housing issues will have virtually no impact on millions of households that have acute housing needs and must fend for themselves in an increasingly hostile marketplace.

Two factors suggest that in the post–welfare reform world, the poor will be less adequately housed by the private market: (1) declining access to a shrinking supply of affordable housing and (2) a weakening inner-city investment environment. Both factors are a function of supply and demand: on the demand side, favorable interest rates and stable home prices have enabled more renters to become homeowners. "Today, the average homeowner now spends a slightly smaller percentage of income on shelter than does the average renter, even while accumulating considerable wealth."[7] One consequence of the rise in homeownership is that rental housing is increasingly occupied by households that have lower incomes, more social problems, and fewer housing choices, and that are more heavily rent burdened. On the supply side, the costs of producing decent housing continue to increase. "Aged buildings need constant repair; some properties still carry heavy debt from the speculation frenzy of the 1980s; taxes and water charges are rising, and expenses must factor in vandalism, security problems, and unpaid rents."[8]

Effective demand for rental housing is declining. Between 1978 and 1993, the number of extremely low income renters (those with incomes below 30 percent of the local median) grew by 47 percent—from 5.9 million to 8.7 million households. This shift, which increased from 22 to 26 percent the share of *all* renters in the U.S. with such low incomes, underscores the growing residualization (concentration of lowest-income households) of the rental market.[9] During this entire fifteen-year stretch, large net additions to the rental supply moderated rent increases, actually enabling overall housing quality to improve.[10] Nevertheless, by 1993, 3.2 million renter households (9.5 percent) still lived in substandard housing.[11]

Significantly, during the latter part of the period—from 1989 to 1993—rents rose more than twice as fast as renters' incomes.[12] As a result, the number of extremely low-income families with dangerously high rent burdens grew to an all-time high: over 5 million households.[13] Reflecting on the fact that 2 million of the 5 million heads of households with severe rent burdens are employed and 1.2 million are working full time, Jason DeParle put his finger on *the* critical housing policy question embedded in the welfare reform puzzle. "Say it proves its doubters wrong," says DeParle of the welfare reform bill, "and those pushed from the rolls find jobs. Where are they supposed to live?"[14]

The deficit in affordable rental housing has been growing during good economic times and bad: between 1985 and 1993 by one-fifth nationally and by about one-third in large metropolitan areas.[15] In just the four years from 1989 to 1993, the number of extremely low-income renters grew by 1 million, while the number of extremely low-rent private-market units for which they were competing with other renters dropped by 250,000.[16] Aggravating the impacts of the loss in effective supply is the worsening competitive market position of the poor. In 1983, extremely low income renters occupied 54 percent of the affordable supply, compared to just 46 percent ten years later.[17]

To enable all Americans to have a decent place to live, most communities have adopted housing codes that set minimum standards for health and safety. However, many lower-income people cannot afford to buy or rent homes that meet these standards. For example, a household in New York City needs an income of almost $15,000 a year to pay just the average maintenance and operating cost ($386/month) of a prewar private rental-housing unit.[18] (This figure does not include the portion of the rent that covers the landlord's mortgage payment or profit.) There are entire New York City neighborhoods in which household income is not nearly enough to pay $386 a month. Moreover, a welfare check alone will not pay the cost of decent housing in New York City—or, for that matter, in any of the 48 contiguous states.[19] In Charlotte, North Carolina, for example, a worker needs an hourly wage of $8.73 to afford a decent one-bedroom apartment and an hourly wage of $9.83 for two bedrooms. As Jason DeParle puts it: "The market can adapt to the poor person's purse by selling cheaper toys or shoes, but there are only so many corners that can be cut in building cheaper housing. To be sure, codes should be simplified and red tape should be cut. But interest, utilities, and taxes—these costs are fixed, regardless of the occupants' income."[20]

In some markets, the economics of low-income housing make it impossible, even for the most experienced and responsible landlords, to maintain their rental housing in reasonably good condition. The bargaining power of tenants becomes inconsequential, and they are often forced by circumstances—and by landlords who recognize that the tenants have few choices—to accept conditions that are unsafe and even illegal. One article referred to the rise of a "shadowy market" where "building superintendents make extra money by quietly squeezing bodies into space next to the boiler; tenants sublease rooms in their own apartments; 'fixers' try to match up desperate tenants with dismal quarters."[21] In buildings that cannot operate at a profit, property owners demolish or board up housing rather than eliminate code violations and threaten to abandon their properties if communities enforce the housing code.[22]

Especially in high-cost cities with large immigrant populations, illegal conversions are also on the rise. One article in a six-part *New York Times* series described how "some New York City landlords have found profit in housing the poor illegally by carving up their buildings and renting out space that is too small and dangerous for those who can afford better, but passable for those with no choice."[23] The problem of illegal conversions also extends to underoccupied office buildings in inner-ring suburbs, such as Hicksville, in New York's Nassau County:

> The solution for the Delagados and their relatives had been to pool their incomes to pay $2,700 a month to house 15 people in an office suite converted into seven tiny bedrooms, two small kitchens, and two bathrooms, one with a row of three sinks. The tenants, who found the complex through word of mouth, all came from Latin America. That is not a coincidence . . . because

immigrants fill many entry-level jobs and have an especially hard time finding housing because of discrimination and the language barrier.[24]

As we look ahead, it is hard to imagine how the housing squeeze will improve without significant policy interventions at all levels of government. Thus far in the 1990s, new-construction rates for multifamily housing have dropped more than 50 percent nationally since the 1980s, and they are lower still in large cities—which means that there is less housing in decent condition to filter down to the poor than there was twenty years ago.[25] And most of the 5.3 million unassisted households that HUD characterizes as having "worst-case housing needs" are already spending more than half of their meager incomes for rent. If rents cannot be raised to keep pace with inflation so that owners can cover basic maintenance and operation costs, conditions will inevitably deteriorate. And as asset values decline, landlords can be expected to adjust their operating practices accordingly. If they cannot upgrade their stock to appeal to a higher-income clientele, they will defer maintenance and convert what remains of their illiquid capital investment into current income. The inevitable result of this endgame strategy is a renewed cycle of housing abandonment, neighborhood decline, and, ironically, higher rents because of the reduction in the available housing supply.

The 20 programs described in this chapter deal with both parts of the preservation challenge: preserving as much of the threatened federally assisted rental inventory as possible and—the quieter crisis—saving affordable unsubsidized rental housing. Most state efforts to improve the economics of federally assisted housing involve financial incentives in the form of tax-exempt financing or an allocation of LIHTCs—although Portland, Oregon's program consists of more stick than carrot. Efforts to preserve the unsubsidized affordable rental stock are also likely to include financial incentives but to combine them with tighter regulatory controls; some such efforts require "going back to basics." In Los Angeles, for example, an ineffective, complaint-based housing inspection system was converted into one that will require city inspections of every apartment unit at least once every three years.[26] To hire inspectors and finance legal action against housing-code violators, the law imposes a $1 per unit monthly fee on landlords. Under the new enforcement plan, the city will hire 50 additional inspectors to conduct routine inspections of all 700,000 units in the city. The ordinance aims to wipe out run-down apartments throughout the city within three years. No exemptions will be made for public or assisted housing.

Milwaukee has added a different wrinkle to its code enforcement program by turning its code inspectors into teachers. Among the 30 percent of property owners who have received training, code violations are reported to be down substantially, and landlords are helping the police reduce illegal drug activity and related crimes associated with the use of the landlords' properties. This is how the city's mayor, John O. Nordquist, describes the landlord training program he has championed:

Milwaukee's inspectors were using up valuable time chasing the same code violators who were renting to the same bad tenants over and over. Then deputy building inspector Marty Collins had the idea for the Landlord Training Program, in which building inspectors teach landlords how legally to screen against bad tenants—those with a history of damaging property, engaging in criminal activity, or not paying the rent. The inspectors also teach that well-kept property attracts reliable tenants. The program provides tips to landlords on how to comply more easily with code requirements. Equally important, the program gives building inspectors an opportunity to learn from landlords.[27]

Programs: State and Local Initiatives Fill the Federal Void

California Housing Finance Agency
State of California

The California Housing Finance Agency (CHFA) was created in 1975 as the state's affordable-housing bank. By taking advantage of the federal tax exemption available on state-issued debt, CHFA can provide housing finance capital at below-market interest rates without adding to state taxpayers' debt burden. CHFA provides single-family loans, multifamily loans, and mortgage loan insurance to meet the housing needs of low- and moderate-income households.

Program Description

In 1998, California's inventory of expiring project-based Section 8 units was estimated at nearly 112,000. According to HUD data, owners of 10,500 of these units opted to leave the program by the end of 1998. Because the tax-exempt financing available through CHFA (from the state allocation of private-activity bonds for affordable housing) was insufficient to address the preservation issue and other affordable-housing needs, CHFA explored other alternatives.

In 1998, CHFA developed three loan products based on taxable bond financing: first mortgages to refinance preservation projects; gap financing to be used with the first-mortgage loans, and an "option purchase" loan for nonprofits to purchase expiring-use projects owned by for-profit organizations. Unfortunately, as of February 1999 there had been no demand for these loan products. CHFA speculates that there are two reasons for the lack of demand: First, CFHA's loan products were simply not competitive in the current market; for-profit owners could refinance on the conventional market more cheaply and convert the units to market rate. Second, given the general uncertainty about operating conditions, for-profit owners were generally disinclined to remain in HUD programs.

However, CHFA's loan products that use tax-exempt financing are available for preservation of affordable housing and have been used for that purpose. For-profits, nonprofits, and public entities sponsoring affordable rental-apartment projects may qualify for CHFA loans at below-market interest rates. At least 20 percent of the units in a CHFA-financed multifamily rental project must be rented to very low income households for the term of the loan. Eligible projects include new construction, acquisition, and rehabilitation. Maximum loan amounts are negotiable but cannot exceed 50 percent of the economic value of the property or 90 percent of the development cost, whichever is less. Interest rates vary according to the term of the loan. In the past year, nonprofit organizations used this financing to purchase two expiring-use affordable-housing projects from for-profit owners, ensuring that over 200 housing units will remain affordable for an additional 30 years. Both projects also qualified for 4 percent low-income housing tax credits.

In addition, CHFA has been approved as one the first state housing finance agencies to participate in FHA's Risk-Sharing Pilot Program, available only to agencies rated as "top tier" by bond-rating organizations. Over a two-year period, FHA will share 50 percent of the default risk for 9,435 affordable rental units representing nearly $250 million in mortgages. The FHA guarantee enhances CHFA's ability to sell securities (bonds) in the secondary market, resulting in a leveraged ability to increase the affordable-housing stock.

Future Plans

In 1999, CHFA plans to introduce a preferentially priced 501(c)(3) bond financing program to enable nonprofit organizations to acquire expiring-use projects. It is also reconsidering its current long-term portfolio philosophy and may incorporate a loan product that would provide shorter-term financing to extend the affordability of at-risk units.

> **Contact**
> California Housing Finance Agency
> G. Richard Schermerhorn, Director of Programs
> 1121 L Street, Seventh Floor
> Sacramento, California 95814
> Telephone: (916) 322-3991
> Fax: (916) 327-5115
> Web site: www.chfa.ca.gov

California Housing Partnership Corporation
State of California

The California Housing Partnership Corporation (CHPC) is a statewide nonprofit that provides consulting services, acts as an information clearinghouse, and maintains a database of assisted properties that serves as an early warning system to identify potential opt-outs. With offices in San Francisco, Los Angeles, and San Diego, CHPC helps to coordinate preservation efforts among various state agencies and between different levels of government.

Created by the state legislature to address the preservation issue proactively, CHPC began in 1989 with half a million dollars in startup funding. CHPC's mission is "to preserve existing affordable housing and to expand the capacity of public, nonprofit, and resident-controlled entities to develop, own, and manage affordable housing."[28]

Program Description

The three subsections that follow describe CHPC's services and activities.

Consulting Services. CHPC provides two types of consulting services: (1) financial and development consulting for multifamily HUD/FHA properties and (2) financial consulting for multifamily developments that are financed through low-income housing tax credits, tax-exempt bonds, or other affordable-housing financing programs. Services provided in HUD/FHA counseling include financial feasibility analysis, preparation of FHA mortgage insurance and capital grant applications, purchase negotiations, and assistance in complying with HUD regulations. Multifamily services include preparation of financial projections, assistance in preparing applications, financial structuring, and negotiations.

Technical Assistance. CHPC provides statewide training and technical assistance to housing providers on a number of topics, including project management, asset management, and housing finance.

Housing Policy. Like preservation-focused organizations in other areas, CHPC maintains a database of HUD-assisted properties that are vulnerable to prepayment or loss of Section 8 contracts. CHPC also (1) maintains and disseminates information on national and state preservation efforts and policy and (2) participates in working groups, task forces, and advisory committees addressing preservation issues. CHPC's role is critical in coordinating preservation efforts among various organizations and facilitating communication among state agencies, local governments, housing and redevelopment authorities, and nonprofits.

Funding Sources

Fees for service make up the bulk of CHPC's revenues; the fees are supplemented by foundation grants.

Accomplishments

CHPC has provided financial consulting services to over 70 organizations, resulting in the preservation and renovation of over 2,500 units.

Contact
California Housing Partnership Corporation
Bill Rumpf, Chief Executive Officer
369 Pine Street, Suite 300
San Francisco, California 94104
Telephone: (415) 433-6804
Fax: (415) 433-6805

Rural California Housing Corporation
State of California

The Rural California Housing Corporation (RCHC) is a private nonprofit organization established in 1967. RCHC's mission is to work in partnership with program participants, other organizations, businesses, and government to improve living conditions for low-income people.[29]

RCHC creates new affordable housing through the construction of self-help homes; develops and operates multifamily rental housing; rehabilitates substandard housing; provides planning assistance to small rural communities; and operates a residents' services program. A focal point for RCHC is working with small community-based organizations and residents' groups to strengthen local empowerment and control.

While RCHC does not have a defined "preservation strategy" for troubled federally assisted properties, such properties are a good match for RCHC's overall target population, development strategies, and emphasis on empowerment.

Program Description

RCHC's development strategies include new construction as well as the acquisition and rehabilitation of blighted existing properties. Participants in RCHC's single-family housing programs must earn less than 80 percent of the median county income, and tenants in RCHC rental housing must earn less than 60 percent of the median county income. Over half of RCHC's tenants receive some form of public assistance, nearly 35 percent are immigrants, and more than 40 percent are single parents.

Project Example: Park Village

Park Village is the only HUD-foreclosed property that RCHC has taken on, although it has also successfully purchased and rehabilitated two Title VI properties.

The Asian Pacific Self-Development and Residential Association (APSARA), a tenant association, and RCHC joined forces with Bank of America Community Development Bank (BACDB) to transform a seriously deteriorated and overcrowded HUD-foreclosed apartment complex. Today, that complex offers a high-quality living environment to 1,000 members of 208 very low-income Cambodian families, including more than 600 children and 50 seniors. The Park Village apartments were reconfigured to accommodate a multipurpose community room with offices and classrooms and 22 four-bedroom units for large families. The remaining 185 apartments feature two-bedroom units. Residents participate in a variety of on-site educational enrichment opportunities organized by APSARA.

The property is owned by RCHC in partnership with APSARA. APSARA has taken the lead in tenant organizing, and RCHC is providing technical assistance to create a business structure to prepare APSARA for the ultimate transfer of sole ownership over the next few years. The visionary leadership of the RCHC-APSARA-BACDB partnership has achieved major victories, enabling a very poor immigrant group with significant cultural and language barriers to build an equity stake in the community.

RCHC played a lead role as developer, providing intensive technical assistance and resources critical to the initiative's success. With APSARA, RCHC formed Park Village Apartments, Inc., the single-asset corporation that owns Park Village. Both organizations have representation on the board of the corporation, and ASPARA will assume all control of the apartments once it has developed the organizational capacity to do so.

To accommodate phased rehabilitation without displacing residents, BACDB provided a construction loan with an extended (24-month) term. BACDB also waived the requirements for cash equity and substantial subordinated financing that would ordinarily have been imposed on RCHC and brought in its own construction and asbestos-mitigation experts for consultation.

When the permanent lender unexpectedly reduced its commitment, BACDB's management team demonstrated extraordinary flexibility and responsiveness. BACDB first extended its construction loan maturity date while working with RCHC to develop alternative financing options. Ultimately, BACDB itself stepped in, providing a full-term loan of nearly $6.7 million; the city of Stockton also provided a deferred $550,000 loan. BACDB's loan was in the form of two mortgage loans, the second of which was structured as an investment in a bank community development corporation. (The project's financial needs exceeded the appraised value of the project. A conventional loan could not be made for that excess amount, so the bank structured the second mortgage as an "investment," with the understanding that RCHC would repay the investment. RCHC treats the investment as a mortgage loan and makes payments accordingly.)

Funding Sources

Project financing is from both private and public sources, including about $80,000 in Community Development Block Grant funding. RCHC also receives monthly management fees from Park Village operating revenues.

Accomplishments

As a developer and operator of affordable rental housing, RCHC has placed 19 multifamily housing developments in service. In the Park Village example, RCHC has provided high-quality affordable housing for 208 families who have taken a major step toward self-reliance.

Contact
Rural California Housing Corporation
2125 Nineteenth Street, Suite 101
Sacramento, California 95818
Telephone: (916) 442-4731
Fax: (916) 442-1701

Solano Affordable Housing Foundation
Solano, California

Solano Affordable Housing Foundation (SAHF) was founded in 1990 to "promote, facilitate, finance, develop, and preserve affordable housing for lower-, low-, and moderate-income families in Solano and adjoining counties."[30] The foundation acts as developer, owner, and manager for its rental projects.

One strategy SAHF uses to meet its objectives is to identify and acquire existing properties that are at risk of being lost as affordable housing.

Program Description

To achieve its affordable-housing mission, SAHF seeks to

- Use all available federal, state, and private funding sources to "bridge the gap" in making housing affordable;
- Request municipal participation only when other sources have been exhausted;
- Incorporate sound real estate principles in the production process;
- Keep within the community as many as possible of the housing production jobs created by SAHF projects;
- Develop an operating budget for its rental properties that includes a full-time, on-site manager; adequate maintenance and utilities funding; and reserves for future repairs.

Amenities such as daycare centers, play areas, athletic courts, patios, and carports are included in many SAHF developments.

Project Examples

The following project examples illustrate SAHF's housing preservation strategy.

Marina Heights, Marina Vista 1, and Marina Vista II. In 1998, creative financing engineered by SAHF resulted in the preservation of a three-building affordable-housing apartment complex in downtown Vallejo, California. The 388-unit complex had been built as affordable housing and was over 25 years old at the time of the purchase. SAHF was the purchaser and developer, and Merit Capital and Pacific Gas and Electric Company took equity positions in the project. TRI Capital Corporation financed the acquisition of the properties for $9.5 million. SAHF assumed a low-interest HUD first mortgage. Using tax-exempt bonds and proceeds from the sale of low-income housing tax credits, SAHF refinanced a HUD second mortgage. The city of Vallejo and the property's seller participated with long-term loans, completing a financing package that allowed SAHF to undertake $1.2 million in needed repairs to the complex.

The property was sold at full market value, and the seller avoided the uncertainty of conversion under HUD's mark-to-market program. The buyer received 100 percent financing that will permit the units to remain affordable regardless of changes to the Section 8 program. The debt coverage on the HUD-insured loans was substantially improved. Tenants will benefit from the improved condition of the property after renovations are completed.

Union Square. In partnership with Wells Fargo Bank and the city of Solano, SAHF created Union Square, a redevelopment initiative that completely transformed a distressed crime- and drug-infested neighborhood. The city first acquired a cluster of eight separately owned apartment buildings for large families, which it then sold to SAHF. With construction financing from Wells Fargo, SAHF rehabilitated and reconfigured the deteriorating 30-year-old properties. With a guarantee from the city, Wells Fargo also made the permanent mortgage loans for the eight buildings, despite the fact that the bank did not have an in-house permanent loan program: the bank's willingness to provide a combined financing package saved its nonprofit partner more than $100,000 in fees. Wells Fargo also agreed to SAHF's use of the loan proceeds for landscaping and the improvement of parking structures on the property of an adjacent landowner.

Funding Sources

The Marina complex required a creative mix of funding from a variety of sources. Union Square project financing is from private lenders who receive public credit enhancements.

SAHF has only two staff members and operates on a small budget. Some of SAHF's revenue comes from the sale of single-family homes that it has acquired and rehabilitated, some from fees for property management. West America Bank provides free office space.

Accomplishments

In the Vellejo project, 388 units will be renovated and preserved as affordable housing. The Union Square initiative successfully consolidated the management of 56 units of affordable housing located on the same cul-de-sac, including SAHF's buildings and another six apartment buildings under separate ownership. This was achieved through the creation of a ten-year master lease between the owner of the six buildings, SAHF, and the city—an agreement that guarantees the owner a fixed amount of cash flow over the term of the lease while ensuring consistent, high-quality management of all 14 properties. Union Square is now operating under a limited partnership ownership structure with SAHF as the general partner. The neighborhood has been stabilized, and families living in Union Square's high-quality affordable housing have a renewed feeling of security and a shared sense of community.

Contact
Solano Affordable Housing Foundation
Dennis McCray, Executive Director
2400 Hilborn Road, Lower Level
Fairfield, California 94533
Telephone: (707) 422-5919
Fax: (707) 422-0631

Atlanta Affordable Housing Fund Limited Partnership
Atlanta, Georgia

Initiated in 1993, the Atlanta Affordable Housing Fund Limited Partnership (AAHFLP) was created to restore and redevelop affordable housing units and help stabilize Atlanta's deteriorating neighborhoods. AAHFLP's first project involved the acquisition and substantial rehabilitation of 2,811 apartments in 11 multifamily apartment communities—the largest multifamily acquisition and rehabilitation project in the city's history. This initial success has led to additional investment and redevelopment by AAHFLP and Bank of America (formerly NationsBank) Community Development Corporation (CDC) totaling more than 4,200 units through 1998.

Participants

AAHFLP is a joint initiative on the part of Bank of America CDC and the Atlanta Neighborhood Development Partnership (ANDP), Inc. Bank of America CDC is a public-purpose, for-profit development subsidiary of Bank of America "dedicated to revitalizing distressed neighborhoods through a variety of roles as developer, equity investor, and facilitator."[31] ANDP is a citywide nonprofit housing and community development intermediary that provides operating funding, technical assistance, and loans to neighborhood-based nonprofits; ANDP also facilitates housing and community development through partnerships and direct investment.

Program Description

The 2,811 units acquired by AAHFLP had suffered serious deterioration and were being held in foreclosure by the Federal Home Loan Mortgage Corporation (Freddie Mac). All 11 properties were located in low- to moderate-income communities within metropolitan Atlanta. At acquisition, 848 of the units were vacant and at least 650 were uninhabitable because of physical deterioration, poor management, and drug and crime problems.

In addition to physically rehabilitating the 11 properties, the partnership attempted to improve the residents' quality of life by adding services and amenities and providing a high standard of property management. The properties now offer playgrounds, community education facilities, and activity facilities; in addition, educational programs (targeted to both young people and adults), educational and social programs, and recreational activities have been implemented.

Project Example: Overlook Atlanta

One example of the partnership's success is the Overlook Atlanta apartment complex, a low-income area of northwest Atlanta. When AAHFLP took over the property, it undertook a comprehensive reworking of the site, including fences, lighting, landscaping, and secured access; it also replaced the small bulletproof window through which residents paid their rent with a spacious leasing office. Central air conditioning and new energy systems were installed in all 512 of the apartments, helping to combat a summertime vacancy rate of more than 60 percent. Boarded-up units were refurbished and occupied units were improved. Today, the property is 98 percent occupied, operates at a very low rate of annual turnover, and turns a profit. At this same complex, the partnership built the first of its "Make a Difference Activity Centers." (There are now a total of eight centers in the AAHFLP portfolio.) The center provides dedicated space and staffing and includes a community room, library, computer lab, kitchen, and tutoring areas. In addition to housing an after-school learning and activity program and summer day camp, the center is used by seniors, Neighborhood Watch, and a 4-H Club. The computers, donated by IBM and Bank of America, are used to help adults and children learn to read and write, to develop computer literacy, and as a tool for completing homework.

Funding Sources

The total original investment in AAHFLP was $35 million—the largest one-time investment in Atlanta's affordable-housing stock ever made. NationsBank (now Bank of America) CDC agreed to purchase the 11 complexes from Freddie Mac for $22 million, which came from the following sources: $10.5 million from NationsBank CDC, $500,000 from ANDP (the limited equity partner in the arrangement), and an acquisition and construction loan for the remaining $11 million from NationsBank of Georgia. NationsBank of Georgia also provided $13 million in rehabilitation costs for all 2,811 apartments. Bank of America CDC intends to turn a profit on the projects and to reinvest its profits in similar projects and in the provision of ongoing improvements to the original properties.

Accomplishments

The rehabilitation of 11 properties returned 2,811 units of affordable housing to Atlanta's stock. Bank of America and ANDP have agreed to maintain the affordability of at least 650 of the units. Today, all of the units are affordable to households with incomes at or below 60 percent of the area median, and some rents are affordable to households with incomes as low as 40 percent of the area median. Since rehabilitation, the overall occupancy rate throughout the 11 properties has risen from less than 70 percent to an average of 96 percent. Collection delinquency has dropped significantly, from 15 percent to below 3 percent.

The acquisition and rehabilitation of a 12th property in 1994 and four other large complexes between 1995 and 1997 brought the total number of distressed units rehabilitated and returned to Atlanta's housing stock to over 4,200, representing a total investment of more than $75 million. AAHFLP was honored in 1994 with a United Nations HABI award, given to honor innovative affordable-housing programs. NationsBank CDC also won a 1995 Social Compact Award for Outstanding Leadership and Innovation; this was the first time that an individual financial institution had been recognized by Social Compact for its leadership and commitment.

Contact

Atlanta Affordable Housing Fund Limited Partnership
Bank of America Community Development Corporation
James Grauley, Senior Vice President
600 Peachtree Street, N.E., Third Floor
Atlanta, Georgia 30308
Telephone: (404) 607-6169
Fax: (404) 607-4359

Community Economic Development Assistance Corporation
State of Massachusetts

The Massachusetts state legislature created the Community Economic Development Assistance Corporation (CEDAC) in 1978 to support nonprofit development activities, with an emphasis on housing. Preservation has become one of CEDAC's priorities, and it has assisted nonprofits and resident groups to purchase expiring-use properties.

Because of the large number of expiring-use properties, rapidly appreciating property values, the demise of rent control, and the relative scarcity of new sites for development, the preservation of assisted housing has become one of the dominant housing issues in Massachusetts. With 27,400 affordable units at risk, the state has one of the largest expiring-use portfolios in the country. Massachusetts has responded with a variety of programs and initiatives aimed at preserving the existing affordable-housing stock. In 1997, although the state allocated 60 percent of its low-income housing tax credit authority for preservation of private and public assisted properties—far beyond the percentage of credits devoted to preservation by other states—less than 40 percent of the preservation applications were awarded credits. In addition to allocating tax credits, Massachusetts has created an "infrastructure" to coordinate preservation efforts, and CEDAC is a primary component of that infrastructure.

CEDAC is a quasi-public entity that functions as an independent agency with its own board and executive director. CEDAC has been involved in a range of preservation issues since 1987, including the foreclosure of assisted properties; the preservation of housing with expiring federal subsidy contracts; the federal Low-Income Housing Preservation and Resident Homeownership Act (LIHPRHA) program; and HUD's mark-to-market program. As the state's "preservation maven," CEDAC has been a leader in preservation policy and practice and acquired a national reputation in the field.

Prior to the creation of LIHPRHA in 1990, the state worked informally with project owners contemplating an opt-out, attempting to obtain pledges that owners would not displace residents and would maintain some level of affordability. While this program had no real teeth, it did slow the rush of prepayments and preserve housing for a period of time. CEDAC disseminated information to nonprofits and tenant groups and helped nonprofits and tenants purchase properties. CEDAC also provided the state and localities with information on the scope of the problem and was active in the development of federal legislative resolutions.

CEDAC's experience with LIHPRHA highlighted the critical need for gap funding in preservation deals. Gap funding was provided under LIHPRHA, but Congress introduced limits on assistance; although rehabilitation costs could be reduced somewhat, an irreducible gap often remained. To address these issues under the second phase of LIHPRHA, the state carved out a special place for preservation deals by (1) providing a tax-credit allocation, (2) dedicating federal HOME funds and other funds for preservation, and (3) clarifying the eligibility requirements for the use of these funding sources for preservation. Also, state-funded general obligation bonds provide soft loans—deferred financing that function more like a grant—targeted to expiring-use properties. These funds all come with long-term affordability covenants. As preservation funding gaps continued to increase, the state continued to fund these programs to address the problem.

Program Description

As previously noted, CEDAC works closely with nonprofit and resident groups to facilitate the purchase of expiring-use properties, providing technical assistance and capacity-building services. CEDAC helped to create Residents to Residents (RtR), an innovative new forum that fosters mentoring relationships between resident leaders of converted properties and residents who are considering acquiring a property.

In addition to providing technical assistance, CEDAC administers revolving loan funds totaling over $8 million for predevelopment and acquisition costs. Nonprofit and resident groups may obtain low-interest, unsecured loans to cover upfront costs related to an acquisition, and the loans must be repaid only if the project moves forward.

CEDAC consults with city and state agencies as well. With help from CEDAC, the Massachusetts Housing Finance Agency (MHFA) is implementing a national preservation pilot program, the Demonstration Disposition program: for this program, CEDAC is providing technical assistance on HUD programs and development assistance to tenant organizations. Under the program, HUD will sell 2,100 units of HUD-owned housing to resident organizations or to developers who partner with residents, with MHFA acting as HUD's administrative agent.

Funding Sources

CEDAC is funded largely through service contracts with federal, state, and local public agencies.

Accomplishments

In 1997, through CEDAC's information and assistance, community-based and resident groups closed on seven LIHPRHA projects containing 894 affordable units, adding to the 2,700 units previously sold to community and resident groups. These projects will retain their affordability for the remaining useful life of the structures.

> **Contact**
>
> Community Economic Development Assistance Corporation
> Vincent F. O'Donnell, Director of Development
> 18 Tremont Street, Suite 1020
> Boston, Massachusetts 02108
> Telephone: (617) 727-5944
> Fax: (617) 727-5990

Expiring Use Friendly Prepayment Program
State of Massachusetts

In Massachusetts, over 10,000 housing units approved under two programs—the federal Section 236 and the state Section 13A (a 236 look-alike)—have passed the 20-year repayment date, and owners of these units may choose to opt out of the affordability restrictions on their properties by prepaying the below-market-rate mortgages. By 1997, four developments had already prepaid their loans, resulting in the loss of 866 affordable units.

To address the potential loss of the most well-positioned properties in the affordable stock, the Massachusetts Housing Finance Agency (MHFA) adopted a unique "triage" strategy, conducting an extensive analysis of every development in the portfolio and ranking the prepayment risk for each one according to three factors: (1) the accumulated equity per unit; (2) the market desirability of the project location; and (3) the extent of capital improvements necessary to obtain market rents. Projects were classified as highly likely, likely, or unlikely to prepay. MHFA then targeted preservation efforts to those properties most in danger of conversion to market rate. Nevertheless, even with the triage approach, MHFA recognized that it would be impossible to preserve all units at risk.

In 1997, Massachusetts created the Expiring Use Friendly Prepayment Program (EUFPP) to address strategically its expiring-use housing problem. In assisted-housing developments that are at risk of converting to market rate because of expiring affordability restrictions, EUFPP preserves the affordability of the units for a minimum of 15 years.

Program Administration

MHFA administers the EUFPP.

Program Description

In addition to ensuring that 20 percent of the units will remain affordable to renters whose incomes are at or below 50 percent of the area median, EUFPP avoids involuntary displacement of low-income tenants. To accomplish this goal, EUFPP issues residents "enhanced" Section 8 vouchers and prohibits landlords from charging rents beyond specified levels until tenants voluntarily vacate their units.[32] Nonrestricted units are projected to convert gradually to market rate over an eight- to ten-year period. On the basis of the MHFA triage analysis, EUFPP targets loans to those projects where the risk of prepayment is highest.

To be eligible, a property must have demonstrated equity in excess of $10,000 per unit, beyond any repair and upgrade costs. Properties may use one or more of the following loan products to restructure underlying debt, pay for capital improvements, or fund equity takeout for the owner:

- *Replacement loan:* Rather than create a new loan, a replacement loan restructures the underlying loan to pay off the mortgage subsidy component, allowing a project to qualify for enhanced rental vouchers. Restructuring avoids redemption of the bonds and allows the unsubsidized portion of the loan to be retained. Typically, the enhanced rental vouchers more than offset the loss of the interest subsidy.
- *Bridge loan:* A 7.1 percent interest-only bridge loan is available for three to five years to cover capital improvements and soft transaction costs. The bridge loan is in the form of a permanent loan. Funds for the bridge loan program come from MHFA reserves.
- *Permanent loan:* The permanent loan program allows owners to take out a bridge loan or to get equity out of a project. Funding for these loans comes mostly from the proceeds of taxable bonds because tax-exempt funds are available only where there is a substantial transfer in the ownership of a property. For property sales (i.e., to a nonprofit), tax-exempt bond financing is available. However, most owners choose to retain ownership of their properties because of the adverse tax consequences of a sale.

The loans offer very attractive terms, including debt-coverage ratios of 1.05 for replacement loans, competitive interest rates, loan-to-value ratios as high as 90 percent, and terms as long as 30 years for permanent loans. According to program staff, the typical permanent loan is $7,800 per unit. At the time of this writing, interest rates were so low that most borrowers were foregoing bridge financing and applying directly for permanent loans to lock into a low long-term rate.

The loans provide for a transition plan in the event that the Section 8 rents are reduced or eliminated. If rent subsidies drop from the "enhanced" fair-market rent level (about 130 percent of fair-market rent) to the fair-market level, the owner must absorb the drop in rent. However, the units convert to market rate when new tenants come in, so rents will gradually climb to market rates for these units. If rent subsidies are eliminated entirely, owners may immediately re-lease units at market rates in order to avoid default.

One problem with EUFPP is that, over time, all but 20 percent of the affordable units are permanently lost. MHFA decided to preserve only 20 percent of the units—the statutory minimum—to ensure that the arrangements would be sufficiently attractive to owners to induce them to use the program.

Funding Sources

Funding for EUFPP comes from MHFA reserves or from the proceeds of taxable bonds.

Accomplishments

As of early 1999, EUFPP had provided $49.2 million in loans for 2,117 units.

Future Plans

In 1998, to increase the number of preserved units beyond EUFPP's 20 percent goal, new legislation created a piggy-back below-market financing program to be used in conjunction with EUFPP. As of this writing, MHFA is awaiting resolution of funding issues to implement the program.

> **Contact**
> Massachusetts Housing Finance Agency
> David Keene, Senior Asset Management Officer
> Preservation and Technical Service Department
> One Beacon Street
> Boston, Massachusetts 02108
> Telephone: (617) 854-1000, ext. 1124
> Fax: (617) 854-1028
> Web site: www.mhfa.com

Affordable Rental Investment Fund
State of Minnesota

Minnesota's Affordable Rental Investment Fund was created in 1995 to assist in the construction, acquisition, and rehabilitation of affordable housing. In 1998, the state legislature appropriated an additional $10 million per year for three years to be set aside for the preservation of federally assisted housing, an allocation that received broad bipartisan support.

Program Administration

The Minnesota Housing Finance Agency (MHFA) manages the Affordable Rental Investment Fund.

Program Description

To make possible the preservation of rural as well as urban projects, the legislation defined the term *preservation* broadly. Participants can receive deferred, no-interest loans for the following purposes:

- Acquisition, rehabilitation, or debt restructuring of federally assisted rental property by nonprofit organizations;

- Equity takeout loans for existing owners who agree to keep rents affordable.

The loans are deferred for 20 years, and borrowers must agree to continue to participate in federally assisted housing programs for the period of the loan deferral. If, for some reason, the federal government cannot support the project, the housing will have to meet the state's definition of affordability for the agreed-upon term. Nonprofits and local housing authorities have the right of first refusal if the housing development is offered for sale. In making funding decisions, MHFA is to give priority to nonprofits and to ensure that federal assistance continues for the longest possible period of time if all other factors (such as the experience level of the sponsor and the amount of money required to preserve a specific housing development) are comparable.

MHFA also works to preserve federally assisted housing through the following means:

- The state's Redefined Equity II Program, which encourages owners of MHFA-financed developments to remain in federally assisted housing programs. Equity II allows owners to redefine their equity annually and qualify for increased returns. Owners must agree to remain federally assisted and not to opt out for at least ten years.
- The state's deferred maintenance and operating loans and grants for developments without adequate reserves; these loans and grants are available to any development in MHFA's portfolio, federally assisted or not.
- HOME rental rehabilitation funds for repairs.
- State Housing Trust Fund and Affordable Rental Investment Fund loans for repair and replacement in preservation projects.
- Allocation of federal low-income housing tax credits.
- Tax-exempt mortgage bond prepayments from agency reserves.

Funding Sources

The state legislature added $10 million to MHFA's funding specifically to create the Affordable Rental Investment Fund.

Accomplishments

MHFA has committed $9.9 million—essentially exhausting the first year's funding—to preserve 1,681 units in projects that were considered at risk of being converted to market rate. Of those units, 1,435 have project-based Section 8 subsidies. MHFA is asking the state legislature for an additional $5 million per year for the next two years of the program.

Contact
Minnesota Housing Finance Agency
400 Sibley Street, Suite 300
St. Paul, Minnesota 55101-1998
Telephone: (651) 296-7608
Fax: (651) 296-8139
Web site: www.mhfa.state.mn.us

Minnesota Housing Partnership
State of Minnesota

The mission of the Minnesota Housing Partnership (MHP), a statewide advocacy and technical assistance group founded in 1989, is "to support the creation and preservation of housing that is affordable to low- and moderate-income people."[33]

MHP is active in preservation issues on two fronts: first, MHP lobbies on behalf of funding bills to support preservation efforts; second, MHP has nine VISTA volunteers working on the preservation of subsidized or unsubsidized affordable housing (six of the nine work on federally subsidized housing).

In fulfillment of its overall mission, MHP provides financial and technical assistance to housing developers, mostly nonprofits. Financial assistance is in the form of predevelopment and capacity-building grants targeted primarily to rural areas. MHP has also distributed funds through HUD's Low-Income Housing Preservation and Resident Homeownership Act (LIHPRHA) program and served as a consultant in the packaging of financing to preserve federally assisted housing.

Program Description

MHP's advocacy efforts and its use of VISTA volunteers are described briefly in the subsections that follow.

Advocacy. MHP provides staff and leadership for the Right to Housing Campaign, the main vehicle for MHP's advocacy efforts. A mix of representatives from public agencies, nonprofit housing organizations, tenant organizations, and faith-based groups from across the state, the campaign gathers and disseminates information and then lobbies for an agreed-upon agenda. Information-gathering meetings are held each summer. During the fall months, the members meet biweekly to share information on research and to develop a legislative agenda for the upcoming session. During the legislative session, campaign participants meet weekly to discuss the group's progress in implementing its legislative agenda. Regular fax alerts and the distribution of meeting minutes allow participants statewide to stay abreast of legislative developments, and MHP's Web page is regularly updated with links to new legislation and research.

Use of VISTA Volunteers. Since 1993, MHP has used the VISTA program to meet a variety of affordable-housing goals. For example, in a project funded by the National Alliance of HUD Tenants (NAHT), two VISTA volunteers work as tenant organizers in privately owned, federally assisted rental housing at risk of prepayment (apartment buildings whose owners may terminate federal subsidies, end the use restrictions attached to those subsidies, and raise rents). The volunteers' goals are to build power among tenants and find ways (e.g., nonprofit buyouts, the provision of incentives to owners) to avert prepayment and the subsequent rent increases. MHP has also placed four volunteers with nonprofit agencies to meet the same goals.

Funding Sources

MHP is funded by a variety of sources including private foundations, contracts with federal and state agencies, grants, and consulting revenues.

Accomplishments

The Right to Housing Campaign has helped to raise awareness of housing issues among rural and urban legislators alike. It has obtained increases in state housing appropriations (over $40 million since 1990) and major reform on issues such as the tax on low-income rental property (the 4[d] property tax classification program described in Chapter 4). The 1998 passage of the $10 million Affordable Rental Investment Fund for the preservation of federally assisted housing, described in the following profile, was a legislative priority for MHP.

> **Contact**
> Minnesota Housing Partnership
> Chip Halbach, Executive Director
> 122 West Franklin Street, Suite 230
> Minneapolis, Minnesota 55404
> Telephone: (612) 874-0112
> Fax: (612) 874-9685

Purchase of HUD-Held Mortgages
State of Missouri

In September 1996, the Missouri Housing Development Commission (MHDC) purchased 26 HUD-held mortgages, allowing approximately 2,220 apartments to remain part of Missouri's affordable-housing stock.

This exchange was the first time that mortgages had been transferred from HUD to a housing finance agency. If MHDC had not purchased these mortgages, HUD would have sold them to private investors, who would have been under no obligation to maintain the affordability of the units. In February 1999, MHDC again purchased two HUD-held mortgages, this time as part of a preservation strategy for a 675-unit complex in St. Louis.

Program Administration

MHDC administers the mortgage purchase program.

Program Description

MHDC was interested in obtaining HUD properties in order to rehabilitate the individual units and to improve the properties overall, creating safe, decent, and affordable housing that would be rented only to low- and moderate-income households.

The 26 mortgages were secured on 19 properties that were originally insured under a variety of FHA programs. The outstanding balance on these units was close to $30 million.

Because MHDC promised to dedicate more than $8 million in rehabilitation loans to the units, HUD sold the mortgages to MHDC for only $10.

When it took ownership of the mortgages, MHDC took on all of HUD's regulatory responsibilities, including servicing the mortgages and administering the Section 8 contracts for the apartments that receive project-based Section 8 assistance. It is anticipated that if the project-based Section 8 contracts are not renewed, tenants will be given Section 8 certificates or vouchers.

MHDC estimates that within the first five years of the project, it will disburse close to $8.5 million in renovation and rehabilitation loans for these units as well as $58,000 each year for initiatives aimed at increasing the self-sufficiency of the residents. These initiatives will include the installation of computer learning centers to help tenants learn marketable skills; the provision of educational opportunities; and the establishment of health and wellness services. The total estimated funding for the project is $15 million, to be disbursed over a 15-year period.

Funding Sources

The majority of the funding for renovation and rehabilitation comes from interest earnings on those of the 26 properties that are operating profitably. MHDC is also using federal interest reduction payments to secure additional funding, and its Housing Assistance Tax Credits Program to solicit corporate contributions. (Missouri's tax credit program is described in Chapter 4.)

Accomplishments

MHDC's first purchase was of 26 mortgages that included approximately 2,200 apartments in 19 properties. In February 1999, the commission completed a deal that will maintain affordable housing in a 675-unit St. Louis complex. The financing package for this project included the purchase of two HUD-held mortgages representing 475 of the total number of units; the purchase of a privately held mortgage; a $6.71 million acquisition and rehabilitation loan; and Federal National Mortgage Association credit enhancement of the bonds used. The deal took about a year and a half to put together, in part because four different partnerships owned various parts of the complex.

Contact

Missouri Housing Development Commission
Pete Ramsel
3435 Broadway
Kansas City, Missouri 64111-2415
Telephone: (816) 759-6600; (816) 759-6656 (Pete Ramsel)
Fax: (816) 759-6828

Programs: Filtering Down, Not Trickling Out— Saving the Unsubsidized Housing Stock

At Home in New Orleans
New Orleans, Louisiana

Initiated in 1998, At Home in New Orleans is a comprehensive, neighborhood-based approach to preserving and rehabilitating the substantial stock of vacant or blighted housing in the low-income neighborhoods of New Orleans. Through this community development lending alliance, vacant or blighted structures are transformed into safe and affordable one- or two-family homes.

In the Esplanade Ridge historic district, a minority neighborhood that was the first area targeted for rehabilitation, about 50 properties are being renovated for resale to homeowners. From the time renovations start, work on each property is expected to be completed within a year. Overall, between 300 and 500 properties are to be rehabilitated, restored, or replaced; the program is expected to cost about $20 million over a five-year period.

Participants

Program participants include the city's division of housing and neighborhood development; the New Orleans Redevelopment Team (a consortium under contract to the city; consortium members are Wallace Enterprises, Gilbane Building Company, and Campbell Tui Campbell Architects); the Federal Home Loan Mortgage Corporation (Freddie Mac); the AFL-CIO Housing Investment Trust; Standard Mortgage Corporation; the 7th Ward Community Services Corporation; Neighborhood Housing Services of New Orleans, Inc.; and Mortgage Guarantee Insurance Company (MGIC).

Program Description

At Home in New Orleans is a creative, collaborative effort designed to address a unique set of challenges. New Orleans faces the housing problems typical of many cities: older, deteriorating, and often vacant housing stock in low-income neighborhoods. However, in New Orleans, a combination of property rights laws and historic preservation regulations has created barriers to revitalization. These laws and regulations make rehabilitation prohibitively expensive; and because the demolition of deteriorated historic structures is not allowed, properties continue to decline.

Each of the eight participating organizations plays a specific role in the initiative. The city of New Orleans, through its division of housing and neighborhood development, acts as a facilitator by identifying and acquiring properties. The division also assists with the permitting process by identifying situations in which the cost of rehabilitation is prohibitive and allowing substantially new construction to be undertaken. The city also assists in marketing the program and provides subsidy funds and credit enhancement to reduce development costs.

The New Orleans Redevelopment Team promotes the program and coordinates property acquisition. The team is also responsible for developing designs and specifications for the homes to ensure that they are in keeping with the historic character of the existing structures and the neighborhood. Finally, the team provides construction management and administrative services.

Freddie Mac offers a menu of affordable loan products tailored to the needs of the program and of potential homebuyers. Freddie Mac will also purchase the loans originated through the program by approved lenders and securitize the mortgage loans into Freddie Mac Gold Participation Certificates (PCs). The AFL-CIO Housing Investment Trust, in turn, will purchase up to $20 million in Freddie Mac Gold PCs collateralized by mortgages originated through the program. The housing investment trust has also pledged to facilitate the support and cooperation of local labor organizations in the renovation of the properties.

The initial participating lender, Standard Mortgage Corporation, will originate and service the mortgage loans, securitizing them through Freddie Mac. Additional lenders will be added as the program grows and the volume of lending increases.

The 7th Ward Community Services Corporation serves as a conduit, taking temporary possession of the properties being rehabilitated until they are sold to individual homebuyers. Neighborhood Housing Services of New Orleans, Inc., provides comprehensive pre- and postclosing homeownership education and counseling. MGIC is providing mortgage insurance to homebuyers participating in the program.

The completed homes must be owner occupied and may have up to two units. Because the initiative is targeting a distressed area for preservation and rehabilitation, there is no income limit for eligible buyers. Purchasers must make a downpayment of at least $1,000 or 2 percent of the home's value, whichever is less. The 7th Ward Community Services Corporation may contribute up to 5 percent, including equity in the land and existing improvements, as an additional downpayment. Borrowers must participate in homebuyer education classes, and prospective purchasers of two-unit properties must attend landlord training courses. Funding sources for the local partners include federal HOME funds and existing community program funds targeted for this effort.

Contact

Freddie Mac
Jacqueline Prior, Community Development Lending Manager
8250 Jones Branch Drive
McLean, Virginia 22102
Telephone: (703) 918-5085
Fax: (703) 918-5291
Web site: www.freddiemac.com

Code Abatement Loan Program
Minneapolis, Minnesota

In the mid-1980s, the Minneapolis Community Development Agency (MCDA) initiated the code abatement loan program to assist property owners who do not have the means to finance the repairs required as a result of "neighborhood sweep" efforts. (During neighborhood sweeps, inspectors evaluate the exteriors of all structures in a given neighborhood and issue citations to those that fail to meet the city's codes.)

Program Administration

MCDA administers the code abatement loan program.

Program Description

Loans of up to $8,000 are available to homeowners or rental-property owners who have received orders from the Minneapolis department of inspections to address code violations. These loans are targeted to applicants who cannot qualify for other financing. Applicants who can afford to make payments but who are refused conventional financing because of bad credit or for some other reason may receive 4 percent loans. Property owners who cannot afford to repay loans are eligible for deferred loans, which are forgiven on a declining basis (25 percent after three years; in six years the loan is completely forgiven). If the owner chooses to sell the property, repayment is due at the time of sale.

Information about the program is listed on all the inspection orders; property owners are also made aware of the program at the time of citation.

Funding Sources

The code abatement loan program is funded through Community Development Block Grant monies.

Accomplishments

Over 1,000 property owners have participated in the program since 1987. Because of the $8,000 lifetime limit on loans, the program has been used less often in recent years.

> **Contact**
> Minneapolis Community Development Agency
> Crown Roller Mill, Director
> 105 Fifth Avenue South, Suite 200
> Minneapolis, Minnesota 55401
> Telephone: (612) 673-MCDA
> Fax: (612) 673-5100

Rental Rehabilitation Loan Program
Minneapolis, Minnesota

Minneapolis's Rental Rehabilitation Loan Program—also known as the "plex" loan program because it targets small-scale rental units—is a matching loan program designed to encourage rental-property owners to repair their properties.

Program Administration

The Minneapolis Community Development Agency (MCDA) administers the Rental Rehabilitation Loan Program.

Program Description

Rental property owners who receive market-rate loans from private lenders may qualify for MCDA matching loans of up to $16,000, at zero percent interest, to make repairs on rental properties of six units or less. (The amount of the matching loan depends on the number of units.) The properties' tenants must have incomes at or below 80 percent of the median Section 8 income guidelines, but MCDA does not set criteria for the amount of rent that can be charged to tenants.

To participate, an applicant must first obtain a loan from a conventional lender. The applicant then contacts MCDA to obtain a matching loan. The applicant makes payments only to the conventional lender, which sends MCDA its share of the payment.

Funding Sources

The Rental Rehabilitation Loan Program is funded through Community Development Block Grant monies.

Accomplishments

Between January 1, 1997, and December 30, 1998, MCDA closed on 16 loans that were used to improve 40 units of housing.

> **Contact**
> Minneapolis Community Development Agency
> Keith Ford, Acting Director
> 105 Fifth Avenue South, Suite 200
> Minneapolis, Minnesota 55401
> Telephone: (612) 673-MCDA
> Fax: (612) 673-5090

Repeat Offender Code Compliance Initiative
Minneapolis, Minnesota

The Repeat Offender Code Compliance Initiative (ROCCI) was one of three efforts initiated between 1989 and 1991 by state and local leaders in Minnesota to shore up ineffective code enforcement systems. Created by the Minneapolis city attorney's office, ROCCI targets the city's worst landlords for stringent selective code enforcement.

The second enforcement effort, sponsored by the state legislature, was a three-county pilot program that established a "housing court" with jurisdiction over issues related to rental property. The court was granted enforcement powers, which had not been available under previous legislation: it could impose fines and criminal penalties, require retroactive rent abatements, and authorize city collection of rent payments to finance repairs that had been neglected by landlords.

In the third code enforcement effort, the Minneapolis city council instituted a program that required all landlords to obtain a license to operate rental property. Granting of the license is contingent on a satisfactory property inspection, and the license may be revoked if violations are not corrected within a given time frame. A scoring system ranks defects according to severity.

These three programs were undertaken because Minnesota faced problems that were similar to those of many other cities: as the housing stock aged and the budgets of local governments became increasingly strained, housing code enforcement became more and more difficult. Housing inspectors often lacked the tracking tools and enforcement power necessary to enforce housing code violations; as a result, citations were simply being ignored. At the same time, lack of coordination between the inspections department and the court system often exacerbated the difficulty of enforcing the code. For example, in cases where strict enforcement was possible through aggressive lien programs, inspectors often had difficulty distinguishing between well-meaning owners who lacked the resources to improve their properties and "repeat offenders"—landlords who were intentionally "milking" properties and allowing them to deteriorate.

Program Administration

ROCCI is administered by two people: an inspector from the Minneapolis Department of Regulatory Services, Inspections Division, Housing Inspections Section; and a prosecutor assigned to work with the inspections department of the city attorney's office.

Program Description

ROCCI targets landlords who own significant amounts of property and who habitually ignore housing code citations out of confidence that the violations will go unpunished. Specifically, the city identifies landlords who (1) own 12 or more properties in Minneapolis; (2) had ten or more housing code violations in at least half of these properties within the past three years; and (3) owned any properties within the city that had any housing code violations within the past year.

The initial screening resulted in a list of 11 landlords, who were then ranked according to additional internal criteria, including the total number of housing code violations, the length of time the owner had managed the property, and the source of the violations (i.e., whether the violations were caused by tenants or by the landlord). On the basis of the ranking, five landlords were targeted by ROCCI.

Under ROCCI, the inspector visits targeted landlords to explain the program and schedule an inspection of all properties. If the landlord refuses the inspection, the inspector may ask the tenants for access to the units. Failing that, the inspector may ask the prosecutor to obtain an administrative search warrant. As a last resort, the inspector will begin the process of revoking the landlord's license.

Assuming that the targeted landlord permits inspection or that a search warrant is obtained, a percentage of the landlord's units (which varies with the size of the property) are inspected and scored, and the landlord is given a date by which all deficiencies must be corrected. (Inspections include not only the interiors but also the exteriors, the grounds, and any common areas.) If obvious hazards or numerous violations are noted, all units on the property must be inspected. The properties are reinspected on the date specified: if violations have not been corrected, a criminal complaint and summons are filed immediately. A landlord found guilty of public safety and health violations may face a fine or a jail sentence of up to 30 days. Landlords exit ROCCI either through satisfactory compliance or through the sale of all their rental properties in Minneapolis.

ROCCI provides a significant negative incentive—the threat of jail time—to gain the compliance of landlords who own significant amounts of property and who habitually ignore citations for code violations. Through technical assistance and through the code abatement program (described in the next profile), Minneapolis also provides positive incentives for well-intentioned landlords who lack the resources to improve their properties.

Funding Sources

ROCCI is funded through the city attorney's operating budget.

Accomplishments

During the initial phase of the ROCCI program, inspectors were remarkably successful in gaining the compliance of some of the city's worst landlords. Participants were cooperative during the process, and more than 60 percent of the units were brought into compliance as a result of the program. One of the most notorious of the five landlords filed for bankruptcy, and his properties were subsequently transferred to a nonprofit organization.

> **Contact**
> City of Minneapolis
> Inspections Division
> George Shellum, Inspector II
> 250 South Fourth Street, Room 300
> Minneapolis, Minnesota 55415-1316
> Telephone: (612) 673-2601
> Fax: (612) 673-5819

Moorestown Ecumenical Neighborhood Development, Inc.
Burlington County, New Jersey

For nearly 30 years, Moorestown Ecumenical Neighborhood Development (MEND), Inc., has developed and managed scattered-site housing in Burlington County, New Jersey, which has a broad spectrum of affordable-housing needs in various kinds of locations—high-cost suburban markets, older residential neighborhoods, and pockets of rural poverty.[34]

According to its 1998 annual report, MEND's mission is to "promote the most responsible programs to provide for the affordable-housing needs of all people of limited income."[35] The organization works to fulfill that mission primarily through the creation or renovation and management of affordable rental housing. MEND's portfolio of housing includes new construction, converted government properties (a courthouse, a firehouse, and a school), and rehabilitated existing housing. Recently, MEND expanded its role to serve as a housing consultant for the Burlington County Community Action Program, assisting that organization to develop a 71-unit facility for senior citizens (MEND will also manage that property).

Program Description

The Chestertowne Village Apartments project is an example of MEND's housing preservation efforts. In partnership with Commerce Bank, MEND transformed a dilapidated property plagued by rising vacancies and rent delinquencies into high-quality housing for 45 low-income families.

Commerce Bank took the lead in assembling a creative financing package that ensured long-term affordability. The bank provided a low-cost permanent mortgage and a bridge second mortgage that was later repaid through an acquisition grant. This financing structure not only covered the purchase of the apartments but also created an operating reserve, allowing MEND enough time—and enough of a financial cushion—to make emergency repairs and to lease up the property while seeking the acquisition grant. After the purchase, Commerce Bank provided grants for further rehabilitation and the construction of an on-site playground. The bank also provided financing assistance that enabled MEND to relocate its offices to the property and—in a demonstration of commitment to MEND's long-term sustainability—bolstered the nonprofit's cash flow with tax-exempt bond refinancing.

As it does with other properties it manages, MEND is working to build bridges with its tenants; it is also encouraging the formation of a tenants' association, which helps foster a sense of shared responsibility among residents.

Accomplishments

To date, MEND has completed the first half of a $1 million renovation of what was once a blighted property. Through MEND's efforts, the Chestertowne Village Apartments have been transformed into high-quality, affordable housing that is a source of stability for the low-income families who live there as well as for the surrounding neighborhood. This achievement would not have been possible without the leadership and vision of Commerce Bank and MEND.

MEND and its affiliates currently own a total of 242 rental units throughout Moorestown, which generate over $120,000 in tax revenue to the community.

Contact

Moorestown Ecumenical Neighborhood Development, Inc.
99 East Second Street
Moorestown, New Jersey 08057
Telephone: (609) 722-7070
Fax: (609) 722-7577

Neighborhood Entrepreneurs Program
New York, New York

New York City's Neighborhood Entrepreneurs Program assists locally based property managers to acquire and rehabilitate deteriorating apartment buildings that have come into the city's possession through tax foreclosures. The program has supported the rehabilitation of apartments in Harlem, central Brooklyn, and the South Bronx.

The Neighborhood Entrepreneurs Program has several goals: to build the capacity of neighborhood businesses to redevelop and manage multifamily buildings; to help reduce New York City's inventory of more than 4,000 substandard buildings; and to increase private sector involvement in the affordable-housing rental market. The program works with nearly a dozen entrepreneurs per year.

Program Administration

The New York Housing Partnership (NYHP) organizes and administers the entrepreneurs program. A subsidiary of the New York Partnership and the New York Chamber of Commerce, NYHP was created in 1982 to mobilize private sector resources to create affordable housing.

Program Description

To select participants for the program, NYHP and New York City's department of housing preservation and development issue a request for qualifications; they then review applications, check references, evaluate each applicant's financial capacity, and visit the applicant's current tenants. NYHP typically selects smaller companies—with a gross worth of no more than $2.5 million and ownership of no more than 250 units—for the entrepreneurs program.

Tenants of the buildings selected for rehabilitation are given first chance at the jobs created by the program, and neighborhood-based nonprofit organizations provide support services—ranging from employment-readiness training to social services and family counseling—to assist residents in qualifying for these positions.

Project Example: West 140th Street

West 140th Street represents one of the first housing preservation projects—and the most difficult—undertaken by NYHP. West 140th Street was chosen as a project site by a central Harlem neighborhood task force created by NYHP. The task force—which included community groups, the local real estate board, planning officials, and block associations—was responsible for assigning priorities to areas in need of rehabilitation. Although the street is known for serious criminal activity and for the dilapidated condition of its buildings, several factors made it a prime choice for redevelopment: the street was home to a newly organized block association; a number of NYHP condominium units had just been sold within two blocks of the street; and a group of historic homes inhabited by middle-class families were located within one block of the street. In addition, a local nonprofit that was just completing the rehabilitation of three buildings on the same block was willing to assist the tenants in the buildings that had been selected for renovation.

For the West 140th Street project, NYHP purchased a cluster of six buildings on the block for $1 each through New York City's property disposition program. During the rehabilitation period, NYHP took title as interim owner. NYHP contracted with Progressive Realty, a small, minority-owned, neighborhood-based company, to develop, manage, and eventually take ownership of the properties. Together, NYHP and Progressive Realty selected a general contractor, who was required to hire local residents. The project's architectural firm, its accounting firm, and one-fifth of its subcontractors were all minority-owned neighborhood businesses.

The total cost of project development was $7.4 million, including $137,145 in acquisition costs, $5.98 million in construction costs, $550,102 in fees, and $747,342 in financing fees and costs. Chase Bank provided a $7.4 million construction loan at 9.34 percent interest. Permanent financing included $1.5 million in tax credit equity provided by the New York Equity Fund; the tax credit equity was used for operating reserves and to cover part of the cost of the project. Project debt of $5.9 million was provided by the city in the form of a 15-year deferred first mortgage at 0.25 percent, which can be extended for another 15 years if the property remains affordable. About $4 million of the mortgage funds came from the city's capital budget, and the remaining $1.9 million came from New York's federal HOME allocation.[36] The per-unit renovation cost for the West 140th Street project came to an average of $51,966.

Through the project, six buildings received interior and exterior renovation, adding the following to New York's affordable-housing stock: three one-bedroom units; 43 two-bedroom units, 42 three-bedroom units, 25 four-bedroom units, and six units with five or more bedrooms. Eighty percent of the tenants occupying these units have incomes at or below 80 percent of the area median; 44 percent have incomes at or below 50 percent of the area median. Three commercial spaces in the buildings contain a launderette, a grocery store, and the management company's office.

Initially, residents of the block—including the tenants of the six buildings targeted for rehabilitation—were concerned by the prospect of having a private agency develop and operate the West 140th Street buildings. To address these concerns, NYHP established a neighborhood task force to discuss the program and project design. The Harlem Congregations for Community Improvement, a local nonprofit under contract to provide tenant services (alcohol and substance abuse counseling, daycare placement, youth activities, healthcare referral, and domestic violence prevention programs), acted as an informal monitor of tenant complaints. In addition, the project was structured so that Progressive Realty did not take legal possession of the buildings until it had managed the property for two years—a time period that allowed all parties to assess the company's performance. To increase their confidence in the project, tenants were provided with written information about their rights and were introduced to staff members of Progressive Realty, NYHP, and the Harlem Congregations for Community Improvement.

Funding Sources

Operating funding for the Neighborhood Entrepreneurs Program came initially from a grant. Current financing is on a per-unit fee basis. The funding for the program is from the city, federal HOME funds, and low-income housing tax credits. Construction financing for the 140th Street project is discussed under the program description.

Accomplishments

The Neighborhood Entrepreneurs Program has completed or is engaged in a total of 29 projects or "clusters." As of March 1999, 1,600 units had been rehabilitated, 1,000 units were currently undergoing rehabilitation, and another 3,000 units were in the predevelopment stage.

Contact

Neighborhood Entrepreneurs Program
New York Housing Partnership
George Armstrong, Director
1 Battery Park Plaza
Fourth Floor
New York, New York 10004
Telephone: (212) 493-7431
Fax: (212) 742-9566
Web site: www.nycp.org

Portland Community Reinvestment Initiatives, Inc.
Portland, Oregon

Portland Community Reinvestment Initiatives (PCRI), Inc., is a nonprofit, community-based, rental property management organization founded in 1991.[37] PCRI was created to address an immediate crisis in affordable housing; it now provides affordable-housing opportunities for low-income households throughout northeast Portland, where there continues to be considerable need for homeownership opportunities and for high-quality, affordable rental housing.

PCRI was created to make the project described in this profile happen: in effect, this project is PCRI's mission and agenda. This unusual circumstance resulted in a brand-new organization with an instantaneous portfolio of 354 housing units; PCRI has since expanded its operations to include the construction of new affordable housing, and it has plans to do more.

Program Description

In 1990, when a Portland investor and mortgage broker was charged with racketeering and fraud, 354 families were at risk of losing their homes. Neighborhood, business, and political leaders saw an opportunity to acquire the investor's portfolio and convert the properties into an affordable-housing resource. PCRI—created as a nonprofit organization to own and manage the newly acquired properties—joined forces with U.S. Bank of Oregon and the city of Portland to craft a strategy for reclaiming these properties. The result would be the largest single-family-home redevelopment effort in the city's history.

U.S. Bank of Oregon played a key leadership role, making available to PCRI a $12.43 million commercial line of credit for purchase and rehabilitation of the 354 properties. The interest rate on the line of credit was reduced by 4 percent through an allocation from the state's tax credit program for lenders. (This program provides lenders with a direct credit from the state for loans made for affordable rental housing; the credit is then "passed through" to low-income tenants in the form of lower rents.) The line of credit has since been restructured into a loan with an interest rate under 4 percent. U.S. Bank made the loan in cooperation with the city of Portland, which provided a loan guarantee (using Community Development Block Grant funds) until the properties were rehabilitated, rented, and could support a real estate loan.

Funding Sources

PCRI receives no government funds; its operating costs are covered by revenue from its rental units. Funding for acquisition and rehabilitation is obtained from private lenders who receive state or local government credit enhancements.

Accomplishments

PCRI, an untested nonprofit when the venture began, has successfully carried out the ambitious goal of acquiring and rehabilitating all 354 properties. Eighty-three homes were sold to low- and moderate-income families through the refinancing of land sale contracts. PCRI rehabilitated the remaining 271 units and retained them as affordable rental housing for families whose incomes are below 80 percent of the area median (the majority of the tenants have incomes that are below 60 percent of the area median). The previous owners of the units—the ones who would otherwise have lost their homes—were given an opportunity to purchase them back or to occupy the rental units. PCRI's pioneering response to an unprecedented housing crisis has not only helped many residents of northeast Portland achieve the stability and economic security that come with homeownership but has also preserved the supply of high-quality, affordable rental properties as a permanent asset for the community.

Contact

Portland Community Reinvestment Initiatives, Inc.
Maxine Fitzpatrick, Executive Director
P.O. Box 11474
Portland, Oregon 97211
Telephone: (503) 288-2923
Fax: (503) 288-2891

Multifamily Affordable Rental Projects
Memphis, Tennessee

The Memphis Division of Housing and Community Development supports the development of affordable rental housing through the provision of gap financing for affordable-housing projects that have exhausted all other public and private sector financing sources yet still need financial assistance.

Program Description

Because of the requirements of the variety of funding sources used, Memphis's multifamily affordable rental projects program generally supports housing for households whose incomes are at or below 80 percent of the area median. Emphasis is on the rehabilitation or conversion of apartment buildings, although new-construction projects will also be considered. Not less than 50 percent of project costs—exclusive of any in-kind or donated value—must be financed from noncity sources. Each project must contain at least ten rental units; however, multiple projects that contain fewer than ten units but that are concentrated in a targeted neighborhood and could be redeveloped under common ownership and management are eligible if the combined number of units exceeds ten.

Financing decisions are made on a case-by-case basis in accordance with request-for-development proposals created by the division of housing and community development. Typically, the division acts as both banker and broker for each project. As a "gap" financier, the division partners with other programs, including historic preservation programs and the low-income housing tax credit program. Each project must target low- and moderate-income renters; partnering funding sources take the lead in establishing specific requirements such as (1) the criteria for tenant eligibility and (2) the duration of the commitment to provide low- and moderate-income housing.

Funding Sources

Financing decisions and sources depend on the individual project. Projects have used Community Development Block Grant funds, Section 108 loans, and—in one case—a loan guarantee for a historic preservation project.

Accomplishments

Since 1995, 900 units of affordable rental housing have been brought on line through the renovation of distressed multifamily projects.

> **Contact**
>
> City of Memphis
> Division of Housing and Community Development
> Ed Cross, Manager, Real Estate Development
> Suite 100
> 701 North Main Street
> Memphis, Tennessee 38107-2311
> Telephone: (901) 576-7300
> Fax: (901) 576-7318
> Web site: www.ci.memphis.tn

Drug Abatement Project
Milwaukee, Wisconsin

Milwaukee's Drug Abatement Project, initiated in July of 1990, combines citizen assistance and police expertise to rid Milwaukee's neighborhoods of drug-related activity.

Program Administration

The vice squad of the Milwaukee police department administers the Drug Abatement Project.

Program Description

The Drug Abatement Project makes use of Wisconsin Statutes 823.114–823.115 regarding the creation of a public nuisance on private property. Under these statutes, any built structure used to facilitate the delivery or manufacture of controlled substances may be declared a public nuisance and is subject to seizure and sale by the government.

The Drug Abatement Project includes four citizen liaison groups, under contract with the city, who cover different areas of Milwaukee. The liaison groups, which were trained by members of the vice squad at the inception of the project, are responsible for receiving complaints regarding suspected drug activity in Milwaukee neighborhoods. The groups report complaints to the police department, and narcotics detectives and beat officers follow up with a thorough investigation. If an investigation reveals drug activity, the detectives and officers report the activity to Drug Abatement Project officers.

Members of the Drug Abatement Project are responsible for sending the owners of the identified properties a certified letter on police department letterhead indicating that the property in question is being used for illegal drug activity. (The police officers assigned to the project must approve the letters, which are sent out from the Police Department.) The landlord is given seven days to respond to the police department regarding the letter and is notified of his or her right to evict the problem tenant with five days' notice. If the landlord ignores this warning and the case ends up in circuit court, the certified letter serves as proof that the landlord had knowledge of illegal activity on his or her property. Such proof is required should the state move to seize the property for sale.

The statute gives the landlord the right to "ask" the tenants to leave within five days. However, eviction cannot be forced; if a tenant refuses, then the normal 28-day eviction process applies. The manager of the Drug Abatement Project reports that 90 percent of the landlords who receive notification of illegal drug activity on their property comply with the request that they evict the problem tenants. Police continue to monitor properties for 60 days after a drug-related eviction has occurred.

Funding Sources

The Drug Abatement Project is funded by U.S. Department of Justice grant funds that are disbursed by the state of Wisconsin. The Drug Abatement Project has applied for fiscal year 1998–1999 funds totaling approximately $1.2 million: $749,978 of these funds would come from the state of Wisconsin federal grant funds, and $467,950 would come from the city of Milwaukee. These funds would support one lieutenant, six detectives, one clerk/stenographer, and one office assistant. Any change in the allocation of funding must be approved by the state.

> **Contact**
> Drug Abatement Project
> Police Administration Building
> 749 West State Street
> P.O. Box 531
> Milwaukee, Wisconsin 53201-0531
> Telephone: (414) 935-7464

Landlord Training Program
Milwaukee, Wisconsin

Since July 1993, Milwaukee, Wisconsin's Landlord Training Program has been assisting landlords to do a better job of being landlords. The training covers topics such as tenant screening, code compliance, and preparation of rental agreements; in particular, the program helps landlords curtail drug activity on their properties.

The Landlord Training Program was originally created by Campbell and DeLong Resources, Inc., of Portland, Oregon, for the Portland Police Bureau. Milwaukee is just one of the jurisdictions that have adapted the program for local use.

Program Administration

Milwaukee's department of neighborhood services (formerly the department of building inspections) administers the Landlord Training Program.

Program Description

Close to 80 percent of Milwaukee's landlords run "Mom and Pop" operations; in other words, they have no formal training in the business side of being landlords. Through the free training program, landlords learn how to *be* landlords: how to achieve code compliance, how to screen applicants, how to prepare proper rental agreements, how to recognize the warning signs of drug activity, and how to respond proactively when they discover that tenants are conducting illegal business on landlord-owned property. The five-hour training session is held on a regular basis during evenings and weekends, and all attendees get a free, 100-page comprehensive manual detailing a variety of legal and business issues related to property management.

The latest innovation in the program is the creation of "landlord compacts"—organized efforts on the part of landlords who own property in the same neighborhood to stop illegal activity in their area. Landlords meet with police and one another to develop and adopt the same screening processes and the same rental agreements; these shared standards set the same expectations for tenant behavior throughout the neighborhood and help prevent problem tenants from simply moving up the block if they are evicted. Landlords put group pressure on (and, in some cases, take legal action against) landlords who are not part of the compact and who do not demand appropriate behavior from their tenants.

Funding Sources

The Landlord Training Program, which operates on a budget of approximately $150,000 per year, is funded through monies from the U.S. Department of Justice, the Bureau of Justice Assistance, the State of Wisconsin Office of Justice Assistance, and the city of Milwaukee. Wisconsin offers four years of startup funds to new programs, and the Landlord Training Program was a recipient of these funds. The Landlord Training Program is funded until June 30, 1999, and will apply for Community Development Block Grant funding beyond that date.

Accomplishments

Since the creation of the Landlord Training Program, individuals from 33 states have been trained to initiate the program on the local level. Approximately 30 percent of Milwaukee's landlords have been through the training (the average number of landlords in the city at any one time is just over 20,000). Because of the success of Milwaukee's program, Madison and

Dane Counties; Racine; Kenosha; Oshkosh; and Green Bay/Brown County have begun programs of their own.

The Landlord Training Program was a semifinalist for the Harvard Kennedy School of Government Innovations in Government Award; it has won the City of Milwaukee's Innovations in Government Award; and it is the only noneducational program to win the Institute of Real Estate Management Award.

Contact
Landlord Training Program
Karin Long, Program Coordinator
Department of Neighborhood Services
841 North Broadway, Tenth Floor
Milwaukee, Wisconsin 53202
Telephone: (414) 286-3367
Fax: (414) 286-8667
Web site: www.ci.mil.wi.us/

Notes

1 Four of the programs profiled in this chapter were originally recognized by Social Compact and described in Suzanne C. Schnell, *1997 Profiles of Partnership Achievement: Street-Tested Strategies for Strengthening Neighborhoods* (Washington, D.C.: Social Compact, 1997). Material that was originally included in the Social Compact volume has been adapted and is used with the permission of Social Compact.

2 *Housing Development Reporter: Current Developments* 26, no. 16 (August 24, 1998): 227.

3 "States Use Tax Credits to Preserve Affordable Housing," *Housing Development Reporter: Current Developments* 26, no. 34 (December 28, 1998): 520–521.

4 "California Acts to Avoid Widespread Opting Out of Project-Based Contracts," *Housing Development Reporter: Current Developments* 26, no. 20 (September 21, 1998): 305.

5 "New REIT to Offer High-Cost Section 8 Projects Haven from Mark-to-Market Consequences," *Affordable Housing Finance* 6, no. 5 (May 1998): 16.

6 National Housing Task Force, *A Decent Place to Live: The Report of the National Housing Task Force* (Washington, D.C.: National Housing Task Force, March 1988), 32.

7 Jason DeParle, "Slamming the Door," *New York Times Magazine*, October 10, 1996, 68.

8 Dan Barry, "For Landlords, Hard Numbers and Obligations," *New York Times*, October 10, 1996.

9 It could be that the decline in the real value of welfare benefits in many states during this period accounts for some of the increase in rent burdens and worst-case needs.

10 Data from the Census Bureau's *Components of Inventory Change* for 1993 show that the total net gain in rental housing from all sources averaged 311,000 units per year from 1980 to 1993, including an average of 443,000 units per year of new construction. From 1978 through 1993, both average rents and the rent component of the consumer price index increased about 45 percent.

11 In 1993, 16.6 percent of all renters whose incomes were less than 30 percent of the area median lived in structurally inadequate units, as did 17.3 percent of low-income Hispanics. Joint Center for Housing Studies, Harvard University, *The State of the Nation's Housing, 1996* (Cambridge, Mass: Joint Center for Housing Studies, 1996), 21, 22.

12 From 1989 to1993, median rents rose almost 15 percent, while the median incomes of all renters rose slightly less than 7 percent, or just 45 percent as much. HUD, Office of Policy Development and Research, *Tabulations of Characteristics of Worst-Case Renters* (Washington, D.C.: HUD, 1996).

13 The threshold for an extreme rent burden is crossed when a household pays more than 50 percent of total income for rent and utilities. Data on extreme rent burdens are from HUD, *Tabulations of Characteristics.*

14 DeParle, "Slamming the Door," 52.

15 HUD, Office of Policy Development and Research, *Rental Housing Assistance at a Crossroads: A Report to Congress on Worst-Case Housing Needs* (Washington, D.C.: HUD, 1996), 43.

16 HUD, *Housing Assistance,* 36.

17 The 1983 figure is from National Housing Task Force, *A Decent Place to Live,* 6; the 1993 figure is from HUD, *Housing Assistance,* 36.

18 New York City Rent Guidelines Board, *Rent-Stabilized Housing in New York City: A Summary of Rent Guidelines Board Research* (New York: New York City Rent Guidelines Board, 1995), p-2.

19 Based on a comparison of HUD's Section 8 fair-market rents and average welfare benefits; cited in DeParle, "Slamming the Door," 55.

20 Ibid., 56–57.

21 Barry, "Hard Numbers and Obligations."

22 See, for example, Karl Vick, "Low-Income Tenants in Maryland Are Fighting Final Curtain," *Washington Post,* December 9, 1996, which describes a wealthy property owner's threat to evict hundreds of tenants from a property that was cited for 881 code violations.

23 Barry, "Hard Numbers and Obligations."

24 Bruce Lambert, "Raid on Illegal Housing Shows Plight of Suburbs' Working Poor," *New York Times,* December 7, 1996, 25–26.

25 Household formation rates remained relatively constant during this period, at around 1.2 million a year. See Joint Center for Housing Studies, *Nation's Housing, 1996,* 1, 30, 31; and tables A-5 and A-6.

26 "City of Los Angeles Backs Regular Inspections," *Affordable Housing Finance* 6, no. 7 (August/September 1998): 20.

27 John O. Nordquist, "How the Government Killed Affordable Housing," *The American Enterprise* 9, no. 4 (July/August 1998): 70.

28 Bill Rumpf, chief executive officer, California Housing Partnership, "California Housing Partnership Corporation Organizational Capability," included with correspondence to author, March 27, 1998.

29 This program description is based, in part, on Schnell, *Partnership Achievement,* 35; use and adaptation are with permission of Social Compact.

30 This program description is based, in part, on Schnell, *Partnership Achievement,* 137; use and adaptation are with permission of Social Compact. The quotation is from Solano Affordable Housing Foundation, *Solano Affordable Housing Foundation: A Nonprofit Corporation* (Solano, Calif.: Solano Affordable Housing Foundation, n.d.).

31 Joseph A. Brown, Atlanta Dvelopment Manager, NationsBank CDC, "NationsBank Community Development Corporation," included with correspondence to author, July 7, 1998.

32 The enhanced voucher is tied to "street rents" rather than to the usual "fair-market rent" standard. The tenant pays what has historically been his or her share and HUD picks up the difference. However, the street rent is locked in at the beginning, and future changes in neighborhood rent levels will not cause further changes in rent subsidies for assisted units.

33 Minnesota Housing Partnership, *About MHP* (from the MHP home page, www.mhponline.org; accessed April 4, 1998).

34 This program description is based, in part, on Schnell, *Partnership Achievement*, 57; use and adaptation are with permission of Social Compact.

35 "MEND: Beginning Our Fourth Decade of Service to Moorestown, 1969–1998," n.d.

36 *Housing and Development Reporter: Current Developments* (August 10, 1998).

37 This program description is based, in part, on Schnell, *Partnership Achievement*, 130; use and adaption are with permission of Social Compact.

6

Welfare-to-Work Rental Assistance

D espite its harsh edges, most Americans support welfare reform, including the provision of assistance to move from welfare to work. For example, in a January 1999 Kellogg Foundation poll, 94 percent of those surveyed supported the idea that people on public assistance who would like to work should be given help to make it possible for them to find jobs.[1] More than three-quarters of those polled believe that when parents on welfare go to work, government should provide help if the parents' jobs do not pay enough to allow them to support their children. Housing policy makers should welcome the finding that in the minds of many Americans, government support of welfare reform should include housing assistance. The Kellogg poll asked respondents to rate on a scale of 1 to 10—where 1 indicates least important and 10 most important—whether government assistance should include "help paying rent as an interim support for persons making the transition out of welfare." While it did not top the list, housing aid in support of welfare reform achieved an average score of 7.2. (In comparison, help paying for child care received an average score of 8.2, and help paying for health insurance an average score of 8.3.)

Overview

Housing policy makers from all levels of government have a stake in helping welfare reform succeed. Despite a 40 percent decline in national welfare rolls since 1994, Brookings Institution researchers found that two-thirds of the 23 cities they surveyed had slower rates of caseload declines than the states in which they were located, and that these "slower" cities are becoming home to an increasing share of their states' welfare caseloads.[2]

Welfare reform can also have significant effects—both good and bad—on neighborhoods. As recently as 1990, more than half of all renters in Detroit, 42 percent of those in Cleveland, and 37 percent of those in Chicago received welfare.[3] The *New York Times* estimated that a $1 billion cut in welfare benefits, proposed by New York's governor George Pataki in 1996, would have eliminated about $15 million in disposable income for households in Ridgewood, Queens; in Manhattan's Washington Heights and Inwood neighborhoods, where greater numbers of welfare recipients live, the total would have been more than $28 million. In the South Bronx, where more people live on public assistance than anywhere else in the city, $47 million would have been drained from the local economy had the cuts been implemented.[4]

Benefit cuts also affect small businesses and, "in low-income housing, the most vulnerable small businesses are small landlords who typically account for a large share of innercity property owners. She might be a retiree who thinks she cannot go wrong with a real estate investment. Or he might be an immigrant building superintendent who believes that to own a 20-unit complex is to own a piece of America."[5] These largely inexperienced and undercapitalized entrepreneurs—who tend to operate less efficiently, to face higher costs, and to suffer greater vacancy and collection losses than their larger and more experienced counterparts—are among the small businesses that could suffer the most as a result of welfare reform.[6]

There is also a great deal of overlap in the populations that receive housing and assistance and those that receive welfare benefits, and the overlap is growing. According to Sandra Newman, a leading expert on the intricate links between housing and welfare policies, the proportion of households living in assisted housing who also receive income assistance has more than doubled since 1966 and is now more than 50 percent.[7] Similar increases, says Newman, have occurred in the proportion of income assistance recipients who also receive housing assistance. Between 1981 and 1995, this fraction increased from about one-fifth to one-third. "Taken together," says Newman, "these changes have moved a significant part of housing policy squarely into the safety net."[8]

Some states have chosen to deal with the inequitable distribution of housing assistance by reducing the welfare benefits of those who also receive housing assistance—or, as the states prefer to describe it, providing larger benefits to welfare recipients who do not receive any housing assistance. Florida's WAGES program sets three payment levels: the highest applies to homeless families or families who pay more than $50 in rent; the middle level applies to families with a shelter obligation greater than zero but less than or equal to $50; and the third applies to families with no shelter obligation at all.[9] Connecticut uses a flat grant to meet all needs, including housing, but decreases the grant by 8 percent for families receiving a housing subsidy. Before the federal welfare reform was enacted, Connecticut had obtained a waiver from the U.S. Department of Health and Human Services that allowed the state to reduce grants awarded to recipients of Aid to Families with Dependent Children (AFDC) if the recipients also received housing assistance. Public housing residents filed suit, obtaining an injunction that prevented the state from implementing the waiver. When AFDC came to an end with the passage of federal welfare reform, the injunction was automatically dissolved, and Connecticut's reduction in cash assistance payments for all residents of public housing and recipients of Section 8 and state rental housing assistance went into effect. Rather than implement a percentage decline, Rhode Island reduces the cash assistance grants to housing assistance recipients by $50 a month; Maryland reduces monthly benefits by $60.[10] Minnesota's grant reduction for families receiving housing assistance has been postponed at least once but is scheduled to become effective in July 1999. Advocates for public assistance recipients are urging the 1999 legislature to delay implementation for another one or two years.

Eliminating welfare entitlements by setting time limits for cash assistance could also profoundly affect the financial circumstances of public housing authorities and other owners of federally assisted rental housing. HUD's preliminary estimate was that because of reduced levels of cash assistance, time limits on benefits, and sanctions on families who violate the rules, welfare reform could cost public housing authorities as much as $2 billion in rental income through 2000. It is thus critical for local housing organizations to participate actively in the development of their state welfare reform plans and to learn how to take advantage of newly available federal assistance to help prepare public housing residents for work.

Despite high levels of welfare dependency in public and assisted housing, more than 60 percent of all welfare recipients live in unsubsidized, privately owned rental housing, which is why HUD's new voucher program for welfare recipients is so important. [11] After failing for three straight year to provide any new money for a single new housing voucher, in 1998 Congress created a special tenant-based rental assistance program to help states achieve their welfare reform objectives. The new welfare-to-work (W2W) program will provide 50,000 special Section 8 vouchers to local housing authorities who create effective partnerships with their state welfare reform agencies; the vouchers will be distributed to families whose unstable housing situations or long commuting times are affecting their ability to find or retain jobs.[12]

Federal funding for 50,000 W2W vouchers is a good first step, and the promise of additional vouchers in fiscal year 2000 is also good news. However, with an average waiting period of 26 months for a housing voucher (longer in many cities), state and local housing policy makers know that they cannot just sit back and wait for the new vouchers to trickle down from HUD. Until they can be assured of a steady flow of earmarked federal funding for this purpose, a number of states and localities have created their own voucher programs to help families move from welfare to work.

For financial and philosophical reasons, states and localities are unwilling to provide welfare recipients with a lifetime entitlement to rental assistance while hundreds of thousands of poor working families who receive no housing aid spend more than half their incomes on rent. Thus, while all HUD-funded W2W vouchers have no time limits, all state and locally funded voucher programs provide time-limited rental assistance and reduce the amount of assistance over the term of the subsidy.

For recipients of public assistance who do not receive housing subsidies, New Mexico increases the payment levels by $100. (Of those receiving Temporary Assistance for Needy Families [TANF], 70 percent are not in subsidized housing.) However, there is a proposal in the current session to eliminate the $100 because it costs over $20 million a year.[13] Minnesota's state-funded rental subsidy program—Rental Assistance for Families—provides a shallow rent subsidy of up to $250 a month for three years to families who receive TANF assistance and have an approved employment plan. Legislation has also been introduced in Minnesota that would create a "school stability initiative" for homeless families with school-age children. In cases where the school has determined that frequent moves caused by the high cost of housing are affecting school performance, the program would provide state-funded housing vouchers to affected families.[14]

The Work First New Jersey Housing Assistance Program provides $6 million ($2 million a year for three years) in temporary rental assistance—enough to help about 400 families. The tenant-based rental assistance, which will be phased out over three years, requires families to spend 45 percent of their income for rent in year one, 55 percent in year two, and 65 percent in the third and final year of assistance. Connecticut's Time-Limited Rental Assistance Program is a two-year, $7.5 million effort funded out of state TANF "maintenance of effort" funds. Rather than gradually reduce the level of assistance, Connecticut's tenant-based rental assistance (TBRA) program pays the difference between 40 percent of income and a state-set maximum rent. Finally, San Mateo County, California, has created a $472,000 TBRA program that is funded through a combination of TANF, county general funds, federal HOME funds, and foundation support. Rental assistance lasts one year, with the recipient paying 50 percent of an approved rent for the first six months and 25 percent for the final six months.

While tenant-based rental assistance is not a large part of the HOME program—representing just 3 percent of cumulative total outlays—at least six jurisdictions have committed a total of $133 million in HOME funds for temporary rental assistance. Because TBRA is limited to 24 months under HOME program regulations, it is generally used either as a bridge to Section 8 (to provide immediate assistance to especially vulnerable households who are on the Section 8 waiting list) or in self-sufficiency programs, where TBRA increases recipients' ability to participate in education and training programs.

Programs

Fremont Housing Scholarship Program
Fremont, California

The Fremont Housing Scholarship Program, initiated in 1987, is an innovative initiative that uses scholarships rather than subsidies to help households on public assistance become self-sufficient. The program combines housing assistance with comprehensive support services to help 20 households a year move toward financial independence.

Program Administration

Fremont's housing department administers the housing scholarship program, which is a partnership between the city and landlords, businesses, and educational institutions.

Program Description

The housing scholarship program combines one-year rent reductions of up to 50 percent with job training, affordable housing, child care, life skill classes, counseling, job placement assistance, and other services as needed to stabilize households while the adults increase their skills and earning potential and become successfully employed. (Priority is given to families with children, but single-person households and households without children are not excluded from participation.) Landlords and developers receiving assistance from the city voluntarily agree to provide rent reductions to low-income households who have demonstrated the necessary commitment and skills to achieve sustainable livelihoods.

Life skill classes, provided by the Mission Valley Regional Occupation Program (ROP), include topics such as budgeting, goal setting, time management, self-esteem, credit counseling, landlord-tenant relationships, parenting and relationship issues, codependency, and problem solving. ROP also provides training in accounting, office management, and in the welding, plumbing, and carpentry trades. ROP provides these services to participants—along with case management and job placement—free of charge.

Local participating training programs refer potential scholarship recipients, who must meet specific criteria and are selected on the basis of income, enrollment in an eligible training program, choice of a realistic career path, and need for adequate housing. Participants must continue to meet performance requirements to proceed in the program. Once a participant gets a full-time job, rents are gradually increased to market rates.

Funding Sources

The housing scholarship program is funded through Community Development Block Grant funds, federal HOME funds, redevelopment funds, and development fees.

Accomplishments

Between 1987 and early 1999, 139 households were assisted.

Housing Opportunities Program
San Mateo County, California

The Housing Opportunities Program (HOP), created in December of 1997 and serving San Mateo County, California, provides support to low-income heads of household as they complete job training and make the transition to employment and self-sufficiency. The program currently provides housing scholarship funds, case management, skills development, and special services for up to 80 families a year.

Program Administration

The Human Investment Project (HIP), Inc., a private nonprofit housing organization serving San Mateo County, created and administers the HOP program.

To meet the families' comprehensive needs, HIP works in collaboration with numerous agencies, including the Regional Occupation Program, the Private Industry Council, Opportunities Industrialized Center West, Shared Undertaking to Change the Community to Enable Self-Sufficiency (SUCCESS) centers, the Child Care Coordinating Council (for child care referrals), and counselors from local community colleges, the Core Services Centers, the Housing Industry Foundation, and the San Mateo County Housing Authority.

Program Description

HOP participants are awarded a housing scholarship for one year. For the first six months, the program subsidizes rent at a rate of 50 percent, which decreases to 25 percent for the second six months. The program provides assistance in locating housing, and the scholarship is awarded after the housing is located. Case management and life skills workshops provide participants with ongoing support and guidance. Whenever possible, scholarship housing units are established in HIP-owned properties.

The program coordinator acts as an advocate with landlords and property managers to secure appropriate housing. Once a unit has been located, the housing quality standards team inspects the unit, reviews the lease, and negotiates with the landlord, if necessary, to rectify substandard conditions or adjust the lease terms. When all standards have been met, the coordinator will connect the participant with resources to assist with moving costs.

Eligibility is based on a referral from an adviser who identifies the applicant as having overcome barriers to self-sufficiency and as meeting several criteria: applicants must be receiving, eligible for, or recently transitioned from CALWORKS (California's welfare-to-work program). They must be homeless, at risk of homelessness, or in housing conditions that are unsafe or overcrowded. Finally, applicants must be enrolled in a job training program; have completed 75 percent of a job training program; have completed a job training program within the past six months; or be earning less than 50 percent of the area median income, with potential for advancement.

Participants are selected on a competitive basis by a panel of community volunteers who assess the applicant's demonstrated motivation, review the income level the applicant needs to support his or her family, and evaluate the applicant's ability to achieve this income level within one year.

The program costs about $950 in administrative and support services per family and $5,000 in housing scholarships per family.

Funding Sources

CALWORKS provides funding for a full-time program director and for the housing scholarships. The county, the city's HOME funds, and foundation grants provide additional funding for scholarships. To supplement the program, a revolving loan fund was established with a grant from a local service club and with memorial donations made in honor of a community leader. This fund supports emergency expenses, continuing education, and unforeseen needs that can undermine participants' progress toward self-reliance.

Accomplishments

As of March 1999, HOP had awarded a total of 69 scholarships. One graduate of the program, a homeless custodial father of two, became a licensed insurance agent.

Contact
Human Investment Project, Inc.
Judy Gaither, Executive Director
364 South Railroad Avenue
San Mateo, California 94401
Telephone: (650) 348-6660
Fax: (650) 348-0284
Web site: www.hiphousing.org

Time-Limited Rental Assistance Program
State of Connecticut

Connecticut's Time-Limited Rental Assistance Program, established in November 1997, assists families by providing rental assistance payments for up to 12 months.

Program Administration

The Connecticut Department of Social Services has contracted with the Connecticut Association for Community Action to provide the rental assistance payments. The association, in turn, has subcontracted with three area community action agencies to implement the program.

Program Description

The housing subsidy is based on the participant's family income. The participant's contribution is 20 percent of monthly household income or 40 percent of adjusted gross monthly income less a utility allowance, whichever is greater. To be eligible,

- The family must have exhausted the 21-month limit on Temporary Family Assistance (TFA);
- The family must not be receiving TFA benefits via an extension;
- The family's income must be greater than the TFA payment standard;
- An adult member of the family must be working at the time of the application for rental assistance;
- The application for assistance must take place within six month of leaving the TFA program;
- The family must be living in privately owned rental housing;
- The family must not already be receiving a rent subsidy.

Case maintenance workers at the department of social services regional office perform exit interviews with all potentially eligible clients as they leave TFA. Families who are eligible for the Time-Limited Rental Assistance Program are mailed a precertification letter explaining the program. The letter serves as proof of eligibility and verification of income. The client (typically the head of household) may then apply for participation in the Time-Limited Rental Assistance Program by mail or in person.

The community action agencies maintain a waiting list of eligible applicants and select participants randomly through a monthly lottery. Not more than 144 applicants statewide are selected through each lottery. Applicants who are not selected remain on the waiting list and continue to be entered into the monthly lottery until they are chosen for participation or their six-month eligibility expires.

Selected participants are issued a time-limited rental assistance certificate and a briefing package that includes a request for lease approval. Participants are strongly encouraged to remain in their current housing unit. When necessary, the community action agency will negotiate the contract rent, approve the lease, execute the housing assistance payment contract, and authorize monthly payments.

Funding Sources

Connecticut's department of social services has set aside over $2 million for rental assistance and administration.

Accomplishments

About 930 households have received assistance during the life of the rental assistance program.

Contact

Connecticut Association for Community Action
Lucille Sciafani
555 Windsor Street
Hartford, Connecticut 06120
Telephone: (860) 560-5846
Fax: (860) 560-5848

Tenant-Based Rental Assistance Program and Security Deposit Assistance
Sioux City, Iowa

To fund a tenant-based rental assistance program, Sioux City, Iowa, and the Siouxland Consortium allocate $138,000 or 25 percent of federal HOME allocations; an additional $42,000 is allocated for security deposit assistance. The members of the Siouxland Consortium—Sioux City, Iowa; South Sioux City, Nebraska; and Dakota City, Nebraska—work cooperatively in the strategic planning and implementation of housing programs.

Program Description

The rental assistance program is based on Sioux City's existing Section 8 voucher program. Assistance is given to families on the Section 8 waiting list maintained by the city public housing authority. Sioux City's program design generally mirrors the federal requirements for the use of HOME funds for rental assistance.

The rationale for the security deposit program is that for many people, the amount of money needed for a security deposit is a significant barrier to housing affordability. The security deposit program offers grants for amounts up to the difference between 30 percent of adjusted household income and one month's rent. Funds must be used to rent a unit under the Section 8 rental assistance program; however, for families at risk of homelessness, funds are also offered to the general public for security deposit assistance on an emergency basis.

Funding Sources

The rental assistance and security deposit assistance programs combined make up 33 percent of Sioux City's federal HOME allocation.

Accomplishments

To date, $371,142 has been expended to provide about 55 families with rental assistance, some since the program first began. Another $163,301 has been used to provide 703 families with security deposit assistance.

Tenant-Based Rental Assistance
State of Kansas

Since 1992, the Kansas Department of Commerce and Housing has made HOME funds for rental assistance available, on a competitive basis, to public housing authorities, nonprofit agencies, and for-profit companies.

Program Description

Although the allocations are made on a competitive basis, the state does not specify criteria for the selection of successful applicants. However, priority is given to programs that are most likely to commit and expend funds. In administering the program, grant recipients must comply with Section 8 standards for housing quality and serve HUD's standards for fair-market rent; grantees must also comply with HOME program goals and pay rent directly to landlords. Rental assistance may be provided for up to 24 months, and the amount of assistance is based on both income level and fair-market rents.

Funding Sources

Successful applicants administer HOME funds through HOME program coupons, which are similar to Section 8 certificates and vouchers.

Accomplishments

In fiscal year 1998, $822,720 of HOME funding was made available.

Work First New Jersey Housing Assistance Program
State of New Jersey

Initiated in August 1998, the Work First New Jersey Housing Assistance Program is a demonstration program that provides time-limited rental subsidies to heads of households who are leaving welfare to begin unsubsidized employment. The temporary subsidies are designed to minimize episodes of financial crisis; stabilize the financial situations of wage earners who are exiting the welfare system; and provide opportunities for lower-wage workers to establish savings—and, when feasible, become first-time homeowners. The program is being implemented in Asbury Park, Camden, Elizabeth, New Brunswick, and Trenton.

Program Administration

The New Jersey Department of Community Affairs, in partnership with the New Jersey Department of Human Services, implements the housing assistance program. The New Jersey Housing and Mortgage Finance Agency (HMFA) is involved in the homeownership component.

Program Description

Over a three-year period, participating households pay gradually increasing percentages of their monthly income toward rent: during year one the household pays 45 percent, in year two 55 percent, and in year three 65 percent. The program pays the balance of the rent directly to the property owner. At the end of year three, the program support ends.

An escrow/savings account is also established for the participants. If, for example, a participant's share of the rent is scheduled to increase because of an increase in earned income, the program places a matching amount into the savings account. When participants complete their obligations under the program contract, they are entitled to the balance accumulated in the savings account, which may be used for a downpayment on a home or for other housing-related costs.

To provide additional assistance, HMFA extends homeownership opportunities to interested households. This program includes 100 percent financing of mortgage loans, extensive homeownership counseling, below-market interest rates, and assistance with closing costs.

Households who are leaving Temporary Assistance for Needy Families (TANF) are selected for the program by the county boards of social services. To be eligible for the program, households must meet three criteria:

- Because the head of household has been placed in unsubsidized employment, the household is no longer eligible for TANF;
- Household income is 150 percent or less of the federal poverty level, but the household is no longer eligible for TANF;
- The household's cash assets do not exceed $4,000 (excluding autos).

Households referred for time-limited rental assistance are assigned priority according to a point system that is designed to respond to need and to reward responsible behaviors.

The New Jersey Department of Community Affairs assists households to locate appropriate housing, conducts case management, inspects housing, negotiates lease and rent-subsidy terms, maintains escrow/savings accounts, determines the length of rental assistance, and refers participants to appropriate counseling services.

Funding Sources

The department of human services has committed a total of $6 million to provide up to $2 million a year for three years to fund the housing assistance program. Ten percent of the funds will be used for administration, and the rest to assist approximately 350 families.

Accomplishments

As of March 26, 1999, 51 families who had found housing were receiving rental assistance and another 80 were searching for housing.

> **Contact**
> New Jersey Department of Community Affairs
> Division of Housing and Community Resources
> Roy Ziegler, Assistant Director
> P.O. Box 800
> 101 South Broad Street
> Trenton, New Jersey 08625
> Telephone: (609) 633-6150
> Fax: (609) 633-8084

Tenant-Based Rental Assistance
State of Washington

Since 1992, Washington State's department of community, trade, and economic development has allocated about 15 percent of its federal HOME funds to the Tenant-Based Rental Assistance (TBRA) program, which is designed to support the self-sufficiency efforts of households receiving rental assistance.

Program Administration

TBRA is administered by the department of community, trade, and economic development in collaboration with local public housing authorities and organizations that have experience in administering Section 8 or tenant-based rental assistance programs.

Program Description

Funds are awarded to public housing authorities or to other nonprofits that can function as housing authorities. The competitive request-for-proposals process rewards flexible program designs that allow grant applicants to meet the needs of households in their service areas. At least 90 percent of the funds must be targeted to households at or below 60 percent of the area median income and the remainder to households earning below 80 percent.

Households (including single-person households) are selected for the program by the TBRA contractor. The contractors are encouraged, but not required, to request that recipients participate in a self-sufficiency program of not more than 24 months duration. The level of rental assistance is determined according to Section 8 rules.

Accomplishments

About $1.2 million was spent in 1998. Since 1992, about 992 households have been assisted.

Contact

State of Washington CTED
Stanley K. Jackson
906 Columbia Street, S.W.
P.O. Box 48300
Olympia, Washington 98504
Telephone: (360) 753-7426
Fax: (360) 586-5880

Notes

1 W. K. Kellogg Foundation, *W. K. Kellogg Foundation Releases Major Survey on Public Attitudes toward Welfare Reform and the Nation's Healthcare System*, news release, January 13, 1999.

2 Bruce Katz and Kate Carnevale, *The State of Welfare Caseloads in America's Cities* (Washington, D.C.: Center on Urban and Metropolitan Policy, Brookings Institution, May 1998), 4.

3 Because the welfare data do not distinguish households living in public housing from those living in private housing, the data in the text overestimate the potential negative effects of welfare reform on private-market rental housing.

4 *New York Times*, February 8, 1996.

5 Dan Barry, "For Landlords, Hard Numbers and Obligations," *New York Times*, October 10, 1996.

6 See, for example, Michael A. Stegman, *Housing Investment in the Inner City: The Dynamics of Decline* (Cambridge, Mass: MIT Press, 1969).

7 Sandra J. Newman, "Introduction and Overview," in *The Home Front: Implications of Welfare Reform for Housing Policy*, ed. Sandra J. Newman (Washington, D.C., The Urban Institute Press, forthcoming), 8.

8 Newman, "Introduction and Overview," 8.

9 Information in this section is posted on the housing/welfare listserv: housingwelfare@lists.cbpp.org.

10 Cited by Barbara Sard in an e-mail to the author, January 16, 1999.

11 For fiscal 1996, the last year of the Aid to Families with Dependent Children (AFDC) program, 0.3 percent of AFDC families were homeless; another 0.9 percent shared group quarters; and for 0.4 percent of families, the

shelter arrangement was unknown. By far the largest group—62.3 percent—rented privately owned housing and received no subsidy. Data from U.S. Department of Health and Human Services, *Characteristics and Financial Circumstances of AFDC Recipients for Fiscal 1996*, cited by Mark D. Schroeder, U.S. Department of Housing and Urban Development, in an e-mail to the author, January 14, 1999.

12 Barbara Sard and Jeff Lubell, *How the Statutory Changes Made by the Quality Housing and Work Responsibility Act of 1998 May Affect Welfare Reform Efforts* (Washington, D.C.: Center on Budget and Policy Priorities, December 1998), 2.

13 Jeff Lubell, Center on Budget and Policy Priorities, in an e-mail to the author, January 19, 1999.

14 Ibid.

Secondary Market Initiatives in Community Development Finance

T his chapter differs from the others in this volume because none of the secondary-market programs described here are, strictly speaking, sponsored by state or local governments. Nevertheless, the programs are included for two reasons: first, they have the potential to compensate for the loss of banks and thrifts in underserved communities; second, as and more peoples' savings are migrating from financial intermediaries covered by the 1977 Community Reinvestment Act (CRA), to other savings vehicles, the amount of money that would otherwise be available to banks to invest in underserved communities is decreasing. It is thus imperative that the affordable-housing community learn how to take maximum advantage of the exciting developments in the secondary-mortgage market.

Overview

Between 1975 and 1995, the interplay of many factors—among them, the deregulation of interest rates in the 1980s, new technology, and growing competition from nondepository institutions—led to a 35 percent decline in the number of financial institutions in the United States, from about 18,600 to 12,200.[1] Many economic studies predict that by the year 2000, this number will shrink by an additional 2,000 to 6,000.[2]

However, a decline in the number of banks does not automatically lead to a decrease in the number of local banking *offices*. During the same 20-year period, the number of branch offices increased by 29 percent. However, virtually all this growth occurred in middle-income areas; low-income neighborhoods saw a 21 percent decline in branch facilities.[3] A recent Deloitte & Touche study predicted that competition with nonbank intermediaries could force banks to close nearly half their branches over the next decade. With more branches being opened in affluent areas, the inevitable implication is that low-income neighborhoods will continue to lose banking offices in significant numbers.[4]

For nearly 30 years, starting with the Home Mortgage Disclosure Act (HMDA), the federal government has encouraged conventional lenders to pay greater attention to the home financing needs of lower-income families and underserved communities. Most prominent in the arsenal of federal laws and regulations addressing this issue is the CRA, which requires federally regulated financial institutions to meet community credit needs. Since passage of the CRA, banks and community organizations have entered into community lending agreements representing more than $400 billion in reinvestment dollars for traditionally underserved populations and communities.[5]

Many reinvestment advocates believe that public accountability has been the secret of the CRA's most recent success. From 1977 through 1992, community groups and lenders negotiated CRA agreements totaling just $42 billion. In the early 1990s, when CRA ratings became public and community groups became actively involved in the bank-merger application process, progress in community reinvestment skyrocketed. From 1992 to the present, over $368 billion of the $410 billion total in CRA agreements was pledged.[6] Recent bank megamergers have resulted in hundreds of billions of dollars in additional affordable-lending commitments. Moreover, in 1992, with the enactment of the Federal Housing Enterprises Financial Safety and Soundness Act, Congress demanded that the Federal National Mortgage Association and the Federal Home Loan Mortgage Corporation (Fannie Mae and Freddie Mac) improve their services to minorities, low- and moderate-income borrowers, and underserved communities.

Given this impressive record, it is no small matter that when the CRA took effect, roughly two-thirds of Americans' long-term savings were in CRA-covered institutions.[7] Today, that figure is less than 30 percent, and the migration from the conventional banking system to mutual funds, money market accounts, and other non-CRA savings vehicles continues unabated. This decline is important because the CRA has spawned a rich array of affordable lending programs that determine creditworthiness by nontraditional means— techniques that measure the circumstances of underserved households more appropriately than established standards.[8]

As demonstrated in Chapter 1, virtually all affordable lending programs feature flexible underwriting, along with risk mitigation measures that minimize potentially higher credit losses. While there is no universally agreed upon set of flexible underwriting standards, most affordable loan products incorporate one or more of the following eight features:[9]

- *Reduced downpayments:* Under flexible standards, downpayments may be as low as zero, versus the 20 percent generally require for a conventional loan.

- *Higher debt-to-income ratios:* Under flexible standards, ratios may be as high as 33 percent for PITI (principal, interest, taxes, and insurance) and as high as 40 percent for total debt to income. For conventional loans, the ratios are 28 to 33 percent.
- *Flexible employment standards:* Conventional loans require continued employment with the same employer; more flexible standards use income stability over time.
- *Alternative credit history:* Conventional loans rely on credit scores from credit-rating companies; a more flexible approach relies on rent and utility payment history.
- *Reduced cash reserves:* Under flexible standards, no cash reserves may be required; conventional loans generally require a reserve sufficient to cover two months of mortgage, insurance, and property tax payments.
- *Reduced interest rates:* To earn CRA credit, banks may offer subsidized interest rates to underserved borrower groups.
- *Private mortgage insurance exemption:* Private mortgage insurance (PMI) is typically required when the downpayment is below 20 percent; under flexible underwriting standards, the PMI requirement may be waived.
- *Reduced points or fees:* Most conventional loans require payment of points and fees at loan origination; for affordable loans, some points or fees may be reduced or waived.

On the whole, despite the potential for higher losses, community development lending has proved to be good business for financial institutions. A recent Federal Reserve study found, for example, that "lenders active in lower-income neighborhoods with lower-income borrowers appear to be as profitable as other mortgage-oriented commercial banks"— which is why the closing of banks and bank offices in low-income neighborhoods is cause for concern.[10] Many community development leaders agree with Nic Retsinas, a former housing commissioner in the Clinton administration, that reinvestment requirements similar to those mandated by the CRA should be extended to "the nonbank institutions that look and behave like banks—to make serving the community part of their mission too." Although the idea lacks significant political support, Retsinas believes that there is no rationale for restricting a community mission only to banks: redlining among insurance companies is just as wrong as redlining among lenders. And while some people may counter that, unlike traditional banks, insurance companies and brokerage houses do not have traditional deposits, notions of what is traditional have become antiquated.[11]

While extending community reinvestment requirements to the "parallel banking system"[12] may be a political pipe dream, creating marketable securities backed by nontraditional, affordable-housing mortgages—securities that provide competitive yields to investors and can be sold and traded in the secondary-mortgage market—is not. Packaging affordable-housing loans for sale in the secondary market is not new. Nearly 20 years ago, the nonprofit Neighborhood Reinvestment Corporation created Neighborhood Housing Services of America to buy small pools of affordable-housing loans originated by local Neighborhood Housing Services programs for sale to socially motivated investors at below-market yields. Packaging affordable-housing loans into low-risk securities priced to yield attractive returns to mainstream institutional investors, however, is a dramatic breakthrough.

Recently, a number of securities backed by CRA mortgages have been brought to market by Wall Street investment-banking firms. In the first ten months of 1998, for example, Bear, Stearns & Co., Inc., managed more than $1.89 billion of securitized CRA loans, including a $396 million bundle from Citibank and $336 million in loans from Mellon Bank.[13]

Since July 1997, Fannie Mae has purchased or securitized nearly $2 billion of seasoned CRA loans in more than 20 separate transactions. In June 1998, Fannie Mae purchased a $750 million real estate mortgage investment conduit composed of seasoned affordable loans originated by Fleet Financial Group and priced by Bear, Stearns.[14] In another recent development, the Federal Home Loan Bank (FHLB) system created a $1 billion mortgage partnership finance program (MPF) to provide a secondary market for mortgage loans for member institutions of the Chicago and Dallas FHLBs. The Dallas FHLB has funded $340 million in affordable loans since joining the program in October 1998. Three other FHLBs are seeking to join the MPF, which has master commitments for an additional $800 million in loans. Along the same lines, the FHLB of Seattle plans to buy up to $25 million in Federal Housing Administration (FHA) loans to finance rent-to-own mortgages for low- and moderate-income households. Although banks must normally accumulate loans in a pool before they can be packaged for sale to the Government National Mortgage Association (Ginnie Mae), the Seattle pilot program allows individual loans to be sold immediately at favorable prices, but with higher servicing fees.[15]

Access Capital Strategies (ACS) Community Investment Fund is another for-profit secondary-market instrument created by the private sector to help financial institutions meet their community reinvestment requirements. ACS is a closed-end mutual fund that will purchase a variety of community development securities backed by CRA loans. Through the fund, banks can invest in CRA securities—thereby earning CRA credit—or sell pools of CRA loans to ACS, thereby freeing up capital in order to originate additional affordable mortgages.

Finally, in a dramatic new partnership, the Ford Foundation has joined forces with Self-Help (a North Carolina–based nonprofit community development organization) and Fannie Mae to expand dramatically the secondary market for CRA loans. With a $50 million grant from the Ford Foundation, Self-Help will expand its innovative affordable home loan secondary-market program nationwide. Since 1994, the program has purchased $100 million in affordable loans from major North Carolina commercial banks that would not otherwise have originated these mortgages. The program has increased access to mortgages among minorities, rural residents, low-income families, and households headed by women. Delinquency rates are also well within acceptable limits, with loan losses of less than 1 percent. Based on the success in North Carolina and a new commitment from Fannie Mae, Self-Help will be able to leverage the Ford grant 40 times over, generating $2 billion in affordable loans for 35,000 low-income buyers over the next five years.

In short, because they enable portfolio lenders to sell CRA loans in volume, the initiatives discussed in this chapter have the potential to increase affordable lending significantly by increasing the secondary market's appetite for nontraditional mortgages. Local housing advocates and policy makers need to exploit the opportunities that these new developments present.

Programs

Community Advantage Home Loan Secondary Market Program State of North Carolina

The Community Advantage Home Loan Secondary Market Program (Community Advantage), created in 1998, is an expansion of Self-Help's current Home Loan Secondary Market Program. By providing participating lenders with a guaranteed market for low-income loans, Community Advantage increases lenders' incentive and ability to make Community Reinvestment Act (CRA) loans.

If successful, the program will demonstrate to secondary-market institutions that affordable loans do not require the type of additional backing that Self-Help provides. With this evidence, secondary-market actors will be encouraged to broaden their purchasing policies to include uninsured affordable home loans.

Participants

Community Advantage is a partnership among Self-Help, a North Carolina–based community development organization founded in 1980; Fannie Mae; and the Ford Foundation. Initial lenders participating in the program include Bank of America, Bank One, Branch Banking & Trust, Centura Bank, Chase Manhattan Bank, First Citizens Bank & Trust, First Union National Bank, Norwest, the North Carolina State Employees' Credit Union, and Wachovia Bank.

Program Description

Conventional lending standards often exclude low-income families (those whose incomes are less than 80 percent of the area median) who seek to become homeowners because conventional lenders often require a higher level of savings and a stronger credit record than low-income borrowers have. To comply with CRA requirements, banks have begun to tailor loan packages to low-income borrowers. Because CRA loans require lower downpayments and have more flexible underwriting standards, they rarely meet the mortgage-purchase requirements of the secondary market. Fannie Mae, for example, will not buy directly from a bank any uninsured mortgage that has a downpayment of less than 20 percent; such loans must be privately insured or guaranteed before Fannie Mae will consider purchasing them. As a result, many banks have amassed in their portfolios a large number of long-term, fixed-rate CRA mortgages; because these mortgages cannot be sold on the secondary market, banks are prevented from offering affordable mortgages to new low-income borrowers.

In 1994, Self-Help created its Home Loan Secondary Market Program to address this problem. Through the program, Self-Help purchased CRA loans and held them in portfolio, assuming the risk of default. Because lenders must agree to reinvest the proceeds from the sale of CRA loans in additional affordable home mortgages, the secondary-market program has enabled an additional 3,000 low-income families in North Carolina to buy their own homes. Since the creation of the program, Self-Help has purchased close to $300 million in affordable home loans from North Carolina's commercial banks.

The new partnership between Self-Help, Fannie Mae, and the Ford Foundation will significantly advance this effort. The Community Advantage program will work as follows: Self-Help will purchase approximately $2 billion in CRA loans over the next five years from participating national or regional banks and will sell these loans to Fannie Mae. Self-Help will retain full recourse for any credit losses for ten years and will be able to guarantee these loans (in part through a $50 million grant from the Ford Foundation). Each participating bank will commit to deliver between $50 and $100 million in CRA loans annually over the next five years and to originate a comparable volume and type of loans in the future.

Community Advantage will expand Self-Help's existing secondary-market program in both size and scope. The $50 million in guarantee funds held by Self-Help should allow Fannie Mae to purchase $2 billion in affordable mortgage loans. With Fannie Mae, Ford, and Self-Help creating a guaranteed market for these loans, banks can originate affordable mortgage loans with the knowledge that they will be able to sell them.

It is estimated that Self-Help's Community Advantage program will assist 35,000 low-income families to become homeowners over the next five years. In addition, Self-Help plans to expand its activities across the country, making a special effort to focus on loans made to members of minority groups.

Accomplishments

As of March 1999, Self-Help had purchased approximately $300 million in loans.

Contact
Community Advantage Home Loan Secondary Market Program
Self-Help
Eric Stein
301 West Main Street
Durham, North Carolina 27701
Telephone: (919) 956-4400
Fax: (919) 956-4605
Web site: www.self-help.org

Rent-to-Own Loan Purchase Program
Regional

The loan purchase program of the Federal Home Loan Bank (FHLB) of Seattle was initiated in August 1998 to promote homeownership by creating a secondary market for the loans used to acquire properties for rent-to-own housing programs.

Program Administration

The FHLB of Seattle administers the loan purchase program.

Program Description

The FHLB of Seattle will purchase FHA-insured loans made by member financial institutions and approved nonmember customers to public housing authorities, local government agencies, and other FHA-approved nonprofit housing development organizations that acquire property for ultimate sale to homebuyers through rent-to-own programs. The purchase program creates an outlet for the sale of these loans on a whole-loan, servicing-retained basis: for the lender, this allows an increase in the amount of lending that specifically benefits low- to moderate-income borrowers and helps meet Community Reinvestment Act (CRA) goals.

The FHLB of Seattle plans to purchase up to $25 million in loans but to manage concentration risks by limiting the number of loans from a given geographic area or from a single seller. The bank is actively seeking loans to purchase.

Eligible loan originators or sellers include member financial institutions and approved nonmember customers who are FHA-approved direct endorsement lenders and experienced FHA loan servicers. All approved sellers must meet the bank's requirements for financial strength and servicing experience and must be members of the FHLB of Seattle. The bank will make an exception for third-party loan originations for properties within its region if a member financial institution first purchases the loan then sells that loan to the FHLB of Seattle.

The loans must be made to HUD-approved public and private nonprofit organizations that operate rent-to-own programs intended to promote low- to moderate-income homeownership. To be considered eligible mortgagors, nonprofit housing development organizations must be approved by the local FHA office. Public housing authorities (PHAs) are considered to be governmental entities, so prior FHA approval is not required. PHAs must demonstrate that they have the authority to borrow and the financial capacity to support the debt, and that they are otherwise creditworthy. The borrowers' rent-to-own programs may include other sources of downpayment assistance—such as secondary financing, gifts, grants, or "sweat equity"—as long as these sources are in addition to downpayment funds accumulated through rent payments. Loans may be made for one- to four-family residences, including condominiums and manufactured housing.

The program will purchase loans that meet FHA maximum loan limits for the region. The loan must have a 15- to 30-year fixed rate, with level payments and interest rates based on the Government National Mortgage Association's secondary-market program guidelines for issuers of mortgage-backed securities that include both single-family and multifamily loans. The collateral for the loan must be the first lien deed of trust, fee simple estate. The selling mortgagee services the loan, subject to the terms and conditions of the master loan purchase and servicing agreement of the FHLB of Seattle. If the loans are delinquent, the servicer must continue to remit scheduled principal and interest payments from its own funds.

The FHLB of Seattle has the option to require repurchase of the loan, at par, if there is failure to obtain or maintain FHA mortgage insurance or if the borrower's payment is more than 90 days delinquent.

Contact
Federal Home Loan Bank of Seattle
Judith C. Dailey, Vice President
1501 Fourth Avenue, Suite 1900
Seattle, Washington 98101-1693
Telephone: (206) 340-8708
Fax: (206) 340-2485

Access Capital Strategies Community Investment Fund National

The Access Capital Strategies (ACS) Community Investment Fund, created in 1998 and based in Cambridge, Massachusetts, acts as a source of long-term, low-cost, fixed-rate capital for low- and moderate-income communities. The fund acts as a vehicle for creating or replenishing sources of capital for community reinvestment.

ACS is a fund registered with the Securities and Exchange Commission and structured as a business development corporation under the Investment Company Act of 1940. This structure allows the fund manager to provide managerial and technical assistance to the issuers of the securities, an important role in serving community development financial institutions and government lenders.

Program Description

ACS is a secondary-market purchaser of a variety of community development securities including home mortgages, mortgages for affordable rental housing, commercial real estate loans, and small-business loans. The fund's objective is to invest in geographically specific private-placement debt securities. The fund has invested primarily in securities designed to support underlying economic activities, such as affordable housing, education, small-business lending, and employment initiatives.

ACS is a closed-end mutual fund that has purchased $28 million in securities backed by community investment loans. The fund offers bank investors the opportunity to invest in Community Reinvestment Act (CRA) securities—and thereby earn CRA investment test credit—and the opportunity to earn a minimum return equal to that of Treasury securities with comparable maturity terms. All ACS investments will carry an AAA credit rating or the equivalent.

As part of the agreement to purchase fund shares, investors must designate a state, a multistate region, a metropolitan area, or the entire United States as the preferred geographic focus for their investment. Once the investor submits a commitment to invest, pays the commitment fee, and chooses a designated target region, the fund manager begins the search and design process for the private-placement debt securities to be created in the designated geographic area.

The fund will invest between 50 and 75 percent of its total assets in securities issued by providers of affordable housing. Affordable-housing investments made by the fund must meet the fund's criteria for return and credit quality and must also support economic activity that would not otherwise be adequately funded through traditional banking or capital markets.

The fund manager will seek and respond to investment opportunities from a variety of channels, including prospective issuers of securities (such as federal, state, and other public sector agencies), investment bankers or financial advisors, and prospective issuers or investment banks that may have or suggest debt securities for the fund to purchase.

To help ensure that the investment and programmatic goals of each transaction entered into by the fund are realized, ACS offers managerial assistance to the issuers of the private-placement debt securities it purchases.

The minimum investment in the fund is $500,000. The maturity term for securities held by the fund will vary by type of investment. Mortgage-backed securities will typically have maturity terms of up to 30 years, while securitized small-business loan transactions may have maturity terms of up to ten years. The fund manager's goal is to raise $1 billion to invest in ten designated target regions throughout the United States.

Accomplishments

The first closing, of $25 million, took place in May 1998; New England was the designated target region.

Contact
Access Capital Strategies Community Investment Fund
Access Capital Strategies LLC
124 Mount Auburn Street
Suite 200N
Cambridge, Massachusetts 02138
Telephone: (617) 576-5858
Fax: (617) 864-5693

The Community Development Trust, Inc.
National

The Community Development Trust, Inc., was created in 1998 for the purpose of providing capital, in the form of debt and equity investments, to projects that meet the requirements of the Community Reinvestment Act (CRA). The trust intends to qualify as a real estate investment trust (REIT) for federal income tax purposes.[16] Operating as a self-managed REIT company, the trust may invest in residential, multifamily, community facility, and commercial properties.

Participants

The Local Initiatives Support Corporation (LISC) formed The Community Development Trust in conjunction with a major initiative to provide a broadened secondary market for community development loans and a source of equity for projects that are not receiving low-income housing tax credits. LISC, along with banks and insurance companies, will be a stockholder in the REIT.

Program Description

The Community Development Trust's goals are to

- Provide stockholders with a competitive return on investment;
- Foster affordable housing and community development;
- Provide a diversity of investment and risk by investing in different cities, communities, neighborhoods, and rural areas;
- Improve the affordable-housing stock, foster community development, and encourage other public and private investment;
- Strengthen the economic and social climate of the areas in which projects are located.

In its debt acquisition activity, the trust will emphasize affordable-housing projects and other community development projects. Its real estate equity investments will concentrate on the acquisition of federally subsidized properties through an "UPREIT" structure (an arrangement in which more than one partnership is "rolled up" in a single REIT offering), which provides the owners of the partnership units with a tax-deferred exchange.

The trust intends to acquire residential, multifamily, community facility, and commercial mortgage loans for investment and securitization. It also intends to acquire equity investments in multifamily real properties on the basis of the properties' potential for cash flow and capital appreciation.

The Community Development Trust will offer its class B common stock in a private placement with a limited number of accredited institutional investors, primarily corporations and financial institutions. Banks can satisfy CRA requirements by investing in the trust. The minimum subscription to the trust is 100,000 shares ($1 million worth) of class B common stock. LISC has invested $1.5 million to acquire all the issued shares of the trust's class A common stock.

Accomplishments

Officials at the trust expect their first closing to occur by the end of 1999.

Contact

The Community Development Trust, Inc.
1350 Broadway, #700
New York, New York 10018
Telephone: (212) 465-1045
Fax: (212) 465-1169

First Union/Bear, Stearns Securitization of Community Reinvestment Act Single-Family Loans National

In October 1997, First Union Capital Markets Corporation (First Union) and Bear, Stearns & Co., Inc. (Bear, Stearns) priced a $384.6 million offering of securities backed by Community Reinvestment Act (CRA) loans. Securitization of CRA loans frees the seller's money for further use in benefiting low- and moderate-income borrowers and enables buyers to obtain CRA investment credit.

Participants

First Union and Bear, Stearns initiated the effort to support First Union's affordable loan program. The offering, First Union CRA Mortgage Loan Trust 1997-1, was formed pursuant to a pooling and servicing agreement among First Union, the seller; First Union Mortgage Corporation, the servicer; First Union National Bank, trust department, the document custodian; the Federal Home Loan Mortgage Corporation, the guarantor; and Norwest Bank Minnesota, National Association, the trustee.

Program Description

First Union implemented its affordable loan program in 1994. This program, like all those established in accordance with CRA guidelines, is intended to benefit low- to moderate-income borrowers. The program allows loan-to-value ratios of up to 97 percent and has no requirements for primary mortgage insurance or cash reserves. Borrowers who wish to buy property that is not located within a low- to moderate-income census tract must have incomes at or below 80 percent of the area median. Those who wish to buy homes in a low- to moderate-income census tract must have incomes at or below 120 percent of the area median.

Under CRA guidelines, banks get credit for originating loans and for buying loans on a whole-loan basis; banks get no credit, however, for holding CRA loans. If a bank sells loans through a securitization process, the buyer may receive CRA investment credit if a percentage of the loans originated in the buying bank's trade area. The sale of CRA loans therefore benefits both the buyer, who can get CRA investment credit; and the seller, who is able to free up capital with which to make additional CRA loans.

The First Union and Bear, Stearns pooling and servicing agreement was the first-ever public securitization of CRA loans. Securitizing these assets enabled First Union to expand its loan portfolio while simultaneously generating additional income from fees. All certificates had an implied AAA rating.

The mortgage loan pool making up First Union CRA Mortgage Loan Trust 1997-1 consists of approximately 5,450 first-lien, fixed-rate mortgage loans evidenced by promissory notes secured by first-lien mortgages, security deeds, or deeds of trust. These mortgages come from 16 states and the District of Columbia. Approximately 97 percent of the loans were originated in accordance with CRA guidelines.

The properties securing the mortgage loans consist of single-family residences that may be detached; part of one- to four-family dwellings; condominium units; mobile, manufactured, or modular homes; townhouses; or units in a planned unit development. All properties are owner occupied. All loans were originated or purchased after August 1988. None of the loans were delinquent (i.e., more than 30 days past due) as of the cutoff date of September 30, 1997. As of the end of September 1997, the average loan balance was $75,458, and the interest rates on the loans ranged from 7.0 to 10.625 percent.

All the affordable mortgages in the trust were originated or acquired by First Union and its subsidiaries. The securitization of these loans should have no impact on customers, who will continue to make payments to and be serviced by First Union.

Contact
First Union Capital Markets Corporation
Agnes Stevens, Corporate Communications Group
301 South College Street, TW27
Charlotte, North Carolina 28288
Telephone: (704) 374-2708
Fax: (704) 374-4197
Web site: www.firstunion.com

Linda Mae Bond Program: Habitat for Humanity National

Through the Linda Mae Bond Program, Habitat for Humanity can package portfolios of mortgages and issue "Linda Mae Bonds," thereby creating liquidity from its existing mortgage base. Linda Mae Bonds are securities issued by Habitat and backed by no-interest mortgages on Habitat-built homes. The money raised will be applied directly to financing the development of additional homes.

Participants

Habitat for Humanity created the Linda Mae Bond Program with assistance from the Local Initiatives Managed Assets Corporation (LIMAC) and the law firm of Wilkie, Farr & Gallagher.

Program Description

Habitat for Humanity, founded in 1976, is a nonprofit corporation whose primary objective is the construction of affordable housing. Under the Habitat program, simple, decent homes are sold at no profit to low-income families who are ineligible for conventional financing. Families finance their homes through a no-interest mortgage from Habitat for Humanity. To receive a house, participating families must contribute between 300 and 500 hours of "sweat equity" to the construction of Habitat homes, both for themselves and for other families. The Habitat program in each community is run by a local nonprofit corporation affiliated with Habitat for Humanity International.

Unfortunately, the number of houses Habitat for Humanity could build has been restricted by the amount of money it could raise from contributors and the amount of money it received from mortgage repayments. While traditional lenders are able to raise money to finance additional homes by selling their conventional mortgages in the secondary market, no such vehicle exists for below-market-rate mortgages made to low-income homebuyers. Because of this limitation, Habitat for Humanity has had to hold its affordable mortgages in portfolio. In an attempt to increase liquidity, many larger Habitat affiliates have tried to develop their own methods of accelerating the recovery of mortgages—either through loans against the payment stream or through the outright sale of mortgages to third-party investors. However, each sale or loan was highly individualized, and returns varied greatly. In addition, affiliates initiating these efforts were forced to devote substantial time and effort to develop very small, isolated programs.

Through the Linda Mae Bond Program, named in honor of Habitat cofounder Linda Fuller, Habitat for Humanity International has met its goal of developing a consistent, nationwide secondary market for Habitat mortgages, greatly increasing its ability to finance additional mortgages. This program will provide both large and small affiliates with a vehicle for raising additional funds at favorable rates.

To participate in the Linda Mae Bond Program, Habitat affiliates must have audited financial statements that show a minimum fund balance of $250,000. The mortgages securing the bonds must not have been more than 60 days past due within the prior 12 months. The interest rate paid to investors ranges from 1 to 5 percent. The term of the bonds is seven years, and they are self-amortizing over the period of the loan. If a mortgage becomes delinquent, the affiliate is required to substitute a performing mortgage for the one that is not performing.

The Linda Mae Bond Program gives Habitat more control over the amount of financing it is able to dedicate to the construction of affordable houses. The more houses Habitat builds and sells, the more assets it will hold to secure additional financing. Habitat affiliates in the United States currently have about $400 million in performing mortgages that are potentially available to secure Linda Mae Bonds.

Habitat expects that the Linda Mae Bond Program will enable it to increase its available capital by 30 percent. The program is expected to issue over $100 million worth of bonds in its first five years of operation. In structuring the Linda Mae Bond Program, Habitat tried to ensure that the program would not violate Habitat for Humanity's underlying principles. In particular, this means that participating affiliates will retain control of the servicing of the mortgages. In addition, no interest cost—direct or imputed—will be borne by the homeowner.

Accomplishments

The first series of bonds, in the amount of $6.5 million, was issued in 1997 as a private placement to a group of socially conscious investors; this group included large banks, insurance companies, and mortgage companies. The initial bond issue was securitized by payments on 250 Habitat mortgages.

> **Contact**
> **Linda Mae Bond Program**
> **Habitat for Humanity International**
> **Aaron Lewis, Staff Attorney**
> **121 Habitat Street**
> **Americus, Georgia 31709-3423**
> **Telephone: (912) 924-6935**
> **Fax: (912) 924-6541**
> **Web site: www.habitat.org**

Notes

1 Robert B. Avery, Raphael W. Bostic, Paul S. Calem, and Glenn B. Canner, "Changes in the Distribution of Banking Offices," *Federal Reserve Bulletin* 83, no. 9 (September 1997): 2. Litan and Rauch report a further decline in the number of financial institutions to less than 10,000 in 1997. See Robert E. Litan with Jonathan Rauch, *American Finance for the 21st Century* (Washington, D.C.: The United States Department of the Treasury, November 1997), 68.

2 Cited by Litan, *American Finance*, 68.

3 Avery et al., "Distribution of Banking Offices," 2, 18.

4 Cited in Susan Headden, "The New Money Machines," *U.S. News ON-LINE*, August 5, 1996.

5 Robert Freedman, "Scores Rise with New CRA Exams," *Affordable Housing Finance* 6, no. 6 (June/July 1998): 34.

6 Ibid.

7 National Association of Community Loan Funds, *Business Plan 1998–2002* (Washington, D.C.: National Association of Community Loan Funds, May 1997), 44.

8 Roberto Quercia, *A Methodology for Assessing the Performance of Affordable Loans* (report prepared for the U.S. Department of Housing and Urban Development, March 1997), 3.

9 Quercia, *Performance of Affordable Loans*, 19–21.

10 Glenn Canner and Wayne Passmore, "The Community Reinvestment Act and the

Profitability of Mortgage-Oriented Banks," Federal Reserve Board Paper 1997-7.

11 Nic Retsinas, "CRA after Glass-Steagall," *Mortgage Origination News* (June 1998).

12 A term frequently used by Mark Pinskey, executive director of the National Community Capital Association, to describe these nonbanks.

13 Mark Pinskey, letter to the editor of the *Wall Street Journal*, January 7, 1999.

14 "Fannie Mae Offers Liquidity for CRA Loans," *Affordable Housing Finance Special Report: Home Buyer Programs* (summer 1998): 6.

15 "Programs Take Aim at Fannie, Freddie," *Affordable Housing Finance Special Report: Home Buyer Programs* (summer 1998): 5.

16 According to W. Brueggeman and J. Fisher, *Real Estate Finance and Investments* (New York: Irwin/McGraw Hill, 1997), a REIT is a real estate company or trust that distributes almost all of its earnings to its shareholders; it also distributes any capital gains generated from the sale of its properties. REITs do not pay taxes on earnings, but the distributions from a REIT are considered dividend income to shareholders and are taxed as such. Distributed capital gains are also taxed at the shareholders' tax rate. A further requirement is that REITs must be passive in nature. Neither trustees, directors, nor employees of a REIT may manage or operate any of the trust's properties.

8

Housing Trust Funds: Growing Old Gracefully

H ousing trust funds were created in response to the Reagan administration's severe cutbacks in federal support for affordable housing. This response was fueled by alarm on the part of housing advocates, who suddenly realized just how vulnerable their plans and projects were to the political winds of change. While the extent of the federal budget cuts alone was probably sufficient to impel states and communities to take action, it was the realization that housing assistance needed to be protected from political machinations that led to the search for dedicated revenues.

Overview

Not all first-generation trust funds have managed to survive over the years; nor have all the survivors succeeded in securing a protected source of revenue—and even when they did, the income streams sometimes proved smaller and more cyclical than their supporters might have hoped. Nevertheless, local control, flexibility, and the ability to make projects work by filling financing gaps—to be the proverbial "straw that stirs the drink"—have enabled housing trust funds to play more important roles in the affordable-housing arena than the absolute size of their budgets might suggest.

Mary Brooks, who has chronicled their rise and accomplishments, estimates that since the mid-1980s, housing trust funds have collectively invested about $1.5 billion to create and preserve close to 200,000 units of affordable housing.[1] In a recent report, Brooks identifies about 110 active housing trust funds—some serving towns with as few as 1,000 people and others covering large cities or entire states—that generate about $315 million a year in dedicated or quasi-dedicated revenues.[2] The revenues vary widely, from as little as $75,000 a year to as much as $122 million. The trust funds' ability to leverage their revenues also varies, from less than $2 to more than $30 of other funds for every $1 of dedicated revenue.

Housing trust funds generate their revenue from a variety of sources, although Brooks suggests that the majority probably rely on recording fees for real estate documents. Other common funding sources include real estate transfer taxes, impact or development fees, and fees negotiated with developers in the course of the local development review and approval process. The flexibility of housing trust funds allows localities to take advantage of whatever potential revenue sources might be available to them. Thus, in Boston, the Neighborhood Assistance Corporation of America manages a trust fund for the Hotel Workers Local 26; revenue for this trust fund comes from an employer-paid increment on members' hourly wages. The state of Arizona dedicates a percentage of unclaimed property deposits to creating and maintaining its trust fund. In San Antonio, Texas, the revenue needed to create a housing trust fund came from the sale of a cable television station. In some areas, a trust fund is created through a temporary source of revenue and a permanent funding source is sought once the program is underway: this was the case in Memphis, where the city used revenue from a cultural exhibit—the Memphis Ramesses Fund—and from the sale of vacant lots to get the trust fund off the ground. Since then, Memphis has dedicated the revenue from unclaimed utility deposits to provide permanent financing for the trust fund.

Trust fund awards may take the form of loans or grants and may be provided to non-profit and community-based organizations, for-profit developers, housing authorities, service providers, or public agencies. Some state housing trust funds, such as Florida's, disburse funds only to established state-run housing programs. Trust funds support new construction, rehabilitation, rental assistance, property acquisition, home purchases, project-based subsidies, and social and supportive services connected with low-income housing.

Most housing trust funds are administered by an existing housing agency or department. Many are overseen by appointed boards whose members are effective advocates for affordable housing, which increases the trust fund's leveraging ability. Some exceptions to this pattern are the Foundation for Home Ownership in Memphis, which is incorporated as a not-for-profit with its own board of directors, and the San Antonio Housing Trust Fund, which is administered by the nonprofit San Antonio Housing Trust Foundation, Inc.

Trust funds distribute awards in a variety of ways. Many disburse funds through an open application process that continues until the funds for a fiscal year have been fully committed. Some programs use a more formal request-for-proposals process or a notification-of-funding-availability process.

Often, housing trust funds coordinate their application deadlines or forms with those of other funding sources, such as the federal HOME program, the Community Development Block Grant program, and the federal low-income housing tax credit program. Programs that focus their efforts on assisting specific populations, such as homeless people or people with special needs, may coordinate their application processes with those of programs that serve the same populations.

Where restrictions exist, they generally pertain to income level: the majority of trust funds require that the people served have household incomes at or below 80 percent of the area median. In addition, many programs have some form of continued affordability requirement as a precondition for funding. Some programs award funding only to projects serving homeless people or special-needs populations, while others require that funds be used to provide rental housing or to assist with home purchases.

The most exciting feature of housing trust funds is that they are designed to meet locally determined affordable-housing needs: this means that the variety of projects undertaken is as diverse as the locations maintaining these funds. The Memphis Community Development Partnership, for example, uses funds for a broad array of purposes including new construction, downpayment assistance, interest-rate buydowns, and predevelopment expenses. Nebraska's trust fund is devoted exclusively to meeting the needs of the state's homeless and near-homeless populations, while Dauphin County, Pennsylvania, uses part of its affordable housing trust fund to provide tenant-based rental assistance that is phased out over time.

While they cannot claim to cover the entire spectrum, the 13 housing trust funds profiled in this chapter provide a good indication of the role that these agile programs play in helping to round out state and local affordable-housing strategies.

Trust Fund Profiles

State Housing Fund
State of Arizona

Arizona's State Housing Trust Fund was established in 1988 to create a flexible funding source for local governments and nonprofit housing organizations seeking to provide affordable housing for low- and moderate-income families. In fiscal year 1999, the application process for trust fund monies was combined with that for federal HOME funds. These combined funding sources are now collectively referred to as the State Housing Fund.

Program Administration

The State Housing Fund is administered by the office of housing and infrastructure development of the department of commerce, which administers several other housing assistance programs.

Program Description

The State Housing Fund has several objectives:

- To assist with the construction and preservation of affordable housing;
- To promote creative and innovative affordable-housing program design;
- To increase the use of federal housing funds;
- To leverage public and private assistance for affordable-housing projects.

Eligible applicants include cities, towns, counties, public housing authorities, tribal governments and housing organizations, nonprofit organizations, and community housing development organizations. By statute, 36 percent of the State Housing Fund's yearly revenue must be used in rural areas.

Funds are awarded in the form of grants or loans and may be used to cover predevelopment and development costs for the construction or rehabilitation of rental housing, housing for purchase, or transitional or emergency shelter. Funds may also be used for rental assistance programs, for the operating costs of emergency shelters or shelters for people with special needs, for fair-housing education programs, for foreclosure- and eviction-prevention programs, or for homebuyer assistance programs. Grants for the development of community housing plans and for project planning are also offered. Funded programs must either serve (1) homeowners whose incomes are at or below 80 percent of the area median or (2) renters whose incomes are at or below 60 percent of the area median. Depending on the level of funding they receive, rental projects must remain affordable for between five and 15 years.

Application deadlines for State Housing Fund awards occur approximately every two months. To be considered eligible, applicants must meet all required thresholds: they must (1) provide a complete and accurate application; (2) be a nonprofit or government agency; (3) meet requirements for the type of property to be funded; and (4) demonstrate that they are ready to receive and use awarded monies. As long as funds are available, eligible projects will be funded.

Funding Sources

The State Housing Fund receives its revenue from a 55 percent allocation of unclaimed property deposits, interest on unexpended funds, loan repayments, and recaptured funds. In 1997, the fund leveraged approximately $9.42 for every $1.00 of dedicated trust fund revenue.

Accomplishments

In 1997, the State Housing Fund awarded over $3.7 million to assist 1,556 households in meeting their affordable-housing needs. Since its inception, the fund has awarded in excess of $31 million dollars, benefiting over 20,000 households.

Contact
State Housing Fund
Arizona Department of Commerce
Office of Housing and Infrastructure Development
3800 North Central Avenue, Suite 1200
Phoenix, Arizona 85012
Telephone: (602) 280-1365
Fax: (602) 280-1470
Web site: www.state.az.us/commerce

State and Local Government Housing Trust Fund
State of Florida

The state of Florida manages the largest housing trust fund in the United States, which is used to support a variety of affordable-housing programs.

Program Administration

The Florida Affordable Housing Finance Agency, created by the Florida legislature in 1980, was made responsible for administering the state and local government housing trust fund. On January 1, 1998, the agency was reorganized and is now called the Florida Housing Finance Corporation.

Program Description

The Florida State and Local Government Housing Trust Fund supports a variety of programs, including the five described in the following subsections.

State Apartment Incentive Loan Program. The State Apartment Incentive Loan (SAIL) program provides developers with second mortgage loans at low interest rates for the purpose of building or substantially rehabilitating multifamily rental properties; SAIL will also fund mortgages at even lower interest rates for similar properties intended for farmworker tenants.

SAIL funds are allocated on the basis of county size and need. Neediness is determined by rental-market studies that assess regions (each of the counties) and groups (families, elderly people, commercial fishing workers, and farmworkers). At least 20 percent of the units in SAIL-funded projects are reserved for very low-income households, although the number of units for very low-income tenants often exceeds this requirement.

State Housing Initiatives Partnership Program. The State Housing Initiatives Partnership (SHIP) program funds "emergency repairs, new construction, rehabilitation, down-payment and closing-cost assistance, impact fees, construction and gap financing, mortgage buydowns, acquisition of property for affordable housing, special-needs housing, matching for federal housing grants and programs, and homeownership counseling."[3]

Florida's 67 counties and 41 Community Development Block Grant entitlement cities all participate in the SHIP program. Funds are disbursed according to population, with each county receiving a minimum of $350,000 per year. Communities are given two years to spend each year's award. Eligible communities are those that have (1) created a trust fund in which to hold disbursements; (2) established a local housing assistance program; (3) determined who will be responsible for administering and overseeing the program; and (4) created a nine-member affordable housing advisory committee made up of representatives from fields related to affordable housing.

Florida Affordable Housing Guarantee Program. By offering guarantees on both taxable and tax-exempt loans, the Florida Affordable Housing Guarantee Program bridges financing gaps for the construction, acquisition, rehabilitation, or refinancing of affordable housing. In 1996, legislation bolstered the program by authorizing the issuance of up to $200 million in revenue bonds to capitalize the program's guarantee fund; these monies are in addition to the allocation the program receives from the State Housing Fund.

Home Ownership Assistance Program. The Home Ownership Assistance Program (HAP) consists of three parts: a permanent loan program, a construction loan program, and a down-payment assistance program. For the first nine months of each fiscal year, 60 percent of HAP revenues are reserved for downpayment assistance, with the remaining 40 percent divided equally between the permanent loan and construction loan programs. During the final three months of the fiscal year, the board can reallocate the remaining funds as necessary.

HAP's permanent loan program assists very low-income families to buy their first home. Qualified families may receive no-interest loans of up to $15,000 for up to 25 percent of the price of their new home.

HAP's construction loan program provides loans at 3 percent interest to nonprofit organizations involved in constructing or rehabilitating affordable housing. The loans reduce the cost of building or rehabilitating housing, and these savings are passed on to the homebuyer. The program also allows a portion of the construction loan to be converted to a no-interest deferred second mortgage for the homebuyer; this converted loan may provide financing for downpayment and closing costs and can lower the principal amount of the first mortgage.

HAP's downpayment assistance program offers a no-interest, 30-year, second mortgage loan in the amount of $2,500 to help with downpayment costs. Repayment is deferred until the first mortgage is paid off or until sale, transfer, refinancing, or rental of the home.

Predevelopment Loan Program. The Predevelopment Loan Program (PLP) offers non-profit organizations upfront financing to construct either single-family or multifamily afford-able housing for low-income Floridians. Eligible participants are awarded funding for site acquisition and land development by means of a quarterly competitive application process. Professional fees for consultants, architects, engineers, and surveyors may be reimbursed under this program. Local governments, housing authorities, and nonprofit organizations are eligible to apply for loans of up to $500,000.

The Florida Housing Finance Corporation holds rulemaking and application workshops for potential applicants at various locations around the state. The corporation maintains a database of interested parties and distributes mailings to inform parties of the workshops.

Funding Sources

Florida initially generated its trust fund revenues through a 1992 increase of $.10 per $100 valuation in its documentary stamp tax, which generated more than $120 million each year for the state's affordable-housing programs. In fiscal year 1996–1997, the stamp tax was increased by an additional $.10 per $100.

Accomplishments

During fiscal year 1996–1997, more than $25.8 million in SAIL funds was awarded to 13 different projects; 13 percent of these projects will serve elderly people, while the remaining 87 percent will provide housing for very low-income families. Since SAIL's inception, the program has helped to fund 14,762 units of housing for low-income households. In fiscal year 1996–1997, the SHIP program disbursed a total of $86.5 million to all of Florida's 108 eligible participants. In total, the Florida Affordable Housing Guarantee program has assisted with funding for the construction of over 4,300 multifamily housing units. During fiscal year 1996–1997, $813,573 was used to enable 89 families to buy their first homes under the HAP permanent loan program, and 327 families received a total of $817,500 in assistance from the HAP downpayment assistance program.

Contact

State and Local Government Housing Trust Fund
Florida Housing Finance Corporation
227 North Bronough Street
Tallahassee, Florida 32301-1329
Telephone: (850) 488-4197
Fax: (850) 488-9809

Illinois Affordable Housing Trust Fund
State of Illinois

The Illinois Affordable Housing Trust Fund was created in 1989 to increase the stock of low- and very low-income housing in Illinois.

Program Administration

The Illinois Housing Development Authority (IHDA) administers the housing trust fund.

Program Description

Illinois's housing trust fund is considered a funding source of last resort. Awards are to be used for gap financing and are provided as grants or loans, typically in amounts of $750,000 or less. Generally, funding goes to nonprofit or for-profit developers; local governments may also apply. The majority of funding is allocated to projects assisting households whose incomes are at or below 50 percent of the area median, and funding may not be used to assist households whose incomes exceed 80 percent of the area median. Trust fund monies support development of both single-family and multifamily homes.

Applications are reviewed by several entities. First, they are reviewed by a loan committee staffed by members of IHDA. Applications are then reviewed by the Illinois Affordable Housing Trust Fund Advisory Commission, which is composed of representatives of governmental organizations. The IHDA board of directors makes the final funding decisions.

Awards are made equitably across the state, though preference is given to projects that leverage additional public and private support.

Potential applicants learn about the availability of financing from the trust fund through the Internet, by word of mouth, or from local government agencies.

Funding Sources

Trust fund revenues are generated from the transfer tax fee charged on all residential real estate transactions. When the fee was doubled—to $.50 per $500 of the sales price of a property—an additional $.25 per $500 was made available to the trust fund. The revenue generated from transfer tax fees varies each year, as does the fund's leveraging ratio.

Accomplishments

In fiscal year 1997, the Illinois Affordable Housing Trust Fund disbursed close to $23 million in awards for 75 projects: 45 single-family units and 30 multifamily projects, which together added 4,327 units to the state's housing supply. Of the total number of units, 3,138 were designated for very low-income households and 1,188 for low-income households; one home sold at market rate. The 75 projects were almost evenly divided between rural and urban areas of the state.

> **Contact**
>
> **Illinois Affordable Housing Trust Fund**
> **Illinois Housing Development Authority**
> 401 North Michigan Avenue, Suite 900
> Chicago, Illinois 60611
> Telephone: (312) 836-5312
> Fax: (312) 832-2167
> Web site: www.ihda.org

Hotel Workers Local 26 Housing Trust Fund
Boston, Massachusetts

After the 1990 amendments to the Taft-Hartley Act allowed unions and employers to provide housing assistance to workers, the 5,000-member Hotel Workers Local 26 negotiated the creation of the first housing trust fund in the country for union members. The trust fund monies are used for programs that help members of Hotel Workers Local 26 become homeowners.

Program Administration

A joint union-management board of trustees hired the Union Neighborhood Assistance Corporation, a Boston nonprofit community advocacy and housing services organization, to administer the trust fund. Union Neighborhood Assistance has since expanded nationally and is now known as the Neighborhood Assistance Corporation of America—NACA. NACA provides both union and nonunion workers with housing benefits, including loans and grants for renting or purchasing housing, assistance in obtaining enforcement of housing codes and rent limits, and homeownership counseling. In addition, NACA works nationally against predatory or discriminatory lending practices.

Program Description

The Hotel Workers Local 26 housing trust fund monies are used to fund homebuyer classes, one-on-one counseling, buyer brokerage, and programs that help provide access to mortgages; for example, trust fund programs include a homebuyer's savings club that matches participants' savings for a downpayment. The fund will also buy down a mortgage to make it affordable.

NACA, the trust fund administrator, has more than $1 billion in mortgage products that are administered from offices throughout the country. NACA targets funding to households with incomes below a certain percentage of the area median and to households that would like to purchase in neighborhoods where access to credit has been difficult. NACA does not require applicants to have a perfect credit history. For borrowers with little savings, NACA offers mortgages requiring no downpayment; for those with some savings, NACA offers mortgages at below-market rates. NACA also lends to households who want to purchase and renovate a property.

Funding Sources

The union members' employers pay $.08 per hour to the Hotel Workers Local 26 housing trust fund. The trust fund balance is currently about $1 million and the trust income about $80,000 per month.

Accomplishments

At least 1,000 families have become homeowners through the Hotel Workers Local 26 housing trust fund.

Contact

Neighborhood Assistance Corporation of America
3607 Washington Street
Jamaica Plain, Massachusetts 02130-2604
Telephone: (617) 250-6222
Fax: (617) 250-6262
Web site: www.naca.com

St. Louis County Housing Trust Fund
St. Louis County, Missouri

The Housing Resources Commission of St. Louis County, Missouri, was created in 1991 to allocate and administer monies from the St. Louis County trust fund to qualified nonprofit organizations for the provision of services to county residents who are homeless or at risk of becoming homeless. The commission's goal is to reduce or eliminate the need for homeless services over time.

Program Administration

The Housing Resources Commission is composed of seven people, appointed by the county executive, who allocate and administer monies derived from the St. Louis County trust fund.

Program Description

The Housing Resources Commission allocates funding to organizations that provide the following services: emergency transitional shelter, programs for the prevention of homelessness, self-sufficiency programs, and coordination of existing services.

To promote the coordination of existing services, the commission funds the St. Louis County Emergency Shelter Homeless Hotline, a centralized intake and referral system. Callers are referred to sources of assistance that can provide shelter, rental assistance, help with mortgage and utility payments, relocation from substandard housing, and community health nursing services. The hot line also collects and maintains demographic data during each call. Data have been collected since 1985, providing a wealth of information for tracking trends, demographics, and resources.

Recipient agencies may use grant funds for salaries and equipment; emergency and transitional shelter beds; assistance with security deposits, first month's rent, back rent, and mortgage payments; housing counseling; life skills and consumer education; home management and community living classes; rehabilitation of existing shelter structures; and compliance with the Americans with Disabilities Act.

Funding Sources

The trust fund is funded through a $300 filing fee that is attached to all real estate documents recorded in St. Louis County. The legislation that initiated the trust fund originated at the state level and was approved for implementation by St. Louis County voters.

Participating agencies must receive at least 25 percent of their funding from sources other than the Housing Resources Commission. To date, the commission has awarded $5.5 million for the provision of services to homeless individuals and families in St. Louis County. These funds have been used to provide shelter for more than 24,000 homeless people and assistance to an additional 5,000 people who were at risk of becoming homeless.

Contact

Department of Human Services
Homeless Services Program
Patricia Ferrell, Homeless Services Supervisor
121 South Meramec Avenue, Fourth Floor
St. Louis, Missouri 63105
Telephone: (314) 889-3453
Fax: (314) 889-3420

Homeless Assistance Program
State of Nebraska

The Homeless Shelter Assistance Trust Fund was created by the Nebraska legislature in 1992 to assist nonprofit organizations to meet the needs of Nebraska's homeless or near-homeless population. In 1996, Nebraska aligned the trust fund application process with HUD's Emergency Shelter Grant Program; this combined application process is known as the Homeless Assistance Program.

Program Administration

Nebraska's Homeless Assistance Program is administered by the department of economic development. An interagency review committee made up of representatives from the departments of health and human services, economic development, and education; the Nebraska Domestic Violence and Sexual Assault Coalition; the U.S. Department of Agriculture and Rural Development; and the Nebraska Association of Community Housing Development Organizations is responsible for reviewing applications and disbursing awards.

Program Description

Trust fund monies are used to assist nonprofit organizations (1) to provide transitional and permanent shelter for homeless people and (2) to support efforts to link housing assistance with efforts to promote self-sufficiency. Fund awards are granted through a regional as well as a programmatic allocation process. Awards are to be used to supplement a nonprofit's budget and may not exceed 25 percent of the organization's total budget.

The Homeless Shelter Assistance Trust Fund requires that funding be disbursed as follows: 35 percent of funds are to be used for food and shelter; 55 percent of funds go to a program pool from which agencies may draw; and 5 percent of funds are reserved for an emergency setaside. The greater Homeless Assistance Program (which includes both trust fund monies and the federal Emergency Shelter Grant Program allocation) requires that its resources be distributed as follows: 50 percent to client services, 20 percent to operations, 20 percent to homelessness prevention, 5 percent to rehabilitation, and 5 percent to investment funds.

Funding Sources

The Nebraska legislature increased the real estate transfer tax by $.25 per $1,000 (to a total of $1.75 per $1,000) to generate revenue for the Homeless Shelter Assistance Trust Fund. (Trust fund revenues are derived from the increase, not from total transfer tax revenues.) Monies are collected by the county registers of deeds and are then remitted to the Nebraska revenue department; as funds are collected, they are kept in an investment trust account until their disbursal. The trust fund collects over $1 million each year.

Accomplishments

In 1998, the Homeless Assistance Program awarded $1.7 million in grants to 60 nonprofit agencies. Over the life of the program, funds have been used for a diverse set of programs, including Liberty Center, Inc., which provides transitional housing for people who have left the regional mental health care center; and The Central Nebraska Community Services, which used award monies to help 30 families relocate when their trailer park was threatened with closure because of health risks.

Contact

Homeless Assistance Program
Nebraska Department of Economic Development
P.O. Box 94666
Lincoln, Nebraska 68509
Telephone: (402) 471-3111
Fax: (402) 471-3778
Web site: www.ded.state.ne.us

Affordable Housing Fund
City of Dayton/Montgomery County, Ohio

The Affordable Housing Fund (AHF) is a private nonprofit organization created in 1991 to bolster the production of affordable housing for low- and moderate-income households. Capitalized through a ten-year commitment from sales tax revenues, the fund acts as a development broker, facilitating discussion and interaction among developers, lenders, providers of housing and services, and government organizations.

In 1989, a group of public officials, business leaders, religious leaders, and housing providers assembled as the Low-Income Housing Task Force of Montgomery County, Ohio. On the basis of its research, the task force concluded that the county (which includes the city of Dayton) needed approximately 10,000 more affordable housing units; it also discovered that more than 11 percent of the county's housing stock was in substandard condition. In response to these findings, the task force suggested the creation of the Dayton/Montgomery County Housing Commission, which was later renamed the Affordable Housing Fund.

Program Administration

AHF is one of the few private nonprofit organizations in the country that manages a housing trust fund.

Program Description

AHF finances two types of activity: (1) development projects involving the construction and rehabilitation of rental or ownership properties and (2) programs that link human services with housing. AHF brokers direct and indirect investment partnerships in local developments and promotes housing development through flexible "gap financing" of new construction or rehabilitation. "As a gap-financing source, AHF will provide subsidized financing only to the extent that it is needed to fill the development gap and meet the needs of the target market."[4]

Both for-profit and nonprofit developers of new or rehabilitated housing for low- and moderate-income groups may apply to AHF for financing. Eligible applicants include corporations, limited partnerships, general partnerships, and limited-liability companies.

All proposals must involve affordable housing and meet local planning priorities. Applications are reviewed by the housing advisory board (made up of local community leaders from both the private and public sectors) and by the AHF board of trustees. Financing decisions are made bimonthly, on a competitive, first-come, first-served basis.

AHF provides loan guarantees, loans, and grants. Loan guarantees are for up to 20 percent of the first mortgage loan for the development of either rental housing or housing for purchase. AHF provides fully amortizing second mortgage loans and may make first mortgage loans if no other form of financing is available to the applicant. Grants of up to $5,000 per affordable housing unit are available through AHF but will be made only after all other funding avenues have been exhausted.

AHF places affordability restrictions on all funded projects: at least 20 percent of rental-housing units must be kept affordable to households at or below 80 percent of the area median income for at least five years, and at least 20 percent of housing built for sale must be sold to households earning 80 percent or less of the area median income. Programs linking housing and human services are given greater consideration if they target households whose incomes are at or below 80 percent of the area median.

Funding Sources

AHF is capitalized with a $1 million annual commitment from the Montgomery County Board of Commissioners. This annual commitment is derived from local sales tax revenue and was to have been made for a total of ten years, beginning in 1991. In 1996, a citizens' committee recommended continued funding of AHF, and the board of county commissioners is reviewing the recommendation. Other revenue sources include loan repayments, interest on the annual commitment, and fees.

The fund charges a commitment fee of .25 percent of the total amount of financing provided and a closing fee of .75 percent of the total amount provided. The fund also charges award recipients for all of AHF's actual costs associated with closing the financing agreement. The fund's administrative costs are met through interest on trust fund revenues, monies from the city of Dayton, contributions, and fees.

AHF has received $7 million thus far and has leveraged more than $100 million of private and public financing. The current leveraging ratio is $11.45 for every $1.00 of trust fund money.

Accomplishments

So far, AHF has disbursed more than $7 million in support of 2,075 affordable housing units distributed evenly between the city of Dayton and surrounding Montgomery County.

> **Contact**
> Affordable Housing Fund
> William Z. Simon, Director
> 6 North Main Street, Suite 330
> Dayton, Ohio 45402
> Telephone: (937) 224-0060
> Fax: (937) 224-3811
> Web site: www.affordablehousingfund.org

Affordable Housing Trust Fund
Dauphin County, Pennsylvania

In 1992, the Pennsylvania state legislature passed the Optional County Affordable Housing Funds Act, which allows counties to fund affordable-housing efforts by increasing (but not more than doubling) their fees for recording deeds and mortgages. State law requires that the funds derived from such increases be deposited in the county's general fund and be used only for affordable-housing efforts ("affordable housing" is defined as housing that is affordable for households earning less than the area median income). At least 20 counties in Pennsylvania have taken advantage of this legislation, Dauphin County among them.

In 1994, Dauphin County passed an ordinance to increase the recording fees for deeds and mortgages; revenue generated through the increase was to be put toward the county's Affordable Housing Trust Fund.

Program Administration

The Dauphin County Housing Fund Board reviews all requests for funding from the Affordable Housing Trust Fund. This board, composed of housing professionals, staff of government agencies, members of the business community, and housing advocates, makes its recommendations to the board of county commissioners, which has final authority over the use of funds.

Program Description

Dauphin County's funds are used to serve households whose incomes are at or below 80 percent of the area median. Funds have been used to create a rental assistance program and a soft second mortgage program.

Rental Assistance Program. Dauphin County's Rental Assistance Program, created in 1996, is administered by Delta Housing, Inc. The program offers families two years of gradually decreasing rental assistance and is intended to help these families make the transition to self-sufficiency. The county has committed $78,000 of trust fund monies to the program so far.

First-Time Homebuyers Second or Subordinated Mortgage Program. The First-Time Homebuyers Second or Subordinated Mortgage Program provides second or subordinated loans of up to $3,500 to first-time homebuyers whose incomes are at or below the county median and whose liquid assets are within program restrictions. Eligible applicants must already have applied for their first mortgage and are required to attend a homebuyer's workshop before applying for a second mortgage.

Monies may be used toward a downpayment or toward closing costs. Applicants must contribute 3 percent of the purchase price or of the appraised value of the home, whichever is less. The loan must be repaid when the property is sold or when the transfer of legal or equitable title occurs. Borrowers who have already received $3,500 from the second mortgage program are eligible to apply to the Pennsylvania Housing Finance Agency for an additional $2,000 toward closing costs.

The planning commission has not found it necessary to formally market the First-Time Homebuyers Second or Subordinated Mortgage Program; potential applicants learn of the program by word of mouth, through the homebuyer's workshop, or through realtors or lenders. In fact, the program was so popular that demand outweighed available funding, and in October 1997, a monthly lottery was implemented.

Funding Sources

Dauphin County's 1994 ordinance doubled existing document-recording fees and dictated that 85 percent of the revenues generated by this increase would be used for affordable-housing efforts and 15 percent for the costs of administering the fund. The document-recording fee currently generates approximately $300,000 per year for the Affordable Housing Trust Fund. Since its inception, the fund has collected nearly $1.4 million.

Accomplishments

To date, Affordable Housing Trust Fund monies have assisted approximately 369 homebuyers to purchase their first homes.

Contact
Affordable Housing Trust Fund
Dauphin County Planning Commission
112 Market Street, Seventh Floor
Harrisburg, Pennsylvania 17101-2015
Telephone: (717) 234-2639
Fax: (717) 234-4058

Memphis Community Development Partnership
Memphis, Tennessee

In 1994, the city of Memphis created the Foundation for Home Ownership, a housing trust fund, to facilitate provision of low- and moderate-income housing; to provide information and technical assistance for activities designed to improve the city's housing stock; and to support efforts to address problems associated with poverty and neighborhood deterioration.

Four years later, an expansion of the foundation's funding and activities led to the creation of the Memphis Community Development Partnership (MCDP). At that time, funding from the Foundation for Home Ownership was combined with a $1 million grant from the Ford Foundation that requires local matching funds from Memphis corporations. Like the Foundation for Home Ownership, MCDP supports the financing and provision of affordable housing (trust fund monies for these purposes are retained within a separate funding pool maintained by MCDP), but MCDP also provides administrative support and technical assistance to Memphis's community development corporations (CDCs) to support their role as the primary catalysts of community development.

Program Administration

Like the Foundation for Home Ownership before it, MCDP is a supporting organization of the Community Foundation of Greater Memphis. In addition to providing MCDP with office and meeting space and administrative support, the foundation is responsible for financial administration of MCDP. The chairman of the foundation approves the selection of members to the MCPD board, which makes all decisions regarding the distribution of awards.

Program Description

Trust fund and other project development monies are used for new construction, rehabilitation, downpayment assistance, interest-rate buydowns, predevelopment expenses, and other costs associated with the development of affordable housing. Both for-profit and non-profit developers have received trust fund monies. To be eligible for funding, projects must serve households with incomes at or below 80 percent of the area median.

Funding preference is given to projects that (1) address an unmet need in the local affordable-housing market, (2) display an innovative and creative use of resources, (3) leverage other funds, (4) are designed to assist low-income people to become homeowners, and (5) include provisions for long-term affordability. The MCDP board gives special preference to projects that involve local residents in the development process.

All funded projects have been sponsored by CDCs, and monies have been awarded in the form of grants and forgivable loans. Recently, an additional $1 million in federal HOME funds was allocated to local CDCs; the funds will be used to rehabilitate or construct 318 single-family homes. In July 1998, the Memphis city council approved the receipt of $2 million in Tennessee Housing Development Agency Bicentennial Neighborhood Initiative funds. MCDP will administer $1 million of these funds, $700,000 of which will be put into a housing rehabilitation pool and $300,000 of which will be kept in a special-projects pool.

Funding Sources

The 1994 city council resolution that created the Foundation for Home Ownership committed several types of one-time funding to the trust fund: $591,550 from the Memphis Ramesses Fund (a cultural exhibit), approximately $160,000 from lot sales, and a $10,000 private donation. Since that time, the foundation has received approximately $100,000 more from the sale of lots; and the city has agreed, when its budget permits, to pass along to the fund approximately $250,000 annually from the savings earned through a new waste-disposal contract.

In 1997, the fund received its first source of dedicated revenue: unclaimed utility deposits from Memphis Light, Gas and Water. The first disbursement—four years of uncollected deposits—was roughly $240,000; future disbursements are expected to be between $40,000 and $50,000 annually.

To meet administrative costs, the Foundation for Home Ownership also receives dedicated revenue and in-kind assistance from the Community Foundation of Greater Memphis.

In March 1998, the Ford Foundation accepted the Foundation for Home Ownership's proposal to become the Ford Foundation's 21st Community Development Partnership in the United States. Ford gave the Foundation for Home Ownership $1 million in seed money and required these funds to be matched by contributions from community corporate partners. Once this funding is in place, MCDP will have $750,000 annually to disburse to neighborhood-based CDCs. By June 1998, 70 percent of the corporate matching contributions had been committed. The city of Memphis is also providing some matching funds.

Accomplishments

Since its inception, the trust fund has disbursed $731,500 to support a total of 390 housing units.

Contact
Memphis Community Development Partnership
Glenn Cox, Executive Director
1900 Union Avenue
Memphis, Tennessee 38104
Telephone: (901) 722-0037
Fax: (901) 722-0010
Web site: www.cfgm.org

San Antonio Housing Trust Fund
San Antonio, Texas

The San Antonio Housing Trust Fund was established in 1988 "to provide decent and affordable housing opportunities for low-, moderate-, and middle-income families, and to effect the revitalization of the neighborhoods and downtown area through housing activities."[5]

Program Administration

A board of trustees, whose 11 members are appointed by the San Antonio City Council, governs the San Antonio Housing Trust Fund. The San Antonio Housing Trust Foundation, Inc., a nonprofit foundation under contract to the city of San Antonio, carries out daily administration of the trust fund. The board of trustees from the trust fund also serves as the board of trustees for the foundation.

Program Description

All funding efforts are targeted to households that earn 120 percent or less of the area median income. Requests for proposals are received during an open, competitive funding round held approximately every 18 months. The board reviews funding requests and makes recommendations for city council approval.

The trust foundation's most innovative project is the Affordable Parade of Homes. This effort, a collaborative initiative on the part of the trust fund, community groups, lenders, and public officials, began in 1996, with the Coliseum Oaks development. Coliseum Oaks consisted of run-down and abandoned housing, and, after much pressure from the Coliseum/ Willow Park Neighborhood Association and the city council member who represented the area, the city foreclosed on the development for back taxes, demolished the existing structures, and sold the site to the San Antonio Housing Trust Foundation for $1. The trust foundation, in turn, sold lots to individual developers for $1 each to encourage participation in the first Affordable Parade of Homes. The trust foundation then helped low- and moderate-income families purchase this first set of affordable homes.

To finance the homes, Christ Is Our Salvation (CIOS), a private foundation, granted the trust foundation an $800,000 loan at zero interest, which was used to leverage an additional $1.4 million in private mortgage financing. Because of the CIOS loan, the trust foundation was able to help qualified homebuyers with downpayment and closing costs, providing $20,000 in 15-year, zero-interest second mortgage financing. All potential purchasers were provided with mortgage prequalification counseling and homebuyer counseling. The 1996 parade of homes was so successful that in 1997, the trust foundation repeated its efforts in a different development.

The San Antonio Housing Trust Foundation is responsible for administering several other housing-related programs in the San Antonio area. The foundation administers the selection process for the federal HOME entitlement setaside for community housing development organizations. In addition, the foundation assists with the Surplus Property Program, through which nonprofit housing developers can purchase surplus city property. The trust foundation coordinates the donation and sale of these properties and performs the necessary environmental assessments. The foundation does not charge administrative costs or fees for its services. Finally, the foundation works in partnership with the Enterprise Foundation to administer the National Community Development Initiative Program in San Antonio to "approve grants for core operating support and award loans for the construction of affordable housing projects." Of the ten organizations receiving $349,000 in 1995–1996, eight continued to receive funding in 1996–1997.

More recent initiatives of the San Antonio Housing Trust Foundation include

- Creation of the San Antonio Housing Trust Finance Corporation, in 1997, which received a $25 million bond allocation for a single-family mortgage program to start in the spring of 1998;
- Co-creation (with the city council and staff) of the San Antonio Housing Trust Reinvestment Corporation to administer tax increment reinvestment zone financing for affordable housing and community revitalization;
- Efforts to expand the city's Surplus Property Program to include properties foreclosed for failure to pay taxes.

Funding Sources

The San Antonio Housing Trust Fund was established with $10 million generated from the sale of a cable television franchise; the trust fund's current value is $10.9 million. Both interest earned on the fund and loan repayments provide revenue for funding affordable-housing initiatives. The trust fund's current leveraging ratio is $11 in non–trust fund monies for every $1 of trust fund money.

Accomplishments

Between 1990 and 1997, the San Antonio Housing Trust Foundation committed over $4.5 million of trust fund revenue to the creation and rehabilitation of 1,122 units of single- and multifamily housing and housing for people with special needs. The Affordable Parade of Homes has produced more than 100 units of affordable housing in the San Antonio area.

Housing Bonus Program and Transferable Development Rights System Seattle, Washington

Seattle's Housing Bonus Program and Transferable Development Rights System were created with the adoption of Seattle's 1985 downtown plan as a means of preserving and constructing housing units affordable to low- and low-to-moderate–income households (households earning less than 50 percent or less than 80 percent of the area median income, respectively). These programs allow developers to add square footage to their downtown commercial projects in exchange for either creating affordable housing units or making a cash payment. Both programs are linked to Seattle's efforts to mitigate the impacts of growth and plan for future growth. Through the programs, developers who would otherwise be limited in their ability to build commercial properties can increase the density of downtown commercial properties while adding to the housing stock as well. Seattle was one of the first cities to create a trust fund through a housing bonus program.

Program Administration

The Seattle Office of Housing, which is part of the mayor's executive department, administers the Housing Bonus Program and the Transferable Development Rights System.

Program Description

As part of the permitting process, developers may choose to participate in the Housing Bonus Program or the Transferable Development Rights System. Developers decide how they plan to achieve additional density at the time the zoning permit is issued. Before the first building permit is issued, developers must either (1) purchase housing bonus credits or transferable development rights (TDRs) or (2) post security to ensure that the credits or TDRs will be produced.

Housing providers, which must be approved by the office of housing through an application process, may use the proceeds from these two programs for construction or permanent financing.

Housing Bonus Program. The Housing Bonus Program is an incentive tool that allows commercial developers to increase the density of a project in exchange for developing housing that is affordable to low- and low-to-moderate–income households.

Housing bonus credits, which allow developers to increase a project's density, can be earned in three ways: First, the developer can choose to build housing as part of a mixed-use development (i.e., on the same site as the commercial development) or at a different downtown location. Second, the developer can contract with a housing developer approved by the office of housing to build enough housing to generate the required number of housing bonus credits. Third, the developer can choose to make a cash contribution to a city housing fund. For each of the downtown zones, the office of housing sets a bonus value that determines the amount of the cash contribution. For example, the bonus value for Downtown Office Core-1 is $20. To calculate the required cash contribution amount, the developer would multiply by $20 the amount of square footage attributable to the housing bonus.

In order to assign a value to the tradeoff between the creation of additional commercial space and the creation of low- and low-to-moderate–income housing, the office of housing maintains a regularly an updated schedule of bonus ratios. The basis for the schedule is a financial model that yields a ratio of square footage of affordable housing to commercial space; the ratio varies according to the level of affordability targeted for the housing. The bonus ratios derived from the model determine the amount of additional (bonus) commercial space that will be approved for construction, which is linked to the type of affordable housing to be produced and the targeted income group. If other public funds (including tax credits) are used, the office of housing calculates the bonus ratio as part of a subsidy review analysis conducted on a case-by-case basis to determine the bonus ratio needed to make a given project financially feasible. Generally, as the amount of other public funds increases, the amount of bonus space approved will decline.

Transferable Development Rights System. The TDR System is a voluntary linkage program that leverages financing to preserve affordable housing for downtown Seattle in exchange for allowing developers to increase project density to the maximum that is permitted in the zone.

TDRs are allowed but unused amounts of floor area that may be transferred between developers, enabling the receiving developer to increase density in a downtown development. Hotel, retail, and office developers who wish to build to the maximum allowable density may do so by purchasing TDRs from owners or developers of low-income housing (housing affordable to individuals whose incomes are at or below 50 percent of the area median) or from the city's TDR bank. (In 1988, the city of Seattle created a TDR bank to purchase and hold development rights; the bank helps bridge the gap between the time that low-income units are determined to be at risk and the time when there is adequate downtown commercial development to cover preservation costs.)

Accomplishments

The Housing Bonus Program and TDR System have provided gap financing to help create and preserve 774 units of affordable housing for the downtown Seattle area. (The TDR bank, which also supports uses other than affordable-housing preservation, has assisted in the preservation of two landmark performing arts theaters in downtown Seattle—the Paramount Theater and the Eagles Auditorium—and contributed to financing the renovation of the landmark downtown YMCA building and the city's Benaroya Hall Music Center, which was constructed to house the Seattle Symphony.)

> **Contact**
> Housing Bonus Program and Transferable
> Development Rights System
> Office of Housing
> 618 Second Avenue, Eighth Floor
> Seattle, Washington 98104
> Telephone: (206) 684-0343
> Fax: (206) 233-7117
> Web site: www.ci.seattle.wa.us/housing/

Housing Levy Program
Seattle, Washington

In November 1995, Seattle voters passed a seven-year housing levy on property taxes. The total anticipated levy of $59.2 million will be used to produce and preserve 1,360 units of housing for low- and extremely low-income households.

Program Administration

The Seattle Office of Housing administers the housing levy program.

Program Description

The Seattle housing levy supports four programs: the Single-Family Homeowner Rehabilitation Program, the Homebuyer Assistance Program, the Rental Housing Production Program, and the Operating and Maintenance Trust Fund Program.

Single-Family Homeowner Rehabilitation Program. The Single-Family Homeowner Rehabilitation program will use $2.9 million in levy funds for a variety of purposes, including the following: preserving and rehabilitating owner-occupied homes; providing financial assistance to prospective homeowners whose incomes are too low to qualify for traditional mortgages; and providing loans to qualifying homeowners who want to share their homes with an unrelated person or family. All single-family homeowner rehabilitation loans will be made to people who earn less than 50 percent of the area median income.

Homebuyer Assistance Program. Another $2.9 million is reserved for the Homebuyer Assistance Program, which is designed to assist low-income families to become homeowners. The program provides downpayment assistance to eligible buyers, supports the development of new housing, and supports the renovation of vacant or deteriorating housing. Applicants' incomes must be below 80 percent of the area median. All potential borrowers must qualify for a first mortgage from a participating lender and must complete a pre-purchase homebuyer education program. Gap financing of up to $25,000 is also available. The Homebuyer Assistance Program was established as a revolving fund, so new loans are made as previous loan payments come into the fund.

Rental Housing Production Program. The $41.5 million that the Rental Housing Production Program will receive from the housing levy will be used mainly to assist working families (especially families with children) who need affordable housing; people with disabilities who require assistance in order to live independently; elderly people who need financial and physical assistance to remain in their homes; elderly people who need assisted living arrangements; and victims of domestic violence. Funds may be used for the construction or rehabilitation of affordable units and are disbursed to nonprofit agencies, public development authorities, the Seattle Housing Authority, and private for-profit owners or sponsors. Generally, tenants must earn less than 50 percent of the area median income to live in levy-assisted rental units.

Operating and Maintenance Trust Fund. The $8.75 million of the housing levy reserved for the Operating and Maintenance Trust Fund was included to "ensure that a portion of the rental production program housing was affordable to extremely low-income households (households with incomes at or below 30 percent of median income)."[6] These funds are reserved to be used for project management, utility costs, property taxes, operating and maintenance reserves, and contract services related to project support.

The office of housing publishes a general notice of funding availability at the beginning of each year. All interested project sponsors must attend a project preapplication conference with office of housing staff, and final project decisions are made by the director of the office of housing.

Funding Sources

The Seattle housing levy is funded by seven years' worth of property tax levies, which will generate $59.2 million by 2002. At that time, voters will have the opportunity to pass another levy. The program costs the owner of a $150,000 house approximately $29 per year. To date, the levy program has leveraged an additional $26.4 million in public and private funds.

The housing levy program includes $3.08 million, or 5.2 percent of all funds, to cover the costs of program administration. The level of funding that can be used to cover administrative costs varies by program.

Contact

Housing Levy Program
Seattle Office of Housing
618 Second Avenue
Seattle, Washington 98104
Telephone: (206) 684-0351
Fax: (206) 233-7117

Notes

1 This essay draws from Mary Brooks's extensive work on housing trust funds in the United States. For an exhaustive treatment of the topic, see Mary Brooks, *A Status Report on Housing Trust Funds in the United States* (Frazier Park, Calif.: Center for Community Change, 1997). The affordable-housing community is grateful to Ms. Brooks for monitoring trust fund activities and chronicling the many ways in which these affordable-housing funding vehicles are adapting to changing times and changing needs.

2 Ibid., 4.

3 Florida Affordable Housing Finance Agency, *Florida Affordable Housing Finance Agency Annual Report, 1996–1997* (Tallahassee: Florida Affordable Housing Finance Agency, 1997).

4 Affordable Housing Fund, *Users Guide to the Affordable Housing Fund* (Dayton, Ohio: Affordable Housing Fund, 1998).

5 San Antonio Housing Trust Foundation, *San Antonio Housing Trust Foundation, Inc., Annual Report 1995–1996* (San Antonio: San Antonio Housing Trust Foundation, 1996).

6 *City of Seattle Housing Levy Administrative and Financial Plan, 1996–1998*, as amended November 1997 (prepared by the Seattle Department of Housing and Human Services), 37.

Geographic Index

The following index is arranged by geographic region (based on the U.S. Department of Housing and Urban Development's regional office designations). The programs are listed alphabetically under the sponsoring state. Regional programs appear as the first listing under each regional category and are also located at the end of this index along with national programs.